The Marketing Edge

The Marketing Edge

Making Strategies Work

THOMAS V. BONOMA

THE FREE PRESS
A Division of Macmillan, Inc.
NEW YORK

Collier Macmillan Publishers
LONDON

*To Elaine, Thomas, Matthew,
Jonathan, and Benjamin*

The Free Press
A Division of Macmillan, Inc.
866 Third Avenue, New York, N. Y. 10022

Collier Macmillan Canada, Inc.

Printed in the United States of America

printing number

5 6 7 8 9 10

Library of Congress Cataloging in Publication Data

Bonoma, Thomas V.
  The marketing edge.

  Includes index.
  1. Marketing.   I. Title.
HF5415.B524   1985   658.8'02   85–1560
ISBN 0–02–904200–3

Contents

List of Exhibits

Preface

THERE IS a story, perhaps apocryphal, about the great master Gauguin. One day the master was approached by one of his apprentices. "Master," said the student, "how do I paint the perfect painting?" It is queries like this that any teacher tries to avoid, because no matter how he answers them he looks bad. If he says, "I don't know," the student mumbles something to the effect that maybe the master isn't quite as great as he's cracked up to be. If he says, "Paint as I do," the arrogance just hangs in the air.

To his credit, Gauguin hesitated not for a second. He didn't even turn around to confront his harasser. Instead, he simply said over his shoulder, "It's easy—become perfect, then paint natu rally."

This is a book about marketing practices and about some factors that can help marketers learn to manage marketing structures and to sharpen their own execution skills to move toward better practices. As in art, "becoming perfect" in marketing is much more a process of approximation or becoming than a state of being. The goal of this book is to provide some guides to practicing marketing better so that eventually execution of its plans, programs, and strategies will at least equal in soundness the formulation of its strategies.

For a number of years now marketing has been strong on strategy and short on implementation. This book addresses the often murky, difficult, politically charged, and person-heavy execution "half" of marketing as an essential element of getting the marketing job done.

I owe so many major conceptual debts for the ideas in this book that it's hard to know where to begin. Certainly the several hundred managers in a number of companies on which I "went to school" deserve a lion's share of any credit for the useful ideas contained herein, for it is from them I learned them. A substantial portion of credit as well must be assigned to my students, for they push me always in useful directions to think harder and better about how this execution business works. Professors Theodore Levitt, Benson Shapiro, and E. Raymond Corey of the Harvard Business School must be classed both as founders of the "practice side" of marketing as a relevant discipline of learning and willing co-conspirators with me over the years that I have fooled with this topic. In his role as Associate Dean of the Division of Research at the school, Professor Corey supported this work financially as well.

My family has been a mainstay through four years of working too hard and being away too much in order to learn something about good practice. In particular my wife Elaine has helped the manuscript immensely, bringing not only copy-editing and indexing skills to its preparation but also her own significant marketing experiences to critique earlier drafts. And my twin sons, Jonathan and Benjamin, by having the poor timing to be born prematurely on a vacation to an isolated spot, taught me some important lessons about getting the job done I won't soon forget!

The data referenced in the book come primarily from thirty-eight case studies I have compiled on marketing implementation, illustrating instances of both good and not-so-good practices. Sometimes, in the latter cases, I have avoided unnecessary over-disclosure in order to make a point without making simultaneously a judgement about the men or women involved. Other times I have buttressed the case data with consulting experiences. These latter references of necessity must remain proprietary. Though most of the references are clearly identifiable as either one of the case studies or as "something else," I have allowed some few ambiguities to persist in one or another place without threatening the data's integrity. The result, I hope, is a set of lessons that teaches without indicting, and thus one that informs good practices better.

When I am pushed past easy rationalization or cocktail conversation about what I teach and research, I will confess that really I teach "driver education" for marketers and general managers. In high school we all learned the theory of parallel parking ("Pull your car up parallel to the car in front of the space until its rear bumper is even with the parked car's bumper. Turn steering wheel full right. Back until your front bumper is even with the parked car's rear bumper. Turn steering wheel full left. Voilà!"), an elegant and concise strategy for parking a car. Nonetheless, most of us found it a theory very difficult to implement in the field!

In a similar way, marketing is long on theory and short on actually helping the manager get that car wedged in between a Lamborghini and a Mack truck. It is with execution that we shall concern ourselves here. Many have taught me some tricks to get the car in the slot—I, of course, remain responsible for any dents left in the finish.

THOMAS V. BONOMA

Boston, Massachusetts
July 8, 1984

CHAPTER ONE

Introduction

There is many a slip 'twixt the cup and the lip.

—Palladas, *Greek Anthology,* Epigram 32

PRELUDE

Despite his recent good fortune, John Stirben was not pleased as he rejoined his business school study group. Just hours before he had been called to the phone from an executive education course he was attending to learn that he had been promoted to vice president of marketing for the $70 million company where he worked. In his hand he was holding a piece of Benco's latest innovation, a triangular and collapsible plastic pipe called "Arch-flow." Early reports showed the arched pipe was 180 percent as effective as anything on the market for draining farmers' fields. Better, the new pipe was only 67 percent as materials-intensive, 50 percent as freight-intensive, and significantly more profitable for dealers to install. Arch-flow was, with little exaggeration, the most significant advance in drainage technology since the industry had moved from clay to plastic pipe.

"And they want to price this pipe low, for volume—in a flat market!" Stirben explained to the six other executives with whom he shared a suite. "Well, they're wrong . . . but they're also right, though not for the reasons they think.[1]

"I can get top management to see that a revolution in pipe design demands revolutionary pricing. We *can* set our prices for Arch-flow high, but it really won't help. No matter what I do in marketing, we can't *implement* a high-priced, value-added strategy for the innovation, because we don't think that way. The *real* problem is how I get this bunch of engineers and lawyers to move from their price-per-pound comfortability to a value-added philosophy?"

Benco competed in the agricultural drainage market and held a 24 percent share of that flat 600-million-foot market. The firm was a third-generation family one. Benco had seen the pipe market go from three competitors and stable prices to fifty vendors and cut-throat pricing over the last five years. The company was the high fixed-cost producer in the industry, but the lowest total-cost producer at full capacity. Management knew its plants had to be run flat out to gain these cost advantages, however.

Every tracking system in the company and, more important, top management attitudes seemed subtly tuned toward maximizing the volume of pipe sold. Salespeople thought and conversed in terms of price per pound of the pipe sold. They called headquarters often for authorization to shave prices in order to meet the many small "garage shop" competitors that were fighting for local market share. Salespeople were paid a base salary plus an incentive for volume. Plant managers' compensation was tied to the quantity of pipe they produced per minute. Even the management accounting system was price-per-pound–based. Given this powerful culture, Stirben was convinced that just declaring a high price on Arch-flow pipe or even formulating some marketing program based on high price and heavy advertising would have only temporary and ineffectual results with management, the sales force, and the market.

"Our history," he noted, "has been to start every fall with great resolve, superior products, and high prices. We wind up every spring cutting price to variable costs in order to compete with the little guys and keep the plants running. I know what the marketing books *say*: revolutionary products command high prices. The trouble is, *how* do we execute that strategy in this company? If we try we'll just cannibalize our regular pipe volume, get scared, and wind up lowering the Arch-pipe prices to keep volumes up. The sales force doesn't have the discipline to stick to value-added pricing when the farmer can buy acceptable plain black pipe for two-thirds of what we might charge for Arch-flow. Do any of those books tell you how to change a price-per-pound culture to make a value-added strategy work?''

INTRODUCTION

Marketing science has made great strides toward strategic maturity in the last two decades. A substantial body of literature and corporate experience is available to help managers formulate marketing strategies. For example, pricing products on the basis of the value-added they provide to customers is an axiom of marketing strategy formulation.

Yet when it comes to guiding the effective *implementation* of strategies, whether recommending a strategy as simple as ''price for value received'' or as complex as managing a portfolio of markets and products, the academic literature is silent and the self-help books ring hollow. What rules are there for marketing *practice* that can help managers effectively translate strategies into market place results?

This is a book about marketing practices. Its central theme is that the key concern of top management in the 1980s lies not so much with the formulation of ''new and improved'' strategies in marketing as with the quality with which plans and strategies are executed. It is, then, a book about *managing* marketing. It assumes that the general or marketing manager often knows quite well *what* he or she wishes to get done strategically. Like John Stirben, however, the manager usually is faced with a set of thorny implementation issues that make executing those strategies problematic.

The critical stimuli for this book, and for the four-year research project that led to it, came from four sources. The first was my consulting contacts with top management in large and small companies. The managers I encountered evinced remarkable clarity about what it was they wanted to do in marketing but often had problems getting the marketing job done despite their strategic certainties. This preoccupation with implementation problems came as a great surprise to me, because I was eminently well prepared to help management find its way out of the strategic darkness but blind as a bat about the factors important in actually getting a strategy executed.

Still, managerial stumbling in marketing implementation seemed evident everywhere. Pricing strategies would go awry because no one thought clearly about implementing them or because management systems frustrated their enactment. Clever new product strategies failed to move the sales force to new selling heights or, indeed, even to involve their interest. Distribution strategies faltered on the shoals of resistance from trade partners who could not appreciate the beauty of their newly reduced margins. And everywhere, management tripped over its own systems and policies. Though put in place to aid the marketing job, they often wound up frustrating it.

The second stimulus came from the academic and trade literature, which seemed strong on strategic marketing but uncomfortably silent regarding *specific* guidelines for how the strategies were to be made to work. When applications stories appeared at all in the literature, they inevitably were puff pieces designed more to impress than to inform. Grand theory proliferated; solid advice on *how* to use these theories in different companies and situations was sorely missed. Worse, marketing, supposedly the science of buyers *and* sellers, seemed to concentrate myopically on the buyers and gave passing attention at best to how the sellers might become more efficient at their marketing practices.

The third impetus came from my students, who were strategic sophisticates. Give them a cocktail napkin and they could design three new "portfolio strategies" quicker than you could finish your drink. Yet they seemed to have trouble, in the words of one unkind recruiter, "organizing a three-car funeral" when it came to getting anything done. Business school training seemed to breed too much of the armchair general's skill at commanding an army from the safety of the rear lines and too little of the master sergeant's ability to take a platoon up a hill under heavy fire and secure it.

The final stimulus was the unique institution at which I teach, the Harvard Business School, which is especially close to the concerns of operating managers. This meant freedom for me to entertain the notion that there might be a codifiable set of rules for *practicing* marketing, as opposed to conceiving it, and to try *teaching* marketing practice.

Closeness to managers was critical throughout this project, for the great bulk of what I've learned about marketing implementation is due to management's willingness in more than thirty firms to let me "go to school" not only on their successes but on their failures as well, to understand the dimensions of marketing implementation.

Mission of the Book

The mission of the book is to inquire if marketing and those who manage it can:

- Come out of the clouds of strategy into the dirt of doing
- Understand where in the corporation marketing is practiced, and what this practice involves
- Uncover what, if any, generalizable rules exist about good marketing practices

This introductory chapter (1) clarifies the relationship between strategy and acts (implementation) in marketing to help managers diagnose the existence of practice problems in their marketing efforts, (2) identifies *marketing* implementation problems as a unique set of concerns to the executive, as opposed to execution problems encountered with other functions in the corporation, (3) explains my research into marketing practices in enough detail to permit critical reading through the remainder of the book, and (4) presents the plan of the book.

MARKETING STRATEGY AND MARKETING ACTS

What Marketing Is and What It Owns

Marketing is the function through which the firm encourages exchanges of goods for money that are profitable to it and satisfying to its customers. Whether marketing is a science or an art form is not clear. Strong disagreement would be found on this point between practitioners and academics. Hence the use of the word "discipline."

The fact that marketing involves exchanges does not sufficiently discriminate it from other firm functions, however. Procurement, for example, also involves exchanges between suppliers and vendors, and the production function "exchanges," or makes tradeoffs between, costs and defect rates that affect customers mightily.

Marketing activities are singled out by two unique identifying features. The first is that marketing is the *revenue-generating function* of the corporation. Looked at this way, all the firm's other efforts are cost centers that are supported by how well marketing is done.[2]

The second distinguishing characteristic of marketing is that, in addition to all the usual cross-functional execution problems encountered within the firm by any management function, marketing's tentacles reach out to and are reached by parties external to the firm. These parties are the trade or distribution channel, and the end users or consumers. Marketing "happens" at this triple interface of company, trade, and customer. Marketing "owns" the customer creation and maintenance function and, as such, embodies the central business purpose of the enterprise.[3]

Exhibit 1–1 shows this relationship among the three parties to marketing practices: company, trade or distributors, and customers. The exhibit shows that marketing practice occurs at the junction of these three special constituencies, and that good execution is therefore dependent on both intrafirm and outside phenomena. This makes the marketer's job at execution both tricky and multiply influenced: "Good practice" in marketing, we might suspect, is a difficult and touchy task involving customers on the one hand and corporate peers on the other.

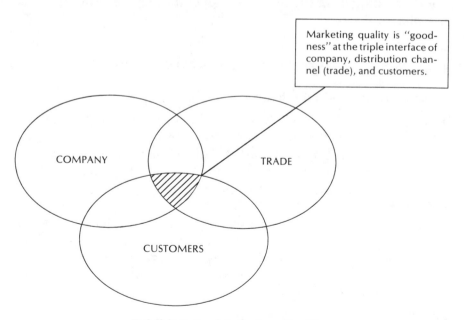

Marketing quality is "goodness" at the triple interface of company, distribution channel (trade), and customers.

COMPANY

TRADE

CUSTOMERS

Exhibit 1–1. Marketing Quality

Strategy and Acts in Marketing

Marketing strategy is the analysis of alternative opportunities and risks to the firm, informed by environmental (e.g., competitive, social) and internal (e.g., production abilities) information, which leads management to choose a particular set of market, product, and customer goals.[4]

Strategic goals posed may be extremely broad, as when a large information-processing firm states its marketing "mission" as "becoming a leader in office automation technology." Or goals may be narrow and time-constrained, as in an annual marketing plan. In either case the object of marketing strategy is to *pose the goals that will direct marketing actions* toward one and away from another set of customers and opportunities. It is these goals, the marketing strategy, that drive all marketing actions.

While it has long been recognized that strategies drive acts in marketing, it is not ordinarily realized that marketing acts, over time, come to constrain and redirect strategies in unintended ways. Consider:

Two donut chains, let's call them A and B, incorporate about the same time, using similar strategies of franchising for distribution breadth. Chain A's managers, wishing to retain as much control as possible over the delivered product, implement their strategy by charging high initial and ongoing royalties from franchisees, and putting in place a rigorous system for spot-checking restaurants by corporate staff. Management in Chain A knows it is "trading off" some greater number of potential franchisees for the higher royalties and tight controls, but it does so gladly. The corporate coffers, fattened by royalties, are used for an intensive franchisee support program to aid the franchised store owners.

Chain B, using the identical franchising strategy, implements it in a quite different manner. B's managers implement by putting one of their stores on every streetcorner. Low initial and ongoing royalties, little to no policing, and little corporate "interference" are sold to their many franchisees. Chain B's implementation route reasons that share of market depends on retail visibility, or "share of outlets," and that management should attend to opening more and more stores.

Things go well for both chains for some period, until headquarters management at both companies becomes dissatisfied with the "share of stomach" that donuts have in the overall menu of fast foods. Looking at consumers' behavior, both managements reason that if there were a broader menu, perhaps of soups and sandwiches, customers might be more likely to stop at their outlets for fuller meals at times of the day when donut demand is low. Expanding the menu requires the addition of stoves and griddles in the franchisee outlets, an expenditure of $3,400 per store. The question is: Which chain will have an easier time getting its franchisees to part with the incremental investment necessary to make the strategic switch?

Clearly Chain A, with its fewer but better managed and perhaps more profitable franchisees, will be more likely to be able to make the strategic move toward a full-line fast food restaurant. Chain B, with its cadre of poorly controlled, independent, and too numerous outlets, which have received little from corporate except a product recipe and a sheaf of forms, may be expected to have a much more difficult time with the strategic switch.

The point of the story, a real one, is that management's implementation moves (even when executing identical strategies) affect, constrain, and otherwise direct strategic changes management may wish to make in the future.

This "practice affecting strategy" cycle often leads to unintended side effects on future strategic flexibility which management does not want and with which it cannot cope. The steel, automobile, and telecommunications industries all have fallen victim to past implementation moves that constrain present strategic flexibility.[5] We shall see some case examples from these industries later in the book. I call the circle or cycle between strategy and implementation the "implementation box:"

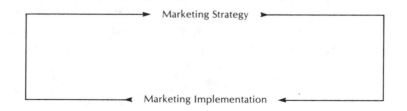

The key relationship between marketing strategy and implementation may be expressed this way: Strategy affects acts, *but acts affect strategy*. Marketing's strategic flexibility often is constrained by execution behavior in a particularly insidious manner, since management does not always recognize the linkage between *how* it does the marketing job and what marketing jobs subsequently can be planned.

The Cascade Phenomenon

There is one final way in which strategy and implementation are interrelated in getting the marketing job done. I call it the "cascade phenomenon," because strategy and implementation seem to form and flow from one to the other down the management hierarchy, much like water does from pool to pool in a Japanese garden.

Exhibit 1–2 shows a "laundered" business plan of a major office automation vendor. At the level of corporate marketing, the chief executive of the firm sets a corporate "mission" (i.e., a very broad strategy statement) of achieving worldwide dominance in office

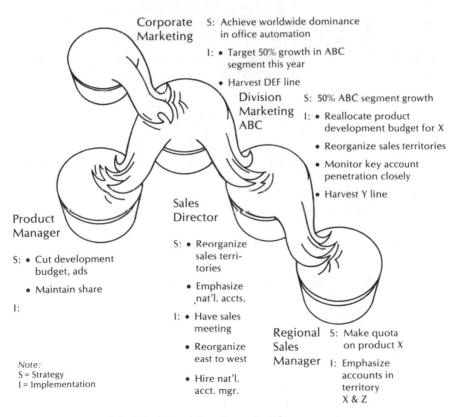

Exhibit 1–2. The Cascade Phenomenon

automation. His "implementation" statement suggests that targeting 50 percent growth in ABC revenues is one way in which the mission will be satisfied, while harvesting the DEF line is another. Clearly, at this level of management even the implementation statements have a heavy strategic and low action content.

Move down one level to division marketing for the ABC segment and note what happens. At this level the divisional manager *takes the implementation moves of the level above as strategy* and devises more specific actions to satisfy them. Thus, the "50 percent growth" implementation suggestion from corporate management is taken as strategy, and key account monitoring is one of the action moves the divisional general manager will institute to achieve this goal. This process of taking strategic direction from the next-higher management level's implementation moves can be tracked all the way down to the regional sales manager for this company.

The cascade phenomenon adds another complication to the strategy–implementation relationship for marketers. It suggests that strategy and implementation cascade from one to the other down the management hierarchy. It implies that strategic analysis without inclusion of the action alternatives of others in the hierarchy will be incomplete at best and misinformed at worst.

DIAGNOSING PRACTICE PROBLEMS

Despite the fuzzy boundary between marketing strategies and marketing acts, it is not hard to diagnose marketing implementation problems or to distinguish them from strategy shortfalls. Indeed, a logical analysis indicates that marketing implementation problems *dominate* strategy concerns in the sense that they must be looked for first. This is because *when implementation is unsound it is impossible to assess the rightness of strategic goals.*

In 1978 Computer Devices, Incorporated, was a $17 million producer of "dumb" terminals for the data-processing market. CDI's terminals, priced somewhat higher than industry leader Texas Instruments', had been experiencing eroding margins because of price pressure from Texas Instruments, which held an 80 percent share of the market. The marketing vice president of CDI hit upon the idea of evolving the dumb terminals into true microcomputers in order to give salespeople, accountants, and other professionals real "portable processing" power in the field. Although CDI did not have the software coding abilities to provide the smart machines with applications software, management had targeted a number of the Fortune 1000 companies that could write their own software for custom applications on the new machines.

A "blitz" sales contest was held to introduce the new microcomputer to the market. On the last day of the eight-week contest period, CDI's fifty-person sales force had managed *collectively* to accrue a *single* bonus point toward the offered prizes. Is the problem with sales force management or with the strategy move to the smart machines?

Assigning CDI's problems to strategy causes doesn't fit the available evidence well (even though the reader rightly will be suspicious about the absence of applications software). The company cannot stay in the "dumb" terminals market for the long term because of eroding margins. Besides, the market for microcomputers was projected to grow by more than 500 percent during the first half of the 1980s, and CDI was well situated to take advantage of this coming boom. CDI's new smart terminal unit itself, while not perfect, was complete, having an on-board modem for remote telecommunications, a built-in printer, and a full memory, as well as reasonable programming power. Whatever else CDI can be accused of, misconstrued strategy is probably not the key complaint.

Assignment of the poor "blitz" performance to marketing implementation causes better fits the situation analysis. The average company sales representative earned more than $50,000 annually from dumb terminal sales alone. On the other hand, reps were uncomfortable selling machines that were software-dependent.

Sales incentives on the new machines were set lower than on the old ones, a puzzling implementation move. This was an especially severe problem because "smart" terminal sales would be made in the operating groups of companies to functional areas like sales forces. In contrast, the "dumb" machines were sold almost exclusively to the data-processing department staff, almost as a commodity good. The dumb terminals, consequently, had a selling cycle one-half as long as the "smart" ones and required neither software knowledge nor support.

The crowning blow, however, was the length of the sales contest. The blitz contest, eight weeks in duration, was only one-half the length of the buying cycle required for the microcomputers it was designed to push! Here is a case where poor execution stifled good strategy.

Though not every situation permits so clear a determination of the relative impact of strategy and implementation on marketing practices, it is (with practice) relatively easy to diagnose implementation problems. More important, as I stated earlier, this diagnosis is if anything *more* important to make initially than a strategy examination, because it is impossible to evaluate strategy when implementation is suspect.

Picture a very simple world where marketing strategies are either appropriate or inappropriate, and the implementation of those strategies is either good or poor. Exhibit 1–3 depicts such a world and demonstrates the dominance of implementation over strategy concerns when diagnosing marketing problems.

The main diagonal cells (appropriate strategy–good implementation and inappropriate strategy–poor implementation) are not the most interesting ones on the matrix, for they are the stuff of introductory marketing examples rather than the scary problems normally faced by practicing marketing managers. Yet they are instructive in their own right.

When strategy is appropriate and implementation good, all that

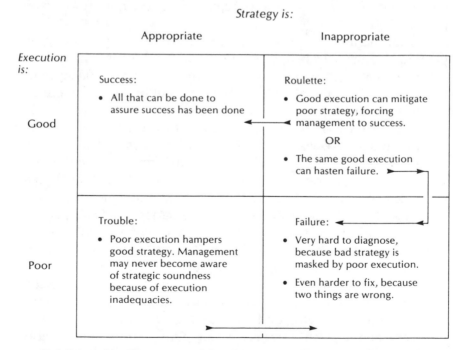

Exhibit 1–3. Strategy and Implementation: Problem Diagnosis

can be done has been done to assure marketing success. This does not mean that success *will* follow, because competitive reaction, customer perverseness, and luck often operate to send even the best planned and executed marketing programs awry. But I label this the "success" cell nonetheless, for the usual outcome is growth, share, and revenues.

When strategy is inappropriate and implementation poor we enter the right-lower cell of the matrix in Exhibit 1–3, called, not surprisingly, the failure cell. This cell, however, has a very interesting dynamic that makes failures due to poor strategy *and* poor implementation especially intractable.

If management remedies its strategy, for instance, its programs still will fail because they cannot be executed. If it fixes up the implementation problems, it will only have gained the ability to execute an inappropriate strategy. Thus, when strategy is inappropriate *and* implementation poor, management will have a difficult time indeed.

It is the off-diagonal cells that show the dominance of implementation diagnoses over strategy ones. When a firm's strategy is appropriate but its implementation poor—what I call the "trouble" cell on Exhibit 1–3—poor implementation will disguise the appropriateness of the strategy. Because management has been schooled by academics and others to suspect strategic rightness first when things go wrong, there is an almost overwhelming impulse to call in the consultants, change the strategy (usually to something *less* appropriate than the original), and then try again with the same faulty implementation structure.

That was CDI's problem. Management decided that its new line of "smart" terminals wasn't so smart after all and that it needed to introduce another series of smarter and even better microcomputers than the first. This redesign, reintroduction, and reabandonment went through several iterations, never leading to market place success. The "trouble" cell is trouble because management, holding an appropriate strategy without the ability to execute it, will be tempted to assume its strategy is inappropriate and change it, often for the worse. *Strategic adequacy cannot be assessed in the absence of management's ability to implement.*

The final cell of the matrix, the "roulette" one, is aptly named, because it is impossible to predict the consequences when implementation is good but strategy poor. Like the engine on a plane in a nose-dive, the ability to implement a poor strategy may just

drive the firm into the ground more quickly. But good implementation may mitigate the effects of inappropriate strategy too, as when
field sales personnel act in the field to "modify" corporate directives they know to be disastrous. The arrows in this cell indicate
this unpredictable dynamic and suggest that it is never certain
what will happen when strategy is poor but implementation ability
good.

Two points to be gathered from this discussion are that (1) it is
possible and usually relatively easy to distinguish problems of
marketing implementation from problems with the marketing
strategy, and (2) it is critically important to do so, for strategic adequacy cannot be assessed without implementation effectiveness.
When in doubt, the analysis recommends, look first to implementation problems and fix *them*, so that strategic adequacy can be
more clearly seen.

THE RESEARCH PROJECT

To learn how managers get the marketing job done, I "went to
school" on managers facing implementation problems in marketing daily. Surveys, questionnaires, or even interviews by themselves didn't seem to be appropriate methods to learn about how
marketing was *practiced* in the field. Such knowledge would come
only from *being* in the field and observing managers as they worked
through execution problems in marketing programs. I therefore
used a clinical investigation method of case research.

Case Research

Cases are familiar to most managers as teaching, not research
tools. A case is a description of a management situation, and its
compilation a joint venture between management and a case
writer. In compiling marketing implementation case studies, our
research team sought out cases in three general areas: (1) where the
marketing strategy of the management team in question seemed
sound but there were operational issues in making the strategy
work, (2) where the firm was reputed for excellence in getting the
marketing job done, and (3) where knowledge gained from one
case study required further testing in another, different industry or
company. Specific case development was dictated by the model of
marketing implementation to be presented in Chapter 2, but these

general guidelines are an accurate overall summary of how cases were chosen for development.

Developing a single case study requires multiple data sources, including a significant amount of time in the field with management. Interviews are conducted as in other management research, but an equally important part of the field time is spent in what is called "naturalistic observation," a fancy term for watching how the managers work, what the organization is like, and how the problem under consideration is dealt with.

In addition to these observations and interviews, company records of all sorts, from financials to internal memoranda, are scrutinized. Industry data are obtained and reviewed, and competitors and outside experts often are consulted to learn about the business. In most cases distributors or other channel partners are seen, and end users often are approached and interviewed. At some of the case sites I "did what the company did" for a time to make sure I understood the business. At Frito-Lay, for instance, I sold Fritos from the delivery truck; at a legal software company, I also "went selling." In short, the case writer makes it his or her business to learn as much as is practicable, including what is confidential or proprietary, about the company, the industry, and the problem under consideration.

All this information is then boiled down to narrative and tabular form, resulting in the familiar "case study" that managers and students analyze in the classroom. Though teaching mileage was gained from the cases, equally valuable knowledge is gained from a research exploration of the same data.[6]

Clearly, the case research process is tedious, time-consuming, and more akin to the explorations of the anthropologist than to the quantitative rigor of the physicist. The net effect of case research, however, is to provide a kind of "deep knowing" that goes beyond mere tabulation toward understanding.

Case Selection for Marketing Implementation

The case problems and companies selected for study in this project were in no way random, as would be dictated by "standard" scientific methods. The research process, rather, was a matter of moving targets, where learning about low-level marketing implementation in, say, the pricing function led to the need to see another pricing problem in a larger or smaller company, in a different industry, or to other research needs. Because of (1) the fact that very little *was* known about practice and (2) the breadth of the model of marketing practice (to be proposed in Chapter 2), the case net was cast especially wide, giving a good cross-sample of companies and industries in both consumer and industrial marketing endeavors. Special attention was paid to observing both small and large firms, for the practice of marketing might be expected to differ between them, and to companies close to start-up status versus mature ones for the same reasons. In addition, multiple case development often was taken up in the same firm, because implementation problems have a tendency to change over time and to require repeated observation for understanding.

The net result of this four-year process of developing cases is shown in Exhibit 1–4 as regards the companies and industries studied. Exhibit 1–5 categorizes some of the topics researched by marketing problem and gives a general location in the book where

Exhibit 1–4. Companies in the Marketing Implementation Data Base

COMPANY[a]	INDUSTRY
Alcan Aluminum Corp.	Siding and roofing
Applicon, Incorporated	CAD/CAM
Applied Materials	Silicon etchers
AT&T Long Lines Dept.	Telecommunications
Atlantic Aviation Corp.	Business jets
Benco, Inc.	Drainage pipe
Binney & Smith, Inc.	Crayons
Boston Whaler, Inc.	Boats
Capital Cities Communications	TV
Cole National Corp.	Optical
Computer Devices, Inc.	Smart terminals
Concept Devices, Inc.	Distributed DP
Frito-Lay, Inc.	Snack foods
Gillete Company	Hair care
Hertz Corporation	Rental cars
Inter-Footwear, Ltd.	Sports shoes
Macon Prestressed Concrete	Concrete
Manac Systems Int'l.	Software
Merrill Lynch	Securities
National Mine Service Co.	Mine equipment
North American Philips	Lighting
United States Zinc Co.	Zinc

[a] Some names are disguised.

Exhibit 1–5. Partial List of Marketing Practice Topics Investigated

TOPIC	WHERE TO FIND IT (CHAPTER)
Advertising management	4
Allocating time, $, people	8
Brand management	4
Competitive behavior	5
Culture and theme in marketing	6,11
Defensive marketing	9
Distributor management	3
Interacting with others/politics	8
Key account selling	4
Leadership	6
Managing consultants	7,8
Marketing auditing	7
Marketing intelligence systems	4
Marketing practices	All
Marketing organization	5
Marketing strategy and plans	2,6,11
Monitoring	9
National account management	4
New product development	3
Organizing	9
Pricing	3
Product management	3,4,8,9
Quality in marketing practices	2,11
Sales control systems	5
Sales management	3
Trade shows	3

they are discussed. The Research Appendix contains a fuller description of the research process, a short abstract of each case, and more information on the cases. Most of the "raw data," the cases themselves, are available for scrutiny; many are contained in the companion volume to this book, *Managing Marketing: Text, Cases, and Readings.*

In quantitative terms the sample consists of thirty-eight case studies developed in twenty-two different companies. The cases involved the participation of more than two hundred managers in their compilation. The marketing practice problems researched ranged from low-level ones about sales force performance, as illustrated in the Computer Devices example above, to global policy issues about marketing "theme" and culture (witness the Benco example with which I started this chapter). The sample is about evenly split between consumer and industrial goods companies and is biased slightly (1) toward high-technology firms and (2) toward products as opposed to services marketing. Each data point is an approximately twenty-page case study, generated by as complete and thorough an anthropological investigation of a marketing implementation problem as could be done. These are the materials from which I attempted to build an understanding of marketing practices.

PLAN OF THE BOOK

The chapters may be divided into four groups: an introductory section, followed by discussions of practice problems in marketing, management skills and marketing fixes, and good practice in marketing.

This chapter and Chapter 2 make up the introductory section. Chapter 2 presents the model of marketing implementation around which the remainder of the book is organized; it attempts also to summarize some of the findings of the research project for the manager looking to find results "all in one place."

Chapters 3–6 make up the "practice problems in marketing" section. Chapter 3, "Blocking and Tackling," deals with executing low-level marketing actions like distribution, pricing, and sales force management. It is a compendium of some things that go wrong when low-level marketing moves are engaged. Chapter 4, "Marketing Programs," discusses practice problems that arise when low-level functions are "blended together" in order to market a product line or penetrate a chosen segment. Programs are the basic building blocks of marketing execution but often are the worst enemies of good practice as well.

Chapter 5, "Marketing Systems," discusses the practice problems fostered or intensified by the systems that management puts in place to serve its marketing efforts, but which often wind up inhibiting them. Chapter 6, on execution policies, talks about identity and direction, theme and culture, and their part in fostering or blocking effective marketing execution.

A primary thesis of the book, explained in Chapter 2, is that the programs and systems management puts in place for marketing execution often cause or at least encourage implementation problems, and good implementation arises from management's substitution of its execution skills to fill gaps in the implementation structure. The third section of the book deals with these skills: Chapter 7 explains in greater detail the notion that skills can bridge the gap in implementation shortfalls. Chapter 8 discusses two of the four management execution skills, interacting and allocating. Chapter 9 discusses the final two skills, monitoring and organizing. Chapter 10 broadens the discussion by presenting some research about managers who are more comfortable at implementation and those who are more able at strategy formulation.

The final section of the book, on good practice in marketing, comprises a single chapter. It is an inquiry into some new ways to think about marketing productivity, including the measurement and inclusion of good execution. It is therefore a foray into what we mean when we use the word "quality" in marketing. It also summarizes some characteristics of good marketing execution found across the sample.

CHAPTER TWO

Managing Marketing

I have thought too much to stoop to action.

—Philippe Auguste Villiers

INTRODUCTION

The following case examples are illustrative of the breadth of problems implicated when we "stoop" to practice marketing, as opposed to just thinking about it.[1]

Lynne Verchere was president of Manac Systems International Limited, a big name for a small (about $2 million) company that sold sophisticated office management software to law firms. Ms. Verchere, a skilled software designer, teacher, and former IBM engineer, started Manac almost as an afterthought to her successful efforts to automate her husband's large law firm.

Manac's software systems for automated time, billing, disbursements, and client accounting outshone competitive systems in performance. They outstripped them in price as well, costing about 20 percent more than other systems on the market. Lawyers, reluctant business people at best, were slow to adopt computerized accounting and control systems, but in the six years since Manac's 1976 founding, more than fifty systems had been installed in Canadian law firms, giving Manac a substantial share of the

Canadian firms large enough to use its system. Manac had grown enough in the years since its founding to permit Ms. Verchere to contemplate a strategy for U.S. entry, but she was reluctant to go ahead with the strategic move because she couldn't see how to make it work.

Her problem was simple: When she was involved in selling Manac's Legal Information System, the $20,000–$30,000 software (plus $20,000–$80,000 more for a computer) sold well. When anyone else took over the selling and marketing activities, sales fell precipitously. Verchere had been through four marketing managers, including sophisticated MBAs, lawyers, and even an ex-football player. How was she to enter the United States, how was she even to continue Canadian sales, unless she could find a way to organize her firm and solidify her management so that somebody other than herself could sell the software successfully?

In another firm a thousand times the size of Manac, management at Merrill Lynch, Pierce, Fenner, & Smith was contemplating the best way to get an overall evaluation of everything done in marketing. The financial services industry was changing rapidly, and though MLPF&S had been an industry and profit leader throughout its history, management was concerned that its retail and institutional activities be kept in line with industry changes and the company's growing diversification activities.

A team of fancy consultants was asked to make an evaluation; they suggested a three-phase "marketing audit" to answer management's questions. In the first phase key managers inside MLPF&S would be interviewed, ML archives would be searched, and outside data would be culled in order to determine the general direction of the financial services markets and ML's role in them. In the second phase everyone through middle management in the company would be interviewed, as would several hundred retail and institutional customers and many competing firms. All of MLPF&S's systems would be scrutinized by the consultants, and complete market share and financial analyses of the firm would also be done. If management gave them several hundred thousand dollars to do this, the consultants proposed, they could "take the pulse" of everything that was going on in marketing at the firm and quite possibly suggest fixes for any problem areas found. Management's concern? How *do* you "take the pulse" of all that's done in marketing? Will a few hundred thousand and consultants do it, or are there other methods that should be used?

Marketing practice problems span the breadth and depth of all of management's concerns, from low-level selling problems to questions concerning everything that is done in marketing. They implicate not only many different practice tasks but all the problems marketing people have dealing with other people as well. What we need is some map that can guide us through this anatomy of action in the same way that decades of development have cleared roads toward better marketing strategies. Sadly, we know much about how to think about *thinking about marketing* and almost nothing about thinking about *doing it*.

Gumptionology for Marketers

In his *Zen and the Art of Motorcycle Maintenance*,[2] Robert Pirsig writes on the traps that sap a mechanic's resolve (he calls it "gumption") to do quality work. He tells, for instance, how a five-cent screw holding an access cover can, if stuck, render a $4,000 motorcycle worthless and the mechanic a frustrated wreck headed for really large-scale mistakes. Pirsig uses the stuck screw as a metaphor for the kind of motivation-sapping "mental stuckness" that strikes all of us sometimes and hinders good practices. Pirsig gives an entire catalog of such "gumption traps," using motorcycles and their repair as a proxy for what causes us to move toward or fall away from quality in everyday life. Only half in jest, he proposes the establishment of a new college course, "Gumptionology 101," to investigate quality-seeking in daily activities.

Like mechanics, managers need a vocabulary for and a catalog of the traps laid for those who practice marketing. My work has led me to such a vocabulary and to a catalog of common marketing implementation problems. The vocabulary forms the basis both for a typology of implementation difficulties and for a model of their resolution. The model in addition sets the plan for the remainder of the book, which is my attempt at a "Gumptionology 101 for Marketing Management."

A MODEL OF MARKETING EXECUTION

Marketing execution takes place at four structural levels in the firm: actions, programs, systems, and policies. Exhibit 2–1 shows an "index card" model of marketing implementation. The idea behind depicting marketing activities as index cards relates to the

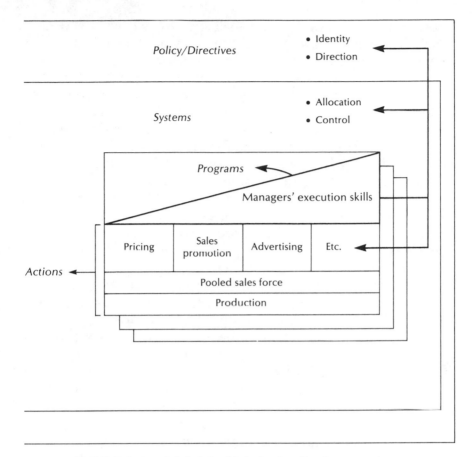

Exhibit 2-1. A Model of Marketing Implementation

way many managers think of marketing, as a number of focused programs they wish to accomplish within available resources.

Starting with the firm's marketing programs (shown as a stack of index cards in the center of the diagram), the exhibit shows how marketing practice's four structural levels relate to one another. As can be seen, marketing programs are managed combinations of marketing and nonmarketing actions or subfunctions, brought together synergistically (it is hoped) to maximize share of a particular product line or maximize penetration of a given market segment. For instance, key account management as it is done in Hewlett-Packard's Medical Systems Division attempts to bring all the firm's low-level marketing actions together to optimize key account penetration. Selling, pricing, service, even H-P's formidable product development activities—all are targeted in one way or another to help management solidify key account relations and therefore maximize its profits from this program.

The low-level actions themselves, of course, are the bedrock of all marketing practices. They include both functions that marketing directly "owns," like pricing, and ones that it only accesses, such as a pooled sales force or product development activities. Regardless of which firm function formally has control of these low-level actions, it is the marketer's job to manage them in the service of customer satisfaction and profits.

Surrounding the programs and low-level functional actions on the exhibit are two other marketing execution levels, systems and policies. Marketing systems refer to the marketing tasks management has routinized in its regular operations, like budgeting or sales force reporting and control. Policies are directives issued by management (not always verbally) that affect the color and character of all that is done in marketing. These usually address either the firm's marketing identity or its basic directions.

Finally, affecting all four structural areas of marketing implementation are the personal execution skills brought by managers to the marketing job. I shall return to these skills in a later section, after the operation of the four structural levels of marketing practice are considered. First, I take up regularly occurring problems and pitfalls at each structural level of marketing execution: actions, programs, systems, and policies.

Marketing Actions: Low-Level Functions

Examples of marketing actions include selling, trade promotion, and distributor management. These low-level tasks are the fundamentals, the "blocking and tackling" of the marketer's job. From my field observations, most firms and many managers have real difficulty with such low-level execution acts. Often the difficulties experienced arise from not addressing marketing's fundamentals in any determined or regular way, as when one CEO we'll meet in Chapter 3 doubted the worth of his trade show expenditures as good marketing communications, but continued to authorize almost $1 million to the trade show program because "we have to be there."

But how *does* management know if its promotional allocations are reasonable or whether sales force dollars ought to be rebudgeted toward advertising? How are products to be priced, absolutely and also relatively with regard to other items in the line and the competition's goods? What constitutes effective selling?

To my surprise, I frequently observed serious problems in the execution of low-level marketing acts. I had expected to see little of sales force management problems, for example, because it is hard to imagine a firm surviving with this function seriously deficient. Yet in my sample problems with this and other low-level marketing functions were the rule rather than the exception.

Most often, actions problems are associated with (1) sales force management, (2) management of distribution channels and the relations found there, and (3) pricing difficulties. Each of these low-level execution problems will be taken up in Chapter 3. Here, I wish to illustrate some of the actions-level *management* problems common to all marketing subfunctions.

Some problems of inability to execute low-level blocking and tackling in marketing could only be labeled "management by assumption." In these instances management simply assumes that the marketing subfunction in question will get executed well by *someone somewhere* in the company, and thus ignores it until a crisis occurs.

In one firm I worked with, for example, management felt that lower list prices, but lower discounts from those list prices would be sound pricing implementation for its line of graphic computers (see Chapter 3 for a fuller account). Certainly management's strategy of undercutting the competition and getting buyers' attention in a crowded competitive field was satisfied by the list price move.

But this manufacturer simply *assumed* a number of things that it should have known about how its clients buy before it chose this low list-price implementation. While the price move was useful in attracting small, single-machine buyers, larger multiple-machine buyers resisted the company's pricing, since purchasing managers in these firms often proved *their* effectiveness to *their* managements by the size of the discounts negotiated from the vendors! The computer firm artificially relegated itself to a small-company customer base when it intended only to make an innovative pricing implementation to get big accounts' attention.

The first actions-level implementation problem, then, is that of *management by assumption*. Unintended consequences result when management assumes things about buyer dynamics or other factors that should inform its marketing moves, goes ahead with those moves anyway, and experiences the often dangerous side effects of substituting assumptions for knowledge.[3] As might be expected, this disease is more prevalent in larger operating units (where management has functional marketing specialists to rely on) than in smaller ones, though managers of small businesses are in no way immune. Because of laziness, faulty logic, or just an abrogation of clear thinking, management often assumes things that may not be true about how its "blocking and tackling" will be received by the customers or by other managers.

A second cause of what goes wrong when marketing functions are mishandled is what I label *structural contradiction*. Here, what occurs at one (higher) level of the execution structure is inconsistent with what management is asked to do with low-level marketing acts.

In a venture start-up firm, for instance, interest in management's promising distributed data-processing technology had produced a thick pressbook and lots of foreign distribution offers for the firm, even though the company had not yet shipped a single unit. Concept Devices' founders had left their former big-company employers and started the fledgling company to get the kind of "customer control" over the distribution chain that would keep their innovative system at the forefront of technology. So far seven stand-alone sales offices had been set up domestically in anticipation of unit shipments; top management felt that the high fixed-cost burden for owned sales offices was the only way to go in order to stay close to the customers.

But a number of foreign computer companies impressed with Concept's ideas recently had appeared on the scene, tempting management with huge bags of money if it would entertain one or another form of indirect distribution in Europe and Asia. One British firm, for instance, had offered $15 million in sales guarantees to become Concept's selling partner in the United Kingdom.

Management was torn. The cash flows were exceptionally attractive at Concept's early stage of development, and management didn't think it had the skills to handle direct selling in Great Britain, much less Japan. On the other hand, however, "customer control" was an important, even emotional issue to Concept's top management. Indirect distribution, or even joint venturing, didn't offer the kind of control over the end user relationship that management hoped to have. In the end the seductiveness of the money won out over the need for independence and channel control.

Management's overwhelming strain toward maintaining channel control was grossly inconsistent with its low-level distribution decisions to execute foreign distribution through indirect and joint venture arrangements. Besides, the marketing organization in this company, a single (though highly skilled) individual, simply did not have the horsepower to manage (1) owned sales offices in the United States, (2) a complex exclusive distribution arrangement in Great Britain, and (3) a joint venture in France.

Yet the seductive specter of foreign opportunity made the conflict difficult for management. Cash flow needs and a shortfall of foreign buyer knowledge seduced it into indirect distribution, while marketing policy dictated owned channels. Management's attempts to balance the contradiction between policy and distribution implementation, along with the "normal" pressures of a rapidly changing market and new venture demands, had explosive results on the cohesiveness of the management team and caused foreign distribution dilemmas.

In the remainder of instances where low-level actions problems short-circuit marketing programs, management seems to suffer from what I call *global mediocrity*. That is, management picks no one marketing subfunction for special concentration and competence, but instead tries to do a good job with each, avoiding hard choices about allocations with a democratic even-handedness that assures the mediocrity of all. Either because of an egalitarian ethic or because of management's good intentions to do well at everything, resources are diffused across marketing subfunctions. As a result the marketing function often comprises pricing, advertising, promotion, and distributor subfunctions, each of them adequate but none outstanding. Customer reaction often parallels this "great leveling" with a matching mediocrity. Interestingly, such firms often are the same ones that engage in too many poorly thought-through programs (see below).

In the firms that are best at low-level execution, by contrast, there is a real facility at handling one or two marketing functions with greatness or at least flair, and competence at the remainder. No marketers are good at everything, but the most able concentrate on doing an outstanding job at a few marketing subfunctions and an adequate job with the remainder. Frito-Lay, for instance, is an example among the companies I studied in which management has refined two "simple" functional skills, selling and distribution, to such heights that they serve as the competitive basis for all marketing practices engaged in by the firm. The Gillette Company's Personal Care Division, another firm in the sample, has made a science of advertising in the same way that Frito-Lay has emphasized distribution. In both these firms resources are allocated, often unequally, to maintain competitive preeminence in the "showcase" functions while doing an adequate job with the remainder. The result is what the consultants call "enduring competitive advantage."

Finally, problems with nonmarketing functions where managers needed cooperation from production, R&D, or other departments were seldom experienced by the managers I worked with. That is contrary to the common corporate wisdom, which has it that marketing is a hotbed of mismanaged internal interactions with production, engineering, customer service, and other firm functions, often causing poor execution. Rather, managers, perhaps very aware that such interactions can be difficult ones in which little leverage is possible, seem to plan, plot, and concentrate their persuasive impacts to good effect. Where low-level marketing actions are concerned, the ones marketing "owns" are problematic to marketing practice rather than the ones it does not. We shall look further into functional-level marketing problems in Chapter 3.

Marketing Programs

At the programs level, management is concerned with blending marketing and nonmarketing functions in a focused attempt to sell a product line or penetrate a target segment. Managing all aspects of the Silkience Conditioner line, for instance, is a marketing program; so is managing a firm's key accounts and *their* special needs. If marketing actions are the blocking and tackling of execution, marketing programs are the tactician's playbook by which the customers are courted and the competition confounded.

One company, for example, wished to install a national accounts program to better serve its key accounts. How, exactly, is this to be gone about? Perhaps the manager should attempt to create a headquarters-based dedicated national account sales force, with the attendant risks that competition with the sales vice president, his superior, implies. Or is he better off working in a dotted-line capacity through the firm's sales managers, attempting no selling or service coordination beyond simple interfunctional persuasion, and running different risks with the customer base? The art of blending functions into programs is poorly understood at best, often left to trial-and-error learning.

This situation illustrates the first of two regularly occurring programs problems that managers encounter. I call it *empty promises marketing*. The firm in question (we'll cover this situation at some length in Chapter 4) made a generalized piece of equipment that served all its industry's segments but did so at some loss in performance to the competition's gear, which was dedicated to specific applications. Consequently, its product appealed to the user who needed multiple applications and could not afford a dedicated system for each purpose. That, of course, was the smaller customer. Service strategies were tailored, it seemed, to these smaller single-site buyers, as was sales deployment. The company's customer base reflected this positioning: Instead of the normal 80–20 rule, where 80 percent of revenues are derived from the largest 20 percent of accounts, in this company only 30 percent of its revenues were generated from large accounts.

Into this environment top management threw a single individual as national accounts manager. He reported to the sales vice president but had no line authority over either sales personnel in the branches or service people. Without either a resource base or authority, he was charged with "putting a national accounts program together" to service the firm's few but important multi-machine accounts. After fifteen months in the job, there had been no progress other than the creation of a national account contract form. Key accounts still were quoted different prices at different operating sites, service was still haphazard, and the accounts were openly dissatisfied.

In short, this firm's national accounts program belied much of what the company was set up to do in marketing. Instead of taking substantive actions to breed a large-account capability (it is moot as to whether that was a good idea, but it *was* the idea), management elected to make no substantive change in its successful small-user marketing mix and instead simply "declared" a national accounts program for which its marketing structure was not suited. As a consequence top management's national accounts program represented only an "empty promise" to its few large users on which the firm could not deliver. Empty promises marketing comes from instituting a marketing program in conflict with the firm's identity on the one hand and its low-level marketing actions on the other.

The second programs-level execution error, which I call *bunny marketing*, arises not from any functional inability to execute program plans but rather from a lack of identity and direction in management's policies for running the marketing effort, a topic we'll take up again in Chapter 6.

One heavy manufacturing firm we'll meet in Chapter 4 continually was frustrated by entering its market late with new products—in an industry where spare parts inventory building and operator loyalties gave the vendor first into market a significant advantage. I traced one product from inception to introduction—almost two years after a major competitor's similar entry. Top management had kept its thin developmental engineering staff busy with a torrent of rework projects for machines already in the field, the new machine itself, and even a significant "blue sky" project it was prototyping under government grant. In essence there was such a profusion of programs going off in all directions that little got done well. This profusion of programs, in turn, seemed to stem from a poor sense of what the firm was and what it did as regards markets and segments. The symptom was program proliferation, or "bunny marketing"; the cause was insufficient clarity in marketing identity.

The presence of many clever marketing programs, a thick "playbook," is not associated with good marketing practice and is often associated with severe execution problems. Where a strong sense of marketing identity and direction don't exist, bunny marketing results. Programs go off in all directions, resulting in diffusion of effort and random results. Where strong functional abilities are not present or run counter to program needs, empty promises marketing results. In this case, clever programs fail for want of the basic subfunctional abilities needed to execute them. Without functional soundness on the one hand and clarity of purpose on the other, management often seems to dream up "Statue of Liberty" plays it has neither the focus nor the functional abilities to make work. We shall inquire into problems associated with marketing programs in more depth in Chapter 4.

Marketing Systems

The marketing systems level includes the formal organization through which marketing is executed as well as monitoring, budgeting, or other "overlays" that foster or inhibit good marketing practices. Systems can be as mundane as voice telecommunications or as pervasive as the one for profit accounting. Of the less pervasive systems, the most problematic for companies are the ones associated with sales force reporting and control.

Of the more pervasive marketing systems, the two most troublesome are those for *allocation* of marketing's scarce resources across programs and those meant to help management *monitor* how its strategies are working in the field. Other corporate-wide kinds of systems, such as personnel, the formal organization, and the like, were no less problematic but seemed easier to get around through the exercise of personal execution skills. In smaller firms allocation systems caused the most problems; in larger ones, control systems. Systems, created to serve managers, wind up driving them, often in less than useful directions.

Systems-level problems are bred from management errors of *ritualization, politicization,* or *unavailability.* Errors of ritual arise when the firm's systems drive it down habitual pathways even when good judgment dictates a different course. At the small construction company used to introduce Chapter 5, for instance, the primary marketing control system was a measure of plant backlog. But the system had some bad effects: When backlogs were low, the sales force "beat the bushes" for jobs no matter how marginal, the estimators (they control pricing in construction firms) shaved margins to the bone, and everyone from the CEO to day laborers was very nervous. When backlogs were high, the opposite prevailed. However, the low-margin business taken in bad times to increase backlog decreased the firm's discipline to take only high-margin business in good times.

When a marketing audit was conducted and a new sales control system was proposed to remedy the problem, the president implemented all the new forms and reports but could not bring himself either to abandon backlog management or to approach profitability by job as a means to more effective segmentation and selling. In this firm it was easier for management to do what was habitual than it was to learn new ways.

The second systems-level error comes from problems of politicization. Nowhere is this more easily observable than when considering sales force reporting and control systems, in particular call reporting. Sales managers frequently "weed" their call reports to tailor intelligence garnered from salespeople in one way or another. Even more dangerous, call reports often lose their intelligence function altogether and become instead a device used to punish sales representatives for submitting "inappropriate" ones. As a consequence, in most firms the cheapest source of marketing intelligence available to managers, sales force reports, is degraded, misused, and rendered worse than useless by politicization of the data or conversion of customer feedback into a sales force reward–punishment system. By protecting themselves or serving other agendas, managers often allow practice to suffer.

The final and most pervasive systems problem is simply *unavailability* of the data needed to do the marketing job. Systems, installed to make managers' lives easier, quickly come to have lives of their own and become unsuited for the kinds of queries managers would like to pose. In all but a handful of companies that I studied, the financial and even sales accounting systems could only be called perverse in their frustration of marketing requests.

The ability to know how well market place results correlate with management's moves might be thought to be readily available to managers in today's data-oriented companies. However, it is rare that marketing management, for example, has any idea of profitability by segment. Rarer still are good numbers on profitability by segment and by product, and only once could I find a system that allowed computations of profitability by account, product, and order. Instead, management is treated to incomprehensible foot-thick printouts of unaggregated data that a cynic would suspect are issued by data-processing staff in order to *discourage* further inquiry. Or else marketing is told that "accounting won't give it to us that way" when making a data request. Unless management has strong individual monitoring skills, the result is that marketing operates in a kind of bell-jar vacuum in which it is impossible to make good decisions. We shall look more deeply into marketing systems in Chapter 5.

Policy Guidelines

At the broadest level of marketing practice are policy directives. Policies encompass a spectrum of management activity from recruiting to termination. However, we will focus in this book on two critical categories of marketing policies: those relating to what the firm *is*, identity policies, and those relating to what it *does* in marketing, or direction ones. By policies I don't mean just written or even verbal statements; indeed, some of the most central policies for marketing's conduct are unspoken.

Problems with *identity policies*, interestingly, occur more often in mature than in young business units. Marketing "theme" and marketing culture are the terms I use to convey the powerful but often unspoken feeling of common purpose that exists in the best marketing practitioners and is absent from others.

Marketing theme, a fuzzy but important term, refers to management's shared understanding of who it is and what it is about in the marketing job. In one firm I observed, for instance, it was obvious from management's interactions that each person had a different sense of "how we do things around here." Some executives thought of the company as a commodity vendor; others felt that the driving force of the firm was in differentiation. The managers, of course, *managed* consistent with their different understandings; the result was a confused and ineffective marketing effort, a sales force that complained of contradictory management signals, and a divisive trade.

By contrast, in another firm I spent time with, management and all its salespeople could repeat (and believed!) that "We are the premier vendor in this country, but we only have two seconds to reach the supermarket shopper, so we live or die on service and shelf displays." Management's shared understanding and continual reinforcement of this theme (through compensation, training, and the like), simple though it sounds, promoted exceptionally effective sales force performance and consistently good customer reactions.

Marketing culture is a broader term than theme. Where themes often can be verbalized, culture is the underlying and usually unspoken "social webbing" of management.[4] It subtly but powerfully channels managers' behavior into its existing paths. Though often unspoken, it can be observed clearly from clues as various as lunchroom conversations to signs put on office walls. For example, when I asked management in one firm why it was planning to build a very large plant when its own market studies showed anticipated sales volumes of half the projected capacity, the marketing vice president responded, "We don't see much sense in trying to chin ourselves on the curb around here." Contrast the risk-prone aggressiveness of this company with the signs to be found at every AT&T installation: "There is no task so urgent we cannot find a way to do it safely."

Direction policies refers to the firm's marketing strategy, one of its guiding forces, and to its marketing leadership, the other. I am not concerned in this book with strategies; but leadership is an important execution variable that is often underemphasized by managers and researchers alike. It has become fashionable in management to blame all shortcomings in practice on "invisible gremlins" like culture. While this is convenient because nobody ever got fired as a result of the *culture's* being bad, it ignores the central role of individual (and responsible) human beings in producing results or failing at the attempt.

It is undeniably true that some top managers and marketers are high-quality leaders, and some aren't. The former are inspiring by their eagerness to get out into the field, clever at designing simple and effective monitoring schemes, and impressive from having driven their understanding of customers and the business to a powerful simplicity. Others are not so good as leaders, being either overly complex conceptualizers or unwilling to leave their leather chairs for the rudeness of the market place. They are inspirational only as models of what their juniors hope not to become. The quality of marketing practices is affected mightly by the quality of marketing leadership.

Time and time again it is the absence of clear identity policies or the weakness of managers leading the marketing effort that results in practice failures. How a strong theme and culture are arranged, whether through personal charisma or by careful orchestration through more formal devices, seems irrelevant. The critical question often is whether these intangibles of "who we are," or identity, and "what we are about," or direction, exist as powerful though unquantifiable forces that impress themselves on observers just as they pervade the firm.

Policies are treated here in two separate ways. Chapter 6 deals with some of the more common problems associated with identity and direction problems when marketing is practiced. Chapter 10 returns to the make-up of the individuals doing the policy setting.

GAP BRIDGING: EXECUTION SKILLS

Reading this litany of structural execution failures, one might conclude that most of my observations were of firms troubled with marketing practices. That is a correct conclusion, though I specifically sought out the excellent implementers as well. Actions, programs, systems, and policies, management's structural formalization of the marketing job designed to make the tasks easy and accomplishable, were often the bane of really *doing* the job and seemed to get in the way of good execution.

What pulled things "out of the fire" more often than not was the exercise of personal, informal, sometimes even "illegitimate" execution skills by the managers themselves, who often had to fight their own marketing structure to do the marketing job well. Indeed, a major theme of the book is that marketing structures often act to cause or foster execution ills, and that the exercise of execution skills by managers often acts to fix these problems. Managers frequently use their execution skills to supplant, subvert, overcome, or otherwise modify shortcomings in the execution structure. Chapter 7, on "gap bridging," explains this relationship between levels and skills in marketing practices more fully.

For instance, I frequently encountered dysfunctional marketing organizations (a formal system) that had been "patched up" to work quite nicely through the exercise of managers' informal organizing skills. Similarly, informal monitoring schemes routinely were created and operated to obtain data the control system couldn't or wouldn't supply to managers, and "budget reallocations" often were designed to subvert formal policy constraints. Managers bring four skills to the marketing job: *interacting, allocating, monitoring,* and *organizing.*

Interacting

Clearly, a first interacting task is to manage oneself to be a good implementer. Some studies I have conducted with top marketers[5] suggest that good implementers are different from those managers more comfortable with strategy in important ways. The implementers were quick to act, proposed more action plans, and were "combat-ready"—that is to say, good implementers are able to make sharp tactical decisions under pressure and often prefer to put out fires that *can* be put out quickly, leaving the bigger battles to be fought another day.

Interacting is important to the marketer in ways other than self-management, however. The marketing job by its nature is one of influencing others inside and outside the corporation. Inside there is a regular parade of peers over which the marketer has no power to impose his or her preferences; horse trades must be struck instead. Outside the marketer deals with a plethora of helpers, including ad agencies, consultants, manufacturers' reps, and the like, each with an agenda and an axe to grind.

Allocating

Regarding allocating skills, the critical tasks of the implementers are to parcel his own and others' time, assignments, and other resources among the marketing jobs to be done. Able implementers seem to have no false sense of charity or egalitarianism, but rather are tough and fair in putting effort and dollars where they pay back. The ineffective, in contrast, continually commit the sin of resolve. That is, they routinely commit too many dollars and people to mature programs with little to be gained "on the margin," and too few to riskier but potentially more promising ones. We take up interacting and allocating skills in Chapter 8.

Monitoring

It is by using his or her monitoring skills that the manager can do the most to reconstruct degraded corporate information and control systems. Good implementers puzzle, struggle, and wrestle with their markets and their businesses until they can simply and powerfully express the critical "back-of-the-envelope" ratios necessary to run the business regardless of control system inadequacies. Poor implementers either wallow in blissful industry clichés or else get mired in awesome quantitative complexities that no one can understand. The general manager of a firm with thirty-eight manufacturing plants and 300,000 customers, for instance, manages everything he considers critical on two 3 x 5 index cards. The sales manager of a company one-hundredth the size of that one, by contrast, generates handtrucks full of computer printouts monthly in his monitoring zeal, only to let them age gracefully like fine cheese until it is time for the next cycle.

Organizing

The final skill, organizing, refers to managers' abilities at what has been termed "networking" by some. Good implementers have an almost uncanny ability to create afresh an informal organization to match each different problem with which they are confronted. They always "know somebody" in each part of the organization (and outside as well) who by virtue of mutual respect, attraction, or some other tie can and will help with each problem. These managers reconstruct the organization to suit each different marketing job that needs to be done. They "customize" their informal organization to allow better execution. Often their organizations and the formal organization chart have little in common. We take up monitoring and organizing skills in Chapter 9.

A TYPOLOGY OF MARKETING PRACTICE PROBLEMS

The decomposition of marketing practice into structural levels and also skills gives not only a useful way of understanding the dynamics of marketing practice but a good way of classifying marketing implementation problems. Exhibit 2–2 shows levels and skills crossed in a four-by-four matrix, where each entry in a cell represents a marketing execution problem. While the matrix makes no pretensions at being exclusive, I think it is exhaustive. That is, any marketing implementation problem encountered probably has elements of more than one level and skill, but in several years of field observations I have not found marketing implementation problems that could not be categorized using this matrix. It thus is a useful diagnostic aid and a kind of "map" of the territory of marketing practice.

CONCLUSION

Marketing implementation is a joint function of the level at which practice occurs and the skills of the managers doing the job. Because of reasons detailed above, marketing structures (actions, programs, systems, and policies) often act to *cause* implementation problems, or else to exacerbate them. The efforts of managers exercising execution skills (interacting, allocating, monitoring, and organizing) often act to "bridge the gap" between inadequate structure and good practice. The close reader will have one question, "Well, that's fine . . . but what *is* good practice in marketing, and how do I know it when I see it?"

In one sense that question requires the remainder of the book to answer, for it is only by comparing good and not so good examples of execution in marketing that relevant differences appear. But in a more general way a response is possible. It is a response that implicates the triple interface of customers, company, and trade that we referred to as the origins of marketing and marketing practices in Chapter 1.

Exhibit 2-2. Marketing Practice: A Taxonomy

Marketing implementation can be analyzed at the level of	Effective implementation is achieved through →			
	INTERACTING	ALLOCATING	MONITORING	ORGANIZING
Actions	*How* are production and R&D colleagues encouraged to devote more time or effort to a single brand?	*How* is sales force territory allocation best done by a printing company?	*How* are salespeople best evaluated and compensated by a bulk chemicals firm?	*How* should the new product planning function of a market follower be organized in a high-loyalty business?
Programs	*How* can sales and marketing effectively collaborate on a new national account program?	*How* should prospects be selected for demonstration rides in a corporate jet?	*How* is a successful ad agency team best managed within a brand group for a new pipe introduction?	*How* should a sales force be reorganized to emphasize a marketing shift from "dumb" to "smart" terminals?
Systems	*How* should ownership of a competitive pricing intelligence system be parceled between sales and marketing in an ethical drug company?	*How* should a regional bank set up centers, lock boxes, and computer services to maximize market share in a new cash management program?	*How* does a mine machinery manufacturer monitor a major trade promotion expenditure?	*How* should customer service engineers be redeployed to avoid hardware–software "buck passing" in a computer graphics manufacturer?
Policies	*How* should a recall of a defective building component be managed by a major steel producer?	*How* should dollars and service resources be allocated to service key accounts by segment and country for a computer-aided design manufacturer?	*How* does a major securities firm regularly audit the marketing function?	*How* should the marketing team be reorganized by a company changing its "theme"?

When all is said and done, quality in marketing practice is not either identical with or a guarantee of good market place results. There's just too much competitive jockeying, luck, and downright customer perverseness involved in the marketing job for such a one-to-one correspondence to emerge. Neither is good marketing practice associated with the *absence* of execution problems and crises; no firm will ever plan so well that things don't go wrong in the field. Rather, the short answer about marketing quality is that good marketing practice means the quality of management's *coping* behaviors when faced with the inevitable execution crises that threaten to blur its strategies. Individually, such day-to-day threats are not much to fear. But taken collectively they are strategy-killers.

Chapter 11 returns to the topic of quality in marketing practices and poses a set of principles observed from the companies studied to differentiate good marketing practices from bad, and to help foster them where they are not yet present.

CHAPTER THREE

Blocking and Tackling—
Marketing Actions

No one can draw more out of things, books included, than he already knows.
A man has no ears for that to which experience has given him no access.

—Gerard Manley Hopkins, *Ecce Homo*

PRELUDE

Kenton E. McElhattan, president and chairman of National Mine Service Company (NMS), surveyed his company's booth at the International Coal Show. NMS, a $127-million producer of heavy mining machinery and a distributor of mine supplies, had reserved 140,000 square feet at the mining equipment industry's quadrennial exhibition of new mining technology.

NMS had trucked in twenty-nine pieces of heavy equipment for the show and had set up displays from its distribution and repair divisions as well. More than one hundred National Mine employees would spend a week manning the booth; company activity had been at a fevered pace for the month before the show. All of NMS's divisions had been busy readying equipment, contacting customers, and developing special advertising materials. The cocktail party to be held on the show's second evening was expected to cost the company some $27,000 alone; in all, NMS would spend $507,000 on its trade show participation, not counting management time.

As he surveyed the booth where yellow mine locomotives sat incongruously on brown shag carpeting, Mr. McElhattan just had to ask his vice president of corporate communications one more time:

"Tim, are you *sure* we get our money's worth from participating in this trade show? We don't *sell* anything here; it's an 'educational activity' from the IRS's and our point of view. That $500,000, dropped to the bottom line, would make us look pretty good in the quarterly stockholders' report. Or $500,000 spent on additional salespeople might increase orders more than any benefit we could get from the show. How will we know we spent the right amount of money in the right way on this activity, or that we shouldn't reallocate the money to other selling or sales promotion jobs?"

How *does* management know if its current choices for "doing marketing" are the right ones at the lowest levels of the job? Usually the firm's emphasis on one or another marketing subfunction, the low-level components of marketing like pricing and advertising, are a combination of historical accident, management "comfort levels," and competitor emulation. How are the tough choices to be made and remade for marketing effectiveness?

In another corporation the vice president of sales had a quite different low-level marketing problem. He was contemplating how to avoid a customer revolt in one of his prime sales territories. Bob Marsh, ethical drug salesman for the Kramer Pharmaceuticals Company, had been terminated by his zone manager. The physicians in Marsh's territory were up in arms, as they considered Marsh an able and experienced salesperson with whom they had had a close professional relationship for eleven years.

The longer he contemplated the dossier assembled on Marsh, the more suspicious the vice president became of Kramer's techniques for managing the sales force. Marsh had been recruited on "amiability" and "dependability," criteria that read like a loyalty oath for the Boy Scouts. Kramer's training looked deficient, and its performance review mechanisms were a litany of subjective judgments. Pay raises seemed to be disengaged totally from performance ratings, and perhaps unrelated to anything else as well: Twice while Marsh was on probation for various alleged offenses against company policy he had received substantial raises.

Worst of all Marsh had been supervised by six different regional managers in the twelve years he was with Kramer. The managers were increasingly "green" over the years, and the vice president couldn't help but note that the younger and more inexperienced the sales manager, the greater the problems reported with Mr. Marsh.

What is to be done? More important, treating the Marsh business as sunk cost, how can the vice president tell whether sales management at Kramer is good or poor? What are the benchmarks for low-level marketing actions?

INTRODUCTION

Low-level marketing execution problems are routinely encountered not only by marketing management but by top management as well. Problems with sales management and with sales promotion activities like trade shows are especially frequent but by no means account for all the blocking-and-tackling implementation difficulties encountered in the marketing function. Pricing, distributor management, new product development, postsale service, and advertising are just some of the down-and-dirty detail work by which a firm gets the marketing job done. Where activities in these low-level subfunctions work smoothly, so does marketing. Where they don't, a common condition, everyone in the corporation feels the results.

Each low-level subfunction in marketing could support a separate treatise on what goes wrong and how to fix it.[1] However, common management patterns run through all marketing subfunctions when execution is mismanaged and also when it is done well. This chapter examines those patterns and uses several of marketing's many subfunctions to illustrate commonalities in what goes wrong when low-level marketing actions are executed.

MANAGEMENT MISTAKES WITH MARKETING FUNCTIONS

Chapter 2 gave a brief outline of three inefficiencies that can arise when low-level marketing actions are undertaken. The first, *management by assumption,* occurs when management assumes that someone somewhere in the corporation will do the low-level homework that pricing, sales promotion, or distribution management implementation decisions require. Often, however, the *someone* isn't *anyone*, and the function in question just gets assumed away until a crisis happens. Management by assumption occurs when *beliefs* about customer, distribution, or competitor response are substituted for *knowledge.*

Structural contradiction is the second inefficiency. Here management sets up its low-level marketing structures to support one kind of endeavor, then requires them to support another, often a diametrically opposed one. The result is a kind of wrenching that neither the subfunction nor management can tolerate.

Global mediocrity, the final inefficiency talked about in Chapter 2, refers to management's strain toward allocative and attentional democracy. Here management attention and budgets are partialed to each subfunction carefully to make sure that "everyone gets something" and that "we try to be good at everything." Those who try to be good at everything are often very good at nothing, and the resulting combination of marketing subfunctions provides the firm with no distinctive competence on which to build its programs and distinguish itself from competition.

The next few subsections look at some of marketing's many subfunctions from the perspective of what goes wrong when low-level marketing acts are executed. While not all of marketing's subfunctions are covered here, what is said is applicable to others as well.

Since it is the *structure* for marketing execution we are concerned with in these early chapters, we shall be looking at how sales management, pricing, and other subfunctional decisions are *routinized* by the corporation. Of course, marketing subfunctions never are independent of the managers doing the job. We take up that concern in later chapters.

Selling and Sales Management

Nowhere are execution problems in marketing more easily observable than in management of the selling function. This subfunction, in one way or another, tends to be problematic for all corporations. Sales management problems are of special concern, because it is in the sales function where the "rubber meets the road" and all else in marketing is consummated.[2]

Management by Assumption in the Sales Management Task. The Kramer Pharmaceuticals case briefly discussed in the "Prelude" is illustrative of a number of *management by assumption* phenomena associated with sales force management. In this case many of the elements of good sales force management simply were assumed away by management in Kramer, including sales force training, performance evaluation, and sales call and reporting systems.

That these components of sales management were assumed away, however, doesn't mean that ways of doing these things didn't become routinized and habitual to management anyway. The structure or "habits" of sales management (or any other sub-function in marketing) develop with or without attention to their good or ill growth. When they develop haphazardly, problems can occur.

One serious problem assumed away by Kramer management was the way in which management dealt with the recruiting, care, and feeding of its own sales management. These were the men and women who were charged with supervising the field sales effort, providing supervisory and developmental resources to field salespeople, and serving as top management's only reliable link to its physician-customers.

Sales managers in Kramer were recruited in the "normal" manner for many corporations: from the ranks of its field sales representatives. As the corporation grew with increasing rapidity, district manager positions became harder and harder to fill with the seasoned men and women that Kramer wanted. Kramer provided little training, formal or informal, for the district managers; it was assumed that their past successes at selling would yield an equivalent success at first-line supervision. As a consequence a succession of younger and younger individuals, most with little or no supervisory experience, were promoted to the district manager position.

Kramer's "lean and mean" sales force management staffing made the district manager's job nearly undoable under the best of circumstances. Each DM had responsibility for fourteen sales representatives, to each of whom were assigned some two hundred active accounts. Assuming a "standard" five calls per day from each representative, the DM was receiving some 350 call reports per week, 1,400 a month, and was supervising 16,800 calls per year! Clearly the DM was so overburdened by paperwork and his/her fourteen-person span of control that there was little time to do anything other than firefighting and filling out reports.

Further, it was Kramer policy that the district manager make ten to fifteen field visits per representative supervised per year. Assuming twelve such visits, a simple calculation shows that the district manager spent over 80 percent of his/her time on the road! How management is to be done in such an environment is not clear.

Kramer's "old guard," though, found the district managers' job doable if not easy. The experienced managers concentrated their time on their "problem" representatives and essentially left the other reps alone. Bob Marsh, who turned in good sales numbers year after year (even though he didn't conform to some of the company's preferences about organizing his records and making sales presentations) fell into the latter class for his early supervisors.

As younger men were promoted to the manager's job, they brought with them a desire to "manage" to all of Kramer's stated sales policies and procedures for each sales representative, perhaps because (old-timers would say) the youngsters didn't know enough to leave things alone or because (newer managers might hold) they were doing the job better. In the latter set of management beliefs, Bob Marsh became a "problem" salesperson.

A "good firing" or not, the case of Bob Marsh shows some deep structural problems in how Kramer manages its sales force, centered on the recruitment, selection, and allocation of district sales management. Further, the rest of Kramer's policies for sales management, from recruiting to performance evaluation, also were in disastrous disarray.

The sales vice president at Kramer, the "deck officer" for the selling function, has allowed first-line sales management in the company to be "assumed away." Apparently management had never asked about or considered the relationships between span of control, type of person recruited to the sales management job, and consequent needs for one versus another kind of sales representative. This vice president has every reason to expect serious consequences from this error—and more Bob Marsh situations.

Structural Contradiction in the Sales Management Task. The Computer Devices case briefly described in Chapter 1 illustrates another sales force management problem, this due to *structural contradiction.* At the time of the case CDI was a small, $17-million producer of "dumb" terminal equipment for the data-processing industry. Its margins were threatened because of competitive pressures, and a strategy was adopted to introduce a line of "smart" terminals, actually full-blown portable microcomputers, that could do complex applications on a stand-alone basis in the field.

CDI held a sales force "blitz" to market the smart machines, which was remarkably unsuccessful. The sales force collectively earned a single bonus point over the duration of the contest! Management was puzzled, but it is not hard to see why the CDI sales force couldn't sell the new "smart" computers. Consider the nature of the products the sales force *could* sell (dumb terminals) against the new ones they were being *asked* to sell ("smart" microcomputers):

	Dumb Terminals vs.	*Smart Terminals*
Products	Terminal, printer, modem	Terminal, microcomputer, printer, modem
Competition	Texas Instruments	Microcomputer firms
Growth	Low	High
Selling cycle	Short	Long
Software	Not needed	Not provided by CDI
Selling skills	Benefits-driven	Applications-driven
Buying pattern	Simple: data-processing dept.	Complex: operating managers

CDI's sales force was ill-equipped to sell the newer machines and ill-structured for the task. Men and women had been recruited to the sales force on the basis of their ability to make features/benefits presentations, not applications sales. Sales representatives' backgrounds, mostly as electronic technicians, made them especially well suited to debate the pros and cons of "baud rates" and other technical hardware details for dumb terminals, but at a loss when a client talked with them about, say, financial auditing applications software.

Worse, the target customers for the two products CDI wished to sell were very different. In the dumb terminals case reps sold to technically skilled and preconvinced data-processing personnel, but for the new microcomputers they had to persuade skeptical managers from many functional areas in the firm.

The sales force historically had been trained, compensated, and expected to go for short-cycle, high-volume, margin-sensitive dumb terminal sales; what management dropped in their laps, two years before microcomputers became plausible as management tools, were long-selling-cycle, software-sensitive, applications-oriented new products they did not know how to deal with.

Exhibit 3–1 illustrates what happens structurally when there are many selling and sales force management problems, as in the CDI

Exhibit 3–1. How the Components of Practice Can Get Out of Whack*

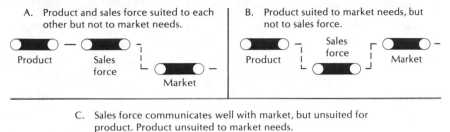

A. Product and sales force suited to each other but not to market needs.

B. Product suited to market needs, but not to sales force.

C. Sales force communicates well with market, but unsuited for product. Product unsuited to market needs.

*I am indebted to Professor Benson P. Shapiro, a colleague at the Harvard Business School, for this diagram.

dilemma. Basically, the sales force gets "out of synch" with either the product being offered to the market place (CDI's dilemma), or with the market itself.

The diagram shows three different ways that the "selling pipeline" of product, sales force, and market can become broken, at least two of which occurred in the CDI case. In the first panel (representative of one part of CDI's dilemma), the sales force was well tuned to dumb terminal selling, but management wished to target a new applications market. A way must be found to "move" the product and sales force pipes to fit the market's needs. In the second panel, we see that CDI's new "smart" terminals potentially fitted their market, but the sales force couldn't sell them.[3]

How the marketing pipeline gets broken often is multiply caused and defines a second element of structural contradiction. Basically, management in CDI did little to prepare the sales force for the new machine introduction.

In CDI's case the new machines were introduced to the sales force without much preparation for their entry and were given to representatives almost a year after they were promised. Further, the new product introduction failed to get the attention of sales representatives, because the commission on each "smart" unit, while higher than that for a "dumb" terminal sale, turned out to be less in actuality because of the difficulty of making a "smart" machine sale. In short, little was done to prepare the sales force for the strategic move being made by the company, even though the product had been in development for three years!

Management by assumption usually causes unperceived problems that simmer until they boil over. With marketing execution inefficiencies caused by structural contradiction, however, management often perceives an incipient problem and thinks it can overcome it by throwing training or compensation dollars at the symptoms. Usually compensation and training alone will be ineffective[4] because there is a plethora of political, organizational, and other roadblocks that serve as harsh constraints upon the exhortations of the trainers or the lure of the marginal pay dollar.

It is the *ritualization* of practice in marketing subfunctions, especially in sales management, that makes for structural contradiction. On the one hand, sales management demands the smart terminal sale. On the other, it has recruited, trained, and paid a sales force for some years *not* to be able to do this kind of selling! Such ritualizations are not susceptible to the easy fantasies painted in training seminars but require a concentrated attack on the *selling structure* in order to be overcome. Indeed, CDI's sales management should have started its program of sales representative broadening toward the selling skills required for smart terminals while the product still was in the developmental phase.

Global Mediocrity in Managing Selling. Global mediocrity occurs in the sales function in two ways. The "standard" way occurs when management is preoccupied with pseudo-democratic allocations of resources across different marketing functions. I'll discuss this below. Another avenue to this trap opens, however, when management becomes so preoccupied with "new ways" to reach its customers that it neglects to manage well the "old ways" of personal selling.

Telemarketing, distributor networks, direct mail, industrial stores, catalogs, direct-order marketing, and national accounts selling all are specializations of the selling function that offer the promise of pinpoint control over segmentation efforts. On the other hand, these new tools also raise the specter of management's need to be good at so many different jobs that the old-fashioned personal interaction with customers is mismanaged.

This is not to mention the plethora of other selling-related vehicles competing for the marketer's attention and the sales budget dollar: trade promotion, end user promotion, advertising, trade shows, and public relations, to name a few. As management tries to pinpoint its selling message by customer segment, selling stage (awareness, interest, desire, adoption, to name one popular model), product type, and available promotion dollars, it is increasingly likely that the marketing group will fail to pick a subset of these available customer-interaction tools for developing the special expertise that can give distinctive competence. Without distinctive competence mediocrity results, with attendant mediocre sales numbers and dissatisfied customers.

Distributor Relations and Sales Support

Hard on the heels of sales force management as a subfunctional execution problem in marketing is the management of channel relations. The distribution channel is and will remain a problematic marketing subfunction for most firms because of the built-in conflicts between manufacturer and reseller. At the margin the manufacturer would prefer to make a narrow product line available to the reseller, invoice goods before they are built, offer cash on delivery terms, and shift all warranty and service problems onto the shoulders of the distributor. The distributor, for his part, ideally would like the broadest product line possible from which to choose stocking items, would like all goods delivered on unlimited consignment, would pay only ninety days after he/she had sold them to the end user, and would want the manufacturer to handle credit checks and do all postsale servicing and warranty work.

These cross-preferences, though I overpaint them a bit, are common in vendor–distributor relations. However, so is the notion of *business partnership* in these same relations; in theory at least, one does not take on a distributor in the expectation of having a war, but rather because there is profit in the connection for both parties.

Yet the cooperative aspects of the manufacturer–distributor relationship can get completely "flooded out" by the competitive aspects. It is my experience that this "flooding" often is due to mishandling of the distributor relationship by management in the manufacturing firm.

Management by Assumption in Distributor Relationships. Consider the following instance of *management by assumption* in channel relationships that recently took place in a high-technology start-up venture. The vice president of marketing in this company was concerned that (1) its four agents were not following up on leads sent to them (one agent had 70 percent of its leads outstanding); (2)

when leads were followed up, closed sales were not achieved as frequently as desired (the agents were closing approximately one out of every ten leads approached); and (3) when a sale was closed, multiple units weren't being sold (an average of 1.1 units were sold per customer instead of the five expected). Basically, though, the vice president had a nagging feeling that there was a significant amount of hostility, "distancing," and other negative elements in the vendor's relationship with its agents that was threatening the distribution arrangement.

When the manager of agent distributors was questioned, the following information was learned. Management's actions to date vis-à-vis distributors consisted of the following: (1) The agents received a quota. While there was some discussion of the quota level, it essentially was set by vendor management. (2) The agents received a book of selling practices and procedures recommended by the vendor. (3) Vendor management traveled around to the distributorships to assure themselves that agent salespeople had indeed read the book.

In plain English, what had been done with agents was to (1) make a demand, (2) give a document, and (3) give an examination on the document! No wonder there were prospecting and closing problems: All the interactive, partnering, and other constructive aspects of the agent relationship had been assumed away by a very busy vendor management in the heat of market entry!

Worse, being in the fortunate position of *having* no ritualizations for how distributors should be managed, vendor management allowed a poor set of practices to develop. The probabilities are high that dysfunctional relationships will be recreated in every new geographical area that the vendor enters, because what was ritualized was ritualized poorly. It is almost easier to forgive management in an established firm with equally suboptimal agent relationships. At least management there can claim it inherited a balky distributor structure.

Structural Contradiction in Distribution Management.   Sometimes structural contradiction arises in distributor relationships because of a *good* development from a strategic point of view. Consider Binney & Smith, a $94-million maker of crayons and art materials.

The firm was faced with a declining birth rate, increasing petroleum costs, and a number of other factors that suggested its basic line of goods, crayons, would not remain a viable growth avenue into the 1980s. Management reasoned that since the firm's greatest asset was its Crayola name, it should distribute its many crayon and art-related products in an integrated "Crayola Fun Center" which would serve as a stand-alone display rack in chain and discount stores.

This move, it was thought, would have the triple effects of (1) solidifying the Crayola image by showing the company's broad, thirty-eight-item line in one place, (2) increasing both the inventory held by chain stores and distributors' profits by inclusion of higher-priced items on the rack, and (3) serving as a jumping-off point for further product diversifications (e.g. into clothes) with retail stores.

The Fun Centers worked beyond management's wildest dreams. Fifteen hundred units had been placed in a year, mostly to large chains like K-Mart. The units were selling as fast as they could be produced. Indeed, conservative projections indicated that the Fun Center line could add some $10 million to corporate sales in the fiscal year.

With burgeoning sales, however, came a problem management had anticipated but couldn't devise a good way to deal with. Large retail chains do not service their own shelves and are particularly averse to paying anyone else to do this job for them. Whatever else the Fun Centers were, Binney & Smith's management was sure that the units were essential to the firm's image development; understocked, vandalized, or otherwise ill-maintained units would only do the firm strategic harm, no matter how good the sales.

Management's problem was that neither its marketing nor its sales group was organized (or felt competent) to manage servicing the Fun Centers. When only a few Fun Centers had been sold, management had retained an outside contract servicing firm to deal with restocking the Fun Centers. This service firm, however, was terminated shortly after it was hired, because the outside firm was not "servicing the accounts assigned to them according to B&S standards." Essentially management experienced trouble interfacing the outside firm with its own territory representatives, felt ill-at-ease about relinquishing control over the customer relationship by using the outside firm, and was not able at managing this type of servicing arrangement.

On the other hand, B&S was not staffed to do its own servicing of the accounts. Territory managers couldn't do it; they had all they could handle selling the firm's six thousand accounts, only fifteen of which accounted for the Fun Center placements. B&S did have a small account servicing force, but its four people in no way could handle a geographic spread of Fun Center units that covered the entire continental United States with only four to ten units in most states.

Never having encountered the problem of regular retail restocking before (crayons are simply unboxed and tossed in a bin), B&S management was ill-prepared *either* (1) to deal with the problem directly or (2) to manage the outside relationships with contract servicers that could do servicing for B&S. In terms of our earlier discussion, no *habits* were in place to manage outside distribution servicers, and there was no *structure* that allowed the firm to do the job itself.

B&S was set up to sell and distribute crayons; it did so exceptionally well. Those very pathways to success for crayons, though, made "migration" to the Fun Center concept all the more difficult.

Global Mediocrity in Distribution Management. One of the most frequent ways that management's attention gets diffused when distributors are managed is that management attempts to make up for poor-quality distribution relationships with more distributors. Instead of fixing its distribution management structures and learning new low-level habits about the "partnering" aspects of distributor relationships, management often just keeps adding distributors in an attempt to get the "right" ones that will have high vendor commitment despite few signs of reciprocity on the vendor's part.

Consider Exhibit 3–2, which shows a graphic representation of ten years' distribution history for a large recreational product supplier. The solid line shows the number of dealers by year; the dashed line shows the average sales per dealer. Management seems to go in "great cycles" on the distribution problem, first overrecruiting marginal distributors, then in subsequent years winnowing out marginal ones. As the list gets winnowed, however, management appears to be dissatisfied still that it has the "right" partners, and rerecruits more distributors to begin the winnowing process again. Each time this happens, distributor sales, on average, go down.

It could be argued that there's nothing wrong with the distribution management tactic paralleling Alex Karras's football one: "Grab everybody, then throw people out until you find the guy

Number/Distributor   Sales/Distributor

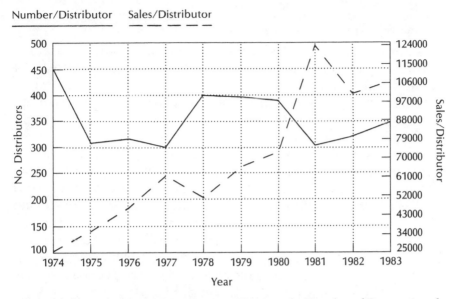

Exhibit 3–2. Nine-Year Distribution History of a Vendor of Recreational Products

with the ball." The difference between football and distributor relationships, of course, is that the former is a purely competitive game and the latter is *supposed* to be a partially cooperative one. Whether management decks its time and money against developing a truly able cadre of quality dealers or spends its limited resources trying to *find* these distributors already existing makes a real difference. The former tactic is likely to work over time; the latter is likely to contain all the seductive promise of middle-aged flirting with most of the same disappointments at consummation.

Indeed, management at this company spent little to no money and gave less attention to building the dealer "commitment" it claimed it so sorely wanted. Instead, it had a total of seven salespeople to manage the entire dealer net, did little training, and gave the salespeople wide latitude in both signing up new dealers and terminating old ones. In essence management ducked the marketing "homework" of making its current distributor relations work over the years by continual distributor replacement; when it recognized this and concentrated on building the commitment it spent so much time talking about, sales per dealer went up remarkably.

Pricing Structures

It is hard to cite examples of management by assumption in the way pricing is done in most corporations. This is not because there are no examples; rather, it is because there are almost no examples where price implementation *isn't* primarily done by sheer assumption!

Consider the following case, which is an instance of clever execution undertaken from very strong assumptions. In 1980–81, both Hertz and Avis experienced moderate market share erosion because of aggressive pricing on commercial accounts by rival Budget Rent-a-Car. Budget, with a military-like strategy to gain share and a corporate policy to be lower-priced than Hertz "no matter what," was a new wrinkle in the cutthroat but stable share battle between Hertz and Avis. The whole problem started when Hertz, in a "signaling" price move, raised its prices to commercial accounts. Avis followed, and Budget didn't.

By March 1981 the other major competitors in the market had lowered their commercial rates to Budget's lower prices (Hertz did not). Budget reacted by establishing a flat rate for all its commercial business. That is, customers were charged a flat rate per day, and unlimited mileage was provided too.

Hertz responded in May 1981 with a "no mileage, ever" campaign targeted at *all* its customers, commercial *and* leisure. The move received wide attention in the media (it was picked up by more than six hundred television stations' evening news programs) and was well-received by customers, Hertz's own personnel, and everyone else connected with the industry (except the competition). The "no mileage, ever" program was successful in boosting Hertz's market share, but it's not clear at what cost.

At the time Hertz made its pricing move, the company accrued 75 percent of its revenues from business users and 25 percent from leisure ones. But in terms of profits the business users provided only 58 percent, while the leisure segment contributed 42 percent! Why would a company, and managers as smart as Hertz has available, apply a near-profitless pricing scheme to its most profitable segment, when all it had to do to become viable again was to meet the competition in the commercial areas with flat-rate pricing?

The president of Hertz himself gives the answer. He notes that Hertz had *always* been "Number 1" in rental cars, and he felt a need to make a pricing move that would reassert the company's industry leadership.[5] But granting this, how could the company make the numbers work?

Hertz essentially made a powerful set of assumptions about the increased volume to be garnered from the pricing move with leisure renters. Management reasoned that although the new business would not be very profitable, they would regain market share and, like the old joke, "would make the losses up on volume." They didn't.

The Benco case described briefly in Chapter 1 also is illustrative of structural contradiction in pricing. Benco invented a new kind of drainage pipe twice as effective as its own or anyone else's brands. The company wished to price the pipe high, consistent with the added value received by users. However, the firm's pricing structure, from the way plant managers were compensated (feet of pipe produced per minute), to sales force planning (the sales force thought in terms of pounds of raw material sold), to management control systems militated against this textbook solution. Indeed the structural contradiction between the firm's commodity orientation and its new invention ran so deeply that the problem for management was as much a *cultural* or *policy* problem as it was a pricing one. We'll return to this case again in the chapter on marketing theme.

Other Marketing Subfunctions

I use sales force management, distribution management, and pricing implementation as extended examples because my research convinces me that these are the most likely marketing actions to go awry when strategies and plans are put into action. Many other subfunctions can be problematical too, though space (and my research base) precludes a full consideration of them.

Advertising, with its peculiar resistance to measurement,[6] sales promotion, and the new product development process are among the marketing subfunctions I've studied that have a diagnosis set identical to that discussed for the sales force, distribution, and pricing. When things go wrong with these subfunctions, they go wrong for one of three reasons:

- Management makes some powerful assumptions about customers', intermediaries', or competitors' responses that seem reasonable on first blush but are not borne out by events. Whether because of its pretensions to superior knowledge, laziness, or just "falling through the cracks," much of the down-and-dirty detail-oriented homework in low-level marketing functions just doesn't get done.

- Management asks its subfunctions to do things for which they were not designed, and which they cannot deliver without massive amounts of preparation, rethinking, and perhaps reorganization. I call this phenomenon "structural contradiction."
- Management tries too hard to do too much, and as a consequence doesn't develop a unique competency in *one or a few* of its marketing subfunctions that can serve the same function that cornerstones do for buildings.

This last phenomenon, "global mediocrity," merits further discussion.

GLOBAL MEDIOCRITY

One of the most difficult realizations for managers (or anyone else) to come to terms with is that there are not enough resources to go around. This is one of those platitudes that is profoundly easy to say and profoundly difficult to *believe.* It is only natural for management to want *all* marketing's subfunctions to be excellent, to be known simultaneously as having a crackerjack sales force, a heavy and effective advertising program, deeper pockets with distributors, flashier trade shows, and lower pricing. With no exceptions that I know, allocating people, money, and time as if this convenient fiction were reality leads to "global mediocrity."

Many managers are uncomfortable with the notion that actions-level excellence in marketing has to be attained piecemeal, one subfunction at a time. Indeed, one executive, commenting on a *Harvard Business Review* article[7] I wrote containing this claim, argued that this proposition was just flat wrong and that managers needed an "arsenal of excellence" across the board in marketing.

There are two pieces of evidence to suggest that this view is dysfunctional to good marketing practice at the lowest levels. The first are my clinical observations of global mediocrity, which suggest across the board that an inability to make tough and inequitable choices among marketing subfunctions often produces the very mediocrity management hopes to avoid.

The second is the way companies who are recognizably *good* at low-level marketing practices do things. Management in the Personal Care Division at the Gillette Company, for instance, shows a genius at advertising. For any one program its product may be only debatably better than the competition's; sometimes its trade relations could stand improvement; once in a while goods are not competitively priced.[8] But always, because of top management focus, attention, and overallocation of time, money, and people, its advertising campaign is brilliant. Indeed, the division's skills at this marketing subfunction serve as a cornerstone for everything else that is done in marketing, and as a market place force that gives it a unique competitive edge.

Similarly, at Frito-Lay, Incorporated, the store-door delivery system requires management to retain more than ten thousand salespeople, an equal number of trucks, and to pay more than 20 percent of every dollar in distribution costs to maintain this unique system. Yet as all commentators, from Peters[9] to me, who have studied the company come to see, what management has built is a unique competency at distribution of goods of a particular sort (short shelf-life, frequent restocking needs, low unit prices) that competitors just cannot match. The trade, a cynical lot, is impressed with the system too, because it requires less work on grocery store personnel's part. The customers, a finicky group, are always provided with a fresh, recently stocked, neat display of FLI products that is the same whether the shopper is in Joplin, Missouri, or Seattle, Washington. The result is a unique competitive advantage that the company has used recently to leverage itself into the cookie business.

None of this is to say that Gillette or FLI doesn't have good products, a good trade show program, or careful pricing. Rather, it argues that low-level marketing subfunctions are a complicated and tricky bag of very different skills, and that those firms best at getting the marketing job done in the trenches are willing to dedicate special effort, attention, and money to becoming good at a chosen subset of these actions, which can become the basis for all that the firm does in marketing.

BLOCKING AND TACKLING

Though I shall have much more to say about good practice in marketing when we reach the "Skills" section of the book, it should not be concluded from this discussion that *all* firms' habitual ways of doing advertising, pricing, distribution, or the like are dysfunctional. Indeed, my clinical observations show many instances of firms that "do things right" when it comes to low-level marketing subfunctions. It is worthwhile considering some aspects of what good low-level marketing practices look like, at least in a summary sense here.

The most important thing to understand about low-level marketing actions is that a "way of doing things" quickly becomes habituated, or structured, in all corporations. Managerial latitude gets restricted by these structures, because the "usual" way of accomplishing pricing or distributor management is the path of least resistance. Structures for low-level marketing actions form whether we want them to or not; the critical question is whether they form to encourage good practices or to inhibit them.

The "cures" to the diseases of management by assumption, structural contradiction, and global mediocrity are not difficult in concept, only in practice. From a number of companies I have studied, the "rules" used by management to get the low-level marketing jobs done look almost absurdly simple:

1. *Top* management must involve itself, mostly by expressing interest (but also by direct intervention where necessary), in the "low-level" trivia it has worked so hard to earn the right to ignore. What is not emphasized by top management will not be done well —period. We shall return to this point in a later chapter.

2. Management by assumption is treated by a continual appeal to the "field" in the best companies, whether that "field" comprises the sales force, the customers, the competition, or distributors. Again, by example, top management gets out to learn what the customers want, not what the marketing staff says customers want. Distributors are *talked to*, not simply dictated to. Competitors are studied, not ignored nor emulated without reason.

3. Structural contradiction is avoided by understanding that there *are* structures in low-level marketing subfunctions and realizing early that, say, a sales force recruited, trained, and paid to sell dumb terminals *will not* be able to sell microcomputers without a significant developmental period and strong changes in compensation, skills, and perhaps even composition. To avoid structural contradiction management must be willing to do "marketing development" while the product is in R&D, so that the subfunctional abilities to sell it will be present when it makes its ap-

pearance. The same arguments could be made for distributor management, pricing moves, and marketing's other subfunctions.

4. Global mediocrity is avoided by management's willingness to make tough choices, the toughest being an executional translation of its strategy into one or a few low-level marketing tasks at which the firm *must* excel. These *must haves* are different from the "want to haves," and the former will receive disproportionate time, resources, personnel, and attention to form the basis for all that the corporation does in marketing.

CONCLUSION

If all of this sounds absurdly simple, the reason is that it *is* absurdly simple. If it sounds as if I think most of the problems we experience with low-level marketing subfunctions can be laid at the door of management, and many at the door of top management, it is because I do so think from my observations. If it sounds as if better management of the structure, more careful thinking, and, most important, a "homework and details" theme in the corporation would solve 90 percent of the problems that I regularly observed when low-level marketing tasks are executed, it is because that is true as well. It all comes back to management.

As we shall learn later, without "subfunctional soundness," the ability to execute those low-level, dirty little subfunctions about which we would all like to forget in our grand rush to formulate the next world-level strategic move to confound the competition, nothing whatsoever works in marketing. It is to the blocking and tackling we must first attend.

CHAPTER FOUR

Marketing Programs

Mountains should be climbed with as little effort as possible and without desire. The reality of your own nature should determine the speed. If you become restless, speed up. If you become winded, slow down. You climb the mountain in an equilibrium between restlessness and exhaustion. Then, when you're no longer thinking ahead, each footstep isn't just a means to an end but a unique event in itself. This leaf has jagged edges. This rock looks loose. From this place the snow is less visible, even though closer. These are things you should notice anyway. To live only for some future goal is shallow. It's the sides of the mountain which sustain life, not the top.

—Robert Pirsig, *Zen and the Art of Motorcycle Maintenance*

RECENTLY I SPENT a couple of days selling high-performance computers with the sales force of a specialty manufacturer. Top management in this company had sought help because it seemed that their company was strategy-less and without even a good planning system that could lead toward a marketing strategy. Their problem, interestingly, had nothing at all to do with strategy and much to do with the subject of this chapter.

What I found from my day selling and some subsequent time with management was an implementation problem, one frequently encountered when marketing programs are executed. Management in this firm had "geared up" special end user marketing programs for its computing machines on *six* separate occasions in the last three years. None had worked.

In one notable example designed to penetrate an end user applications market, sales representatives familiar with the application were hired across the company's sales branches, special brochures detailing the advantages of the firm's computers were written, demonstration software was compiled, but a product promised for this program was never delivered by headquarters. In a second instance, a program to penetrate the graphics market, corporate headquarters terminated its attempt *one week* after the demonstration units had been received by the sales force, and even before prospects could be invited in to see the unit (sufficient margins could not be generated from the program, management believed). In each case some different low-level marketing function had "gone wrong" and fouled up well-laid plans.

In this *and all the rest of the six cases,* management had pulled back on its plans within nine months and declared the marketing program a failure (leaving specialized reps in place who were at a loss as to what to do for a living). Only shortly thereafter corporate marketing announced yet another program to penetrate a different segment with yet another package of tailored marketing innovations.

Had this phenomenon occurred once, twice, or even three times, it might have been a consequence of poor program design or the lack of strategy the firm claimed (if anything, it seemed the company suffered from *too much* strategy!). But the six-in-a-row statistic, which included ventures as diverse as a work station that wouldn't communicate with the firm's larger machines and an operating system innovation that was not applied consistently across the firm's products, leads even a casual observer to suspect that the problem wasn't with marketing's programs at all.

Rather, there was the distinct feeling that two very different things were going on to cause repeated program failures. First, it seemed that the marketing actions discussed in Chapter 3 were problematic for the firm. In other words, it was not the programs themselves that were weak or ill conceived, but rather the organization's inability to execute the pricing, product, and other low-level components of those programs that was causing the repetitive problems.

In addition, there seemed to be a clear lack of management *resolve* when each new program was undertaken. It was almost as if management had no clear sense of who it was or where it was going in marketing, and so tentatively engaged a number of different programs that were abandoned at the first sign of less-than-overwhelming market acceptance.

Interestingly, management seemed to take some succor from its failures at each of these programmatic ventures. It underinvested in them to begin with (as if it didn't believe they would work). Then, having shown a propensity for engaging in programs it couldn't execute, management seemed to *congratulate* itself with each failure on having had the wisdom to commit itself tentatively in the first place. Finally, it set about happily designing the *next* program it could not execute.

It was the happiness I found fascinating. It seemed not at all unlike that displayed by my two-year-old, whose towers of blocks inevitably topple not because the concept of the tower is faulty, but rather because his motor skills are too gross to permit the manipulations necessary to execute the design. His resolve, from moment to moment, has no staying power. Like this management, he keeps on building what will not stand.[1]

MARKETING PROGRAMS

If marketing actions are the low-level blocking and tackling by which the essentials of the marketing job are executed, *marketing programs* are the tactical playbook integrating low-level marketing functions in the service of a brand or a special segment.

Programs are the most natural "unit of analysis" to the marketer. It is with these formally or informally tailored combinations of product, pricing, promotion, and distribution[2] that the marketer hopes to add unique value to his firm's offerings and differential satisfaction to the customer. When programs work, they provide focus, competitive differentiation, and high consumer satisfaction quotients, which allow increased profit-taking. When they do not, which happens frequently from my observations, the damage done to the marketing effort is profound.

Programs in marketing are of two types. *Product-focused programs* construct custom combinations of the firm's low-level marketing abilities centered around a product, product line, or service. Brand management as it is done in many consumer companies and not a few industrial ones is a prime example of product-focused programmatic marketing. The brand or product manager has responsibility for integrating product development, advertising, packaging, research, pricing implementation, and other low-level functions to maximize market share of his or her brand of goods. Even where sales is done in a pooled fashion, it is the brand manager's job to tailor the selling effort through special promotions and persuasion of sales management so that the brand managed receives the specialized attention it deserves.

Customer-focused programs are those combinations of low-level marketing actions where the marketing goal is to tailor the "marketing mix" of the company better to a special segment or customer group. When firms set up special national account management groups, it is an example of a customer-focused marketing program. Special products may be offered to key accounts at special prices, promoted in distinctive ways, and vended by a dedicated sales force. Often access to the special products and selling team cannot be obtained by other customers of the company. Though national account programs are a prime example of customer-focused marketing programs, *any* customization of the "marketing mix" for special segments qualifies as a customer-focused marketing program.

Whether product- or customer-focused, the goal of marketing programs is to tailor the nature of the offering to the end user or distribution channel by creatively and synergistically combining low-level marketing actions. This chapter looks at marketing programs and what goes on when they are executed. Both product-focused and customer-focused programs are examined later, though a similar set of management processes is at work in the implementation of both.

The central argument of the chapter is that marketing programs constructed by management often *appear* coherent but actually are empty shells that promise much and deliver nothing. This is because declaring marketing programs is easily done, *whether or not* management has in place the low-level marketing structures to execute such programs or the high-level resolve to consummate them. Programs, meant to be coherent combinations of good low-level marketing structure, can too easily become only convenient substitutes for the absence of the low-level structures that management is too busy to construct right. Or they can mirror management's policy-level confusion as to what marketing is about.

Having *named* or *declared* a program to accomplish the task in question with a relevant product or segment, management then can convince itself that it has done its job and need worry no further about its inability to execute the program's components. Since such programs, of course, do not work, management finds it convenient to declare still more programs. These do not work either, for the problem lies not in the presence or absence of programs but with the low-level execution abilities or the overall direction management may be missing.

The declaration of programs that fail can become a vicious circle, so that management winds up with a very thick playbook of marketing programs that are continually invented, revised, implemented, and then falsely blamed for the market failures that result. In this view marketing programs often serve as a kind of "flashiness" or "trendiness" in marketing, when the company has neither the low-level marketing structures to make its strategies work nor the top-level discipline to recognize this fact.

I have found this phenomenon of program formulation without the ability to execute so frequently that I have invented names for different ways in which the phenomenon occurs. Much of this chapter explores the variations on this unhappy phenomenon. The last section talks about better practices when programs are executed.

PROGRAM MANAGEMENT AND MISMANAGEMENT

Empty Promises Marketing

John Hayes, marketing director at North American Philips Lighting Corporation (NAPLCO), had an unenviable job. Philips's recent program to get Norelco-branded light bulbs on the grocery shelves, dubbed "Project Shopping Cart," had been a failure on almost every dimension. Yet Hayes's management and corporate management at parent North American Philips were committed to the strategy of making Norelco-branded bulbs the third major force in the consumer light bulb business after G.E. and Westinghouse. Hayes was charged with trying yet again to make it all work.

NAPLCO was a small ($30-million) subsidiary of giant N.V. Philips. The division primarily produced and sold industrial lighting equipment and also produced a line of private-label and promotional goods sold under supermarkets' own brand labels as off-price competition to G.E.'s and Westinghouse's well-known national brands. Because upper management feared that NAPLCO's niche as a private-label manufacturer was not secure from entry by the giant light bulb makers, it formulated a strategy to put Norelco bulbs on the supermarket shelves as a third national brand.

The light bulb market appeared ripe for such a creative strategic move. The grocery store share of total light bulb sales had been in slow decline over the last five years, while hardware and discount store sales had picked up. Light bulbs were the grocers' most profitable store item per linear foot of goods stocked. The market was dominated by General Electric, with approximately 60 percent of the market; next was Westinghouse, with over 20 percent of bulb sales. NAPLCO management figured that with its proven capabilities at making quality bulbs, the strong Norelco name, and the profits a third line of bulbs potentially offered supermarkets, it would be a snap to gain a small but profitable portion of the market for the firm.

Project Shopping Cart was structured to make this conquest. A new and clever gravity-fed display was designed on the basis of consumer research, as was a novel transparent and protective package for the bulbs themselves. The display held twelve of the most popular light bulb types (fifty were ordinarily carried by supermarkets and double that number constituted a "full line"). NAPLCO set about "selling in" this program to retailers across the country.

At the end of two and one-half years of effort, the company had grossed only $1.1 million, against its forecast revenues of $7.5 million. A minuscule 0.3 percent market share had been achieved, and $600,000 had been lost. Management currently was sitting on more than $500,000 of the special racks and light bulb packages. Project Shopping Cart, in short, failed miserably.

A look at the program suggests many plausible reasons for the failure. First, the line offered to the supermarkets probably was too narrow, and the clever new display rack consumed too much space to allow easy trial by retailers. The program used heavy "push" money to try to get the bulbs on retailers' shelves but almost no "pull" advertising or other consumer appeals to get end users into the store demanding Norelco bulbs. Indeed, NAPLCO's largest consumer promotion came in the form of recruiting Bruce Jenner to pose on posters used at the point of purchase; no other advertising was done.

The program was rolled out nationally as opposed to regionally, demanding management resources NAPLCO didn't have. Worse, NAPLCO, having no direct sales force capable of servicing and selling the supermarket chains, was forced to rely on brokers, who could give the line only intermittent attention and who had real troubles convincing supermarket managers *why* they needed a third brand of bulb. The trade's reaction was that if more shelf space for bulbs would garner more profits, they might as well add to their existing shelf footage with known brands.

While any of these reasons is a good explanation for what went wrong with Project Shopping Cart, none is sufficient. Rather what seems to have gone on is that management of an industrial lighting group tried to launch a full-blown consumer marketing effort that the low-level marketing structure in NAPLCO hadn't the vaguest idea of how to execute. Management essentially created a program that contained many elements of good thinking to get Norelco bulbs on the shelves but failed to realize or ignored the fact that the low-level marketing structures of their division had none of the experience or familiarity with the tasks necessary to get the job done.

No advertising had been done before to any degree in the division, so management just *didn't* advertise in Project Shopping Cart. No supermarket sales force was available, so brokers were used, as they had always been used to sell the private label goods. The brokers, who handled multiple lines and were perhaps better at account servicing than new product sell-ins, were ineffective in distributing the bulbs. It was unclear what sort of line to offer the supermarkets, so a unilateral product assortment decision was made. In short, Project Shopping Cart was an ''empty promise'' for NAPLCO's management, its distribution channel, its supermarket triers, and its potential end users. It promised what the company could not deliver from a low-level execution point of view.

Empty promises marketing, as the case example points out, occurs when management creates programs it does not have the subfunctional capability to execute. The marketing functions in this industrially and generically oriented company were unable to supply the retail blocking and tackling that top management simply assumed would "be there" to implement its well-conceived plans. The result was an empty promise for all concerned.

Had this firm and this management attempted a marketing program more in line with their considerable subfunctional skills at marketing, say with industrial key accounts or even for "off-price" promotional goods, I suspect they would have succeeded. Empty promises marketing does *not* mean that NAPLCO did not have good low-level marketing structures in place; rather, like structural contradiction discussed in Chapter 3, the structure was not equipped to deliver on the tasks asked of it.[3]

Empty promises marketing is not limited to product-focused programs but is equally likely to occur when customer-focused programs are implemented. Applicon, for instance, a growing graphics computer vendor, wished to install a national accounts program to serve better its small but rapidly growing number of key accounts. Management recruited a highly regarded national account manager from another company and gave him a secretary and a mandate to put a key accounts program together. After a year and a half in the job, top management reported it was dissatisfied with the new man's performance; key account coordination programs continued, and the only visible progress they could cite was a seven-page key account contract. The new program seemed to promise much but deliver little.

The firm, a rapidly growing one, made CAD/CAM equipment which was useful in automating many drafting and design tasks. Interestingly, most of its current purchasers were small, single-site users. Indeed, with the exception of its recently declared national accounts program, every marketing act the company took seemed to gear the firm as the vendor of choice for small users but as an unattractive source for large, multisite accounts.

The sales force was deployed toward smaller accounts and better suited to serve them. The computer-design machine itself did everything adequately but served no single application outstandingly, making it more suitable to those with a broad set of needs. Company pricing on the machine offered lower list prices than the competition but correspondingly lower discounts from book price during negotiations. This practice too was biased against key account sales, where buyers often were measured on the depth of discount from list prices they were able to negotiate. Finally, postsales service pricing on the company's offering was set some

10–20 percent above that of the competition, with no discounts for a larger installed base of machines.

The new manager was given no authority over the sales force and, indeed, reported to the sales vice president. His position in the firm was largely one of coordination and "moral suasion," trying to convince otherwise unready sales and service arms that the machine offered to a key account company ought to be priced, sold, and serviced differently from the identical unit for a smaller account. The sales and service forces, not surprisingly, were somewhat resistant to this notion.

The national accounts program in this company served as a simple declaration of comfortability to management: It could not work as structured and was only an "empty promise" made by management to itself and to its key accounts. The firm and the management in question were competent at serving the smaller user and, had it attempted a marketing program here, probably would have done very well indeed. But just declaring a program and appointing an individual to staff it is not enough to make the firm's subfunctional execution suitable for key accounts.

Bunny Marketing

The difference between empty promises marketing and bunny marketing is that in bunny marketing programs are created intentionally or unintentionally *as a cover* or self-deception for the absence of strong and shared marketing implementation policies, like clear marketing theme or strong leadership. In empty promises marketing sound subfunctional structure is present but is misdirected by program demands.

I shall devote a later chapter to marketing implementation policies, but a brief preview is in order to allow understanding of bunny marketing's causes. As Chapter 2 noted, there are two kinds of critical implementation policies: those of *identity* and those of *direction*. The former are inculcated by management's actions to set a clear marketing *theme* in the organization and engender a felicitous marketing *culture*. The latter are inculcated by top management's strength of *leadership* and, of course, by the marketing strategy. Where there are weak leaders at the top, or where there is no clarity of theme and vision to give the entire marketing organization and all its tactical acts a driving, resonating single-mindedness, bunny marketing is the likely result. In bunny

marketing[4] a profusion of marketing programs is employed, usually unintentionally, as a "mask" for these unclear marketing
policies.

A heavy manufacturing company in my sample was continually
frustrated because it introduced its new products late into a market
where spare parts inventories and operator loyalties gave the first-
in vendor significant advantages. One of its key products, a
machine for special conditions, was introduced almost two years
after the competition's entry, even though the firm's own machine
had been in development a year earlier.

For years management had kept its thin engineering and
development staff busy with a torrent of projects, some to rework
designs already in the field, others to make minor modifications to
accessory equipment. There was also a major R&D project to design a prototype machine under government contract that would
not be commercially feasible for a decade. The engineers were
asked to respond to all these demands *and* design the new
machine.

The chairman of the corporation, a design engineer himself,
seemed to encourage the diffusion of attention in product development because of his own strong interest in each and every one of
the projects on the drawing boards. All were important in his view,
all were significant, and all correctly captured the essence of the
firm.

Yet it wasn't clear to anyone in the company, especially not to
sales or the development engineering staff, just *what the company
was as a marketing entity.* Did it stand mostly as a firm reworking old
technologies to make them better, as an R&D shop that worked on
government grants that could not be commercialized for decades,
or as a market follower that introduced machines significantly better than the competition's too late to capture any share? Worse,
none of this was clear to customers, who were confused by the
firm's claims that its machines were suited primarily for tough applications but seemed to break down with more frequency than
other brands.

In essence, top management in this firm failed to set a clear
direction and focus for marketing's "front end" efforts, confusing
its own developmental engineering staff, the sales force, *and* the
customers at once. The entire marketing structure consequently
seemed to lack a clear sense of who the firm was and what it did in
the market place. The result was a kind of "identity disarray" that

kept the development effort lagging and relegated the firm to a low-share, follower position.

The specialty computer vendor discussed at the beginning of this chapter illustrates additionally the "bunny marketing" phenomenon when it stems from lack of clarity about marketing purpose *and* less than sound subfunctional structures. Here, the weak sense of marketing identity, or "theme,"[5] inculcated by management fostered less than complete commitment on its part to anything it did, while weak actions-level structures made failure all the more probable.

TOWARD GOOD PROGRAMS PRACTICE

Not every marketing program is a victim of empty promises or bunny marketing. But more programs are victimized than are not by those phenomena, if my observations are any indication. I should first like to bring some of what was discussed above together in one place as a set of diagnostic aids for the marketer wishing to evaluate his/her firm's marketing programs. Then I'll write more positively about the factors implicated in the good execution of marketing programs.

Diagnosing Programmatic Ills: "Negative Rules"

Consolidating what has been discussed above in summary fashion, it is possible to give a brief set of guidelines for the manager to look for when marketing programs seem not to work the way they are expected to. These diagnostic aids are formulated here in the form of what I call "negative rules"; where signs of these are present, it is probable that there will be trouble with programs execution.

- It is not true that the firm with the most or even the most clever marketing programs is the best at program execution. Rather a profusion of programs frequently (but not always) means that these are being used to disguise a shortcoming somewhere else in the marketing execution structure. Usually the shortcoming is either in a mismatch of the low-level execution abilities of the marketing structure, the actions, or in the clarity of theme and vision for marketing that has been set up by top management, the policies. Negative Rule 1 is this: **The presence of many clever marketing programs, a great** tactical "playbook," is no indicator of good marketing practices. Indeed, it may be an indicator of execution problems.

- More often than not, the real culprit when marketing programs fail is not the programs themselves, which are coherently chosen combinations of marketing's low-level subfunctions like pricing, advertising, and product development. Rather, **when programs go awry, the usual culprit is the low-level marketing actions themselves** (Negative Rule 2).

Either the low-level marketing structure is being asked to do things for which it was not constructed and with which it cannot cope, or else the firm's marketing blocking and tackling abilities are weak and cannot respond to even reasonable requests. In the first instance, of course, empty promises marketing results. In the second, bunny marketing makes an ugly appearance.

- When the programs are not working and no problem can be found with low-level marketing actions, look to high-level marketing implementation policy directives (see Chapter 6). Negative Rule 3 states, **where a profusion of failing programs is discovered, a suspected cause should be top management's failure to provide a clear marketing theme and strong marketing culture, an "identity" for all that is done in the marketing job.**

Good Program Practices

I shall have more to say about good program practices in the "Skills" section of the book when management interventions in faulty structures are discussed. Here, though, are some observations about the program *structures* I found in companies that seem able to conceive and consummate marketing programs with good market place effects.

First, and not surprisingly, these companies often show (by just counting) fewer simultaneous programs than companies having marketing program problems. It seems as if the managements in question in the better firms show a strong strain toward what I have come to call "program pickiness." The *main* marketing programs engaged by the company are relatively few in number and are pursued with a vengeance by management[6] because they are the core of the marketing organization.

But coupled with "program pickiness" comes allocation extravagance. Having been especially careful and focused about *which* programs get into the marketing mainstream and having said no to many others, the managements in the better execution shops then invest heavily in their choices. Nothing is stinted for a program that has management's commitment; not time, not its best people, not money. There is a sense of commitment to the "rightness" of the program that keeps management in there plugging, sometimes after others would have abandoned the business.

The example at Frito-Lay with GrandMa's Cookies is a case in point. For a number of reasons that seemed to make excellent sense, in 1980 FLI management decided to "export" its well-known salty snack consumer franchise to the cookie business, a slow-growth category that seemed ripe for the picking. An entire line of single-serve cookies and snack bars was created under the GrandMa's label, a brand and technology with a strong regional (Western) reputation that FLI had acquired. A full marketing push was undertaken to get GrandMa's on the grocery store shelves and achieve significant market shares. Indeed, management planned to create a $120-million business out of thin air in little more than two years.

Unfortunately, the trade did not agree with FLI's plans, or at least portions of them. FLI's line of cookies and snack bars met with good acceptance among the many "up and down the street" accounts, the smaller delicatessen owners, but with strong chain store and supermarket resistance. Supermarket owners just didn't want to allocate the additional space to FLI's new entry, because they didn't think single-serve cookies would sell well. While management eventually ran the business up to about a $50-million annual level through good small account sales, the goal of penetrating the supermarkets was not met, and FLI management considered the program a real failure.

Instead of abandoning its commitment or accepting a business volume others would have been grateful for, FLI management reformulated its product, rethought its business concept toward head-to-head competition with Nabisco, and went back out with a second program in 1982 to put bulk-packaged ready-to-eat cookies on the supermarket shelves. While it is too early to tell what the results of these "cookie wars" will be, FLI currently has good retail distribution, a quality product, and, most important, a program it "picked" carefully and then allocated to "extravagantly" to make work.

The keys to good marketing program management, then, can be captured in a single-phrase generalization: program pickiness with allocation extravagance. Of course there are many other requirements for marketing program success. The firm's subfunctions need to be capable of getting the job done. Marketing systems, the bane of many marketers' existence, have to work or at least get out of the marketer's way so that the job *can* be done. Marketing policies, especially those of identity and direction, need to be remarkably clear in order for the programs to be construed well in the first place. But these topics are the subject of other chapters.

Moving the Organization to New Endeavor

Much of what has been said in earlier sections about empty promises marketing or bunny marketing can be construed to mean that it is very hard to get marketing structures to do things for which they were not designed. That is true, and it is worth some discussion to detail just how innovation in marketing is well managed.

Companies excellent at the marketing job are not less innovative than their more programmatic but less competent peers; in fact they are more so. But, as the sword swallower notes, ''it's *how* you do it that makes the difference.''

The foregoing discussions give some hints for good innovation management. First, program pickiness implies that management has the discipline to say no to many interesting, indeed, potentially highly profitable programs that just don't meet (1) the organization's current low-level marketing abilities or, more likely, (2) top management's vision and theme for the marketing organization. But even with these clear constraints, there will be a need for old marketing organizations to learn new tricks in some instances.

The critical difference between those programs that work and those that don't, however, is a kind of gradualism that allows the organization to learn *how to manage* the new endeavor before everything is ''on the line,'' when a single action spells the difference between success and failure. FLI's initial entry into cookies with single-serve items is a case in point. Though I suspect management did not *plan* for its single-serve cookie business to fall short of goals, the product introduced (single-serve cookies) by its nature was a less risky program for management to start with than a head-to-head competition with Nabisco in the ready-to-eat market. Going the former way allowed management (1) to learn some things about the cookie business, (2) to learn how to adapt its considerable store-door distribution skills to a business that looked similar but was in fact rather different, and (3) to minimize the managerial consequences of not achieving objectives. Had FLI gone first to bulk ready-to-eat cookies, I doubt that the firm would be in the cookie business now.

Contrast this gradualism with the specialty computer vendor, or the other computer vendor that wished to put in a national accounts program. In both instances highly public, risky, and precipitous program decisions were taken with no time for the organization to figure out what it was doing or how to manage the "new marketing direction." In both instances the programs caused unfavorable reactions, and even resistances, among the firm's own marketing personnel, who were not unwilling to learn new tricks but were exposed daily to the implementation glitches that top management had not thought through before making its pronouncements.

CONCLUSION

Marketing programs should be seen as the synergistic combinations of low-level marketing skills that they are. Just because an athlete is a good skier and a good rifleman does not mean that he or she can compete in a biathlon (an Olympic event for skiing cross-country, then stopping and shooting at targets) without some time to practice putting the skills together. Turning on a dime is a good ability for new cars and for venture start-ups with little or no structure; it is a physical impossibility for most established marketing organizations.

Marketing programs often are mistaken for the heart of marketing practices. Actually they are only the *outcomes* of other, more fundamental things management does in marketing. These include the low-level blocking and tackling of subfunctions and the guidance of policy directives as affected by marketing's systems. It is to the systems, then the policies, that we now turn.

CHAPTER FIVE

Marketing Systems

I know that age to age succeeds,
Blowing a noise of tongues and deeds,
A dust of systems and of creeds.

Alfred, Lord Tennyson, *The Two Voices*

PAUL JONES, PRESIDENT of Macon Prestressed Concrete Company (MPCC), wasn't sure he had gotten his money's worth from the consultants. The consultants, for their part, weren't sure Macon could ever be dragged, even kicking and screaming, into the twentieth century.

MPCC was a regional vendor of concrete products competing in the Sunbelt. The firm had experienced the not unusual violent swings in revenues that often accompany construction-based industries. After living through the most recent bad period, Jones had resolved to improve his marketing systems to try to forestall the effects of the next downturn.

Consultants were retained. They studied every aspect of the MPCC marketing process and found much wanting in the way MPCC managed its marketing efforts. While financial measures in MPCC were very sophisticated (the firm looked at return on managed assets by plant location), the selling process largely was unmanaged, in the opinion of the consultants.

The firm managed its selling to accrued backlog, a not uncommon tactic when future revenues are unpredictable. However, this meant that the firm seemed to reap the benefits of smart marketing in neither good times nor bad. In bad times the sales force beat the bushes for business, any business, that would increase backlog regardless of margins or (sometimes) appropriateness to MPCC's skills. But even in good times there wasn't enough "loose" business available to keep backlogs high enough to make management comfortable. Macon, in a word, was always scrambling for business and often wound up trading margins for the certainty of future bookings.

No notion of segmentation was employed in Macon, either for the firm's key highway and bridge accounts (government) or for its more frequent but smaller orders. While it was recognized that business put out for bid always was less profitable to Macon than business that was negotiated, jobs were not tracked on this variable or on several others that could be used to inform future selling efforts. The only selling rule used by the corporation encouraged "beating the bushes" for work[1] in an attempt to keep backlog at maximum levels.

The consultants recommended a system of controls to remedy these problems. First, increased attention to key account selling and to sales call planning and control was recommended. Second, an attempt was to be made to allocate costs to jobs in a way that allowed a determination of profit by job, the first step in a job-tracking system. The consultants also designed a *post hoc* segmentation system so that MPCC could learn to differentiate highly profitable business from that which was not so profitable on a job category basis, then direct its selling activities accordingly.

Jones was comfortable with the notion of key account emphasis and even liked the idea of reforming call reporting and sales call patterns. But he felt an almost visceral resistance to the notions of tracking profit-by-job and segmentation of the marketing effort. The former idea, he felt, required revamping the job accounting system in a way that required too much effort for the information returned. The latter idea seemed to him "too sophisticated" for a firm of Macon's size; he wasn't sure that running a construction company involved anything more than just getting out there and trying to talk people out of *all* their pending construction jobs. Do that well, he thought, and the profits would take care of themselves.

Paul Jones was not unsophisticated; he was a good general manager. Mostly he was *comfortable* with the systems, the rituals, he had in place to handle the relationships between the consequences of the firm's selling efforts and the profits of his corporation. He was willing to do some fine-tuning of the selling effort but unwilling to undertake drastic revisions of the way MPCC went after business that might have made a major difference in the next downturn. Comfort, habit, and ritual had produced an information set for MPCC that did not make available to management information that might have helped run the business better.

SYSTEMS IN GENERAL

William James rightly called habit the "great flywheel of society." Habits are to individuals what systems are to marketers. They act to routinize certain repetitive acts so that they happen automatically and without the application of much thought on the part of the actors. James wrote at length in his *Principles of Psychology* about the felicitous effects of our tendency to wear ruts in our behavior so that we are not only an orderly people but predictable as well. Systems—the routinization of tasks—make orderly action possible in the corporation in the same manner as habits make them possible for individuals.

With equal insight but opposite conclusion, Ralph Waldo Emerson called the sometimes foolish consistency in behavior that results when systems direct acts the "hobgoblin of little minds." Emerson, had he lived in a later age or been a student of management, might well have added management systems to his list of consistencies that "grind and grind in the mill of a truism, and nothing comes out but what was put in."

Systems, set up to serve managers, often wind up driving management in dysfunctional directions. Whether because of the comfortableness of current systems (as in the Macon example above) or the frequent negative encounters managers have with systems apparently designed diabolically to obfuscate rather than inform, marketing systems often seem to inhibit good marketing actions.

How are we to understand the ritualizations of routine marketing activities in systems, with their simultaneous capacity to remove the drudgery of repetitive decision-making on the one hand and their pernicious ability to lock us into potentially dysfunctional behavior patterns on the other? What modes of assessment are available when general management wishes to know, in Mayor of New York style, "How am I doing?" vis-à-vis marketing systems? Marketing systems and their effects on the quality of the marketing job are the subject of this chapter.

SYSTEMS IN MARKETING

Marketing systems are the formal or semiformal devices management has available to inform, control, or facilitate its marketing decision-making. Depending on the firm in question, its history, and its management, there may be few or many systems marketers can call on to improve decision-making. A high-technology venture start-up with second-round venture funding but no sales may have few if any marketing routinizations in place; a company like Procter & Gamble or IBM often is claimed to allow little that *isn't* routinized in its marketing endeavors.

Broadly speaking, marketing systems may be divided into two groups: those which focus on marketing operations *internal* to the firm and those which look to the effects of marketing actions on *external* parties, like customers or distributors. Again, the universe of marketing systems can be cross-cut by whether the system in question is primarily employed to supply information to management or designed to allow the exertion of control[2] over measured phenomena.

Exhibit 5-1 shows this two-by-two classification and gives some examples of marketing systems classified as internal versus external ones and informational versus control systems. As the chart shows, many systems under the control of other firm functions are of high informational interest to the marketers—credit approvals, for instance, may be unaffectable by the marketing group because this system is "owned" by finance, but it is critical to marketing success. Clearly, systems that affect marketing often do not neatly fall into one of the four cells given on the chart. Nonetheless, the four-way classification is a useful one for understanding marketing systems.

Exhibit 5-2 shows a list of a number of systems commonly implicated in doing the marketing job and categorizes them in terms of Exhibit 5-1's categories. As is always true in the real world, a number of systems in marketing serve both informational and control purposes and sometimes concern phenomena inside and out-

Designed For:

	Information	Control
Focused On: Internal Phenomena	Systems giving information, but little control. For example: • Personnel systems • Order entry systems • Credit approval systems	Performance information measures concerned with efficiency control. For example: • Marketing productivity systems (sales-to-staff ratios) • Sales call tracking system
External Phenomena	External tracking systems for data management needs to know but cannot control: • Industry tracking system • Competitive analysis system	Systems to measure and control marketing effectiveness with the customers and the trade: • Segment profitability system • Key account tracking system

Exhibit 5–1. A Matrix of Marketing Control Systems

Exhibit 5–2. Examples of Marketing Systems

LEVEL	SYSTEM	CATEGORIZATION
High		
	Organization structure Job definition/design Management compensation Sales force compensation Performance evaluation	Internal control
	Decision support system	Int./ext. information
	Competitive intelligence . . .	External information
	Customer intelligence system	External information
	Sales call reporting . . .	Int./ext. control
	Order entry Billing Accounts receivable	Internal control
Low		

side the corporation at the same time. Exhibit 5–2 cross-categorizes the listed marketing systems by whether the system in question is a high-level one affecting much of marketing or a low-level one from a marketing point of view. Note the wide diversity and proliferation of systems that affect the marketing effort in even the smallest firm.

The marketing organization is perhaps the broadest-level example of an internal system meant to lend control to managers over marketing acts.[3] Yet the marketing organization, a formal marketing system, seems almost never to work, if by "work" we mean facilitate the marketing effort. Indeed, many managers suspect the organization in their firm was set up diabolically late one night by some mad manager to *keep* them from doing their jobs. Others, facing a "matrix organization" made popular in the 1970s, are befuddled by not being able to figure out who their boss is or what it is they're supposed to do! Marketing organization will be taken up in greater detail below.

Compensation, performance evaluation, and even the writing of job descriptions are internal management information and/or control systems that normally are not thought of as part of the marketing function (job design is supervised by the personnel department), but they have powerful effects on how well the marketing job is done. Unfortunately there is little knowledge, beyond anecdotal evidence, about the operation of these systems over time, and about how they can go haywire to discourage effective action in marketing. Yet for many managers it is frustrating to see the wrong people regularly assigned to the wrong jobs and then apparently paid in such a fashion as to discourage quality action.

Moving down a level of generality from corporate to marketing-wide systems, there are a number of devices intended to regularize the flow of information to the marketers and to facilitate better decision-making. The competitive intelligence system, the customer intelligence system, and even the sales reporting system are all formalized (or not so formal) devices by which management attempts to routinize its knowledge-gathering endeavors about the "outside world" in order to maximize its implementation actions. Often, however, such systems either resemble a black hole in what management knows about the market or else seem to misdirect the marketing effort in ways that can only be called perverse. We shall look at the sales force reporting and control system further to inform ourselves on these types of systems.

Finally, at the lowest level of systems generality are a number of systems not "owned" by marketing that nonetheless affect what is done in marketing mightily. Order entry, credit approval, billing, and accounts receivable—none of them controlled by marketing staff—often remain unaffected by actions taken by marketers. Yet each is part of the company's interactions with the customers, and each can pose problems for effective execution of plans, programs, and strategies.

Clearly the sheer number of systems that impact or are impacted by marketing activities requires a book of its own for adequate treatment. However, my research is clear that two of the many categories of marketing systems have farther-reaching effects than others on the quality of marketing practice. Those are systems concerned with the *allocation* of scarce resources across the many marketing jobs needing to be done and systems concerned with *monitoring* what is going on in marketing. The marketing organization, for example, is both a monitoring *and* an allocation system; reporting is channeled by way of organizational control, but assignment of people across marketing jobs is clearly an allocative function. It is on systems of this sort that I concentrate here, because they strike at the heart of marketing implementation.

How Systems Facilitate and Impede Effective Marketing

Whatever else they may be, it is clear that marketing systems (and all management systems, for that matter) represent a routinization of management activities. This routinization is like a snapshot taken of the world at any point in time; the photo "concretizes" reality and freezes it within a certain perspective. As long as the world doesn't change radically and the photographer has an inclusive perspective, the snapshot will be a fair representation of what is going on; reading the *National Geographic* will suffice instead of traveling.

But pictures frame certain events *inside* them and leave others out. Besides, the world changes over time, so that what was a good representation of reality yesterday can be an impediment to action today. It is change in the corporation or in the customers that partially determines whether marketing systems will impede or facilitate the overall marketing effort over time.

This simple fact—that the world "slips away" over time from any system designed to inform on it or to offer "control" over its phenomena—is the source of much of what goes wrong when marketing systems are considered.

Exhibit 5–3 shows the strength of various marketing systems implemented in the firm cross-cut by the rate of change of the phenomena the system is concerned with measuring or controlling. As the chart shows, when the rate of change[4] is low, management has the opportunity to routinize much of its decision-making effectively with strong systems for marketing organization, decision support, and intelligence gathering (upper-left cell). However, such routinization will be an aid to getting the job done *only when* management's clarity of theme for marketing serves as a guiding hand on system design and use.

The McDonald Corporation, for example, is a company well known for its continual substitution of systems for personnel skills in retail service delivery.[5] At the retail level, at least, the firm is able to tolerate over 50 percent turnover in employees and pay relatively low wages while still delivering a quality product that keeps the customers coming back. Want to know how long to leave french fries in the vat at McDonald's? It's easy—wait till the buzzer rings! Want to know how many fries to put in a bag? It's easy—use the scoop! McDonald's narrow product line (hamburgers and fries, largely), short contact with the customer, and low rate of change in meat-and-potatoes fast-food consumption patterns allow the corporation to standardize systems in a way that would drive a high-technology firm out of business in a year.

Rate of Change

	Low	High
System Strength Strong	Appropriate: But requires clarity of vision and strong marketing theme to work.	Trouble: Structures quickly become inappropriate and often impede execution efficiency.
Weak	Depends on execution skills: May be inefficient in any case since low change rate invites systems routinization.	Appropriate: Appropriate if managers are highly skilled at execution; otherwise, moves to Trouble cell.

Exhibit 5–3. Marketing Systems and Rate of Change

Most important, though, is a clear marketing theme at McDonald's, which employees express as QSC/TLC, first propounded by Ray Kroc and since inculcated in every graduate of Hamburger University in Florida. The theme: Quality, Service, Cleanliness/Tender Loving Care. This is implemented down to the level of phone booths (prohibited) and posters in the retail store windows (prohibited); it even governs employee grooming (black shoes only) and stock politeness phrases used with customers! We shall learn more about theme in the next chapter. Without it even low-change industries go awry in systems implementation.

It's the same with marketing systems. What allows P&G to systematize in the marketing effort or Frito-Lay to systematize selling so rigorously simply is (1) a relatively low rate of change in the phenomena with which the systems are concerned, and (2) a clear vision and strong marketing theme serving as ''systems insurance'' as well as implementation direction. In the top-left cell of Exhibit 5–3, strong systems can be used to drive management, with appropriate cautions, but in the other three cells of the chart there is the possibility of trouble with marketing systems. When the rate of change is high in a market, a distributor group, or even a sales force, strong systems with their powerful ''locking in'' effects cause definite trouble for management. Essentially the installed systems may act to impede, rather than facilitate, execution efficiency. It is just this phenomenon, systems that wouldn't let management react appropriately to market or other changes, that I observed frequently in my research. Where change was low, on the other hand, lack of clarity in theme often caused system problems for management.

The lower row of the matrix is concerned with what happens to marketing effectiveness when systems are weak. Clearly, when marketing systems are weak managers have to rely on their personal execution skills for interacting, allocating, monitoring, and organizing, for they cannot rely on the organization (one system) or the budgeting process (another one) to make their choices for them. We shall devote the next part of this book to execution skills and learn what marks of good implementers allow the carrying of weak structures.

For the present it is enough to recognize that systems often breed problems, either because there is no clarity of vision in management (upper left-hand cell) or because the rate of change in the market or other phenomena measured make the systemic "snapshot" an impediment rather than an aid to getting the marketing job done (right-hand column).

Exhibit 5–3, then, summarizes one argument of this chapter. Often marketing systems *get in the way* of good marketing because it is inappropriate to routinize the nonroutine decisions being made. Or else, when change is low, routinizations of action are allowed to "flood" the organization because clarity of theme and strength of vision are not prominent in the company. Systems so encountered can become obstacles to effective action instead of aids.

Like the frightening interactions played out in Joseph Heller's fine novel about a marketing executive, "something happens" to marketing systems when they are used by human managers in the service of decision and control. The systems get concretized, become politicized, or just flat don't work for what they were designed to do.

Everywhere in my field work I was confronted with managers who on the one hand were supported with multimillion-dollar "decision support systems," clever sales force reporting and control systems, and fancy matrixed marketing organization systems designed (I'm sure) to help them do a better job. But very few of these executives knew the profit per account, per segment, or per product they vended! Sales force reports routinely were discarded as unusable because they were "tainted" somehow, and decision support systems seemed to obfuscate rather than clarify the parameters of problems under consideration. The fancy organizations seemed designed mostly to keep the manager from interacting with others that could help him or her in doing a needed job. In general the bureaucracy seemed constantly to get in the way of the people, rather than the other way around.

Like Frankenstein monsters, marketing systems take on lives of their own. We create them to serve us, but over time they become our masters. One example of this uncomfortable characteristic of marketing systems keeps coming to mind. A sales vice president in a mature business reacted to my query about how well informed he was on his sixty-person sales force by reaching into a credenza and taking out a computer sales report so thick it was an OSHA hazard wherever it was laid. As he dropped it on the desk with great effort, he said, "See? We're fully computerized around here. The problem is, I can't figure this damned thing out before I get the next one from the data-processing people!'' The list of ''something happened'''s is taken up in the next section.

MANAGEMENT FAILURES WITH MARKETING SYSTEMS

Chapter 2 argued that three regularly recurring management difficulties can operate when marketing systems are troublesome, even when routinization of marketing decisions is appropriate. I called these errors of ritual, errors of politicization, and errors of unavailability. This section looks at each of those errors over several exemplary marketing systems. Of particular interest are the marketing organization, the customer/competitor decision-support system, and sales force monitoring.

Errors of Ritual

As the Macon Prestressed Concrete Company example given in the introduction to this chapter shows, how things are ''ordinarily'' done in marketing can become a powerful force for how they *should* be done, even when conditions change or the old ways don't work. Marketing systems, because of the comfort we all take from repetitive ritual, can become a bloody bed of Procrustes where situations, analyses, and marketing responses are ''lopped off'' to fit what makes management comfortable.

In a firm I cannot identify here, management approached me to help with cost reductions in its $1-plus-billion sales budget. The reason management thought it needed help with the costs was that competition in the industry, once almost absent, was heating up to a fevered pace. The firm was facing severe price pressures in the market.

Management felt, for a number of reasons, that it was important to continue to serve ten distinct segments of the market with key account services, even though four of these were producing distinctly suboptimal sales per staff assigned and new product sales; three of the remainder showed promise to deliver much better than their already high ratios if additional people and money would be allocated to them.

When the sales allocation and budgeting system was discussed, it was quickly learned that the relevant vice president had since the beginning of his tenure pursued a policy of routinely ''dividing up" available resources relatively equally among the segments, because he knew that *all* were important to the firm. Allocations were made on the basis of a complex formula that essentially rewarded sales staff for using more people (central staff groups' work was not charged back to the segment managers, and so on) and time than necessary to get the job done. The scheme for assigning budgets at its most basic level was a quota system that implicitly built in the poorer segment managers' difficulties in lower management expectations.

This system was pursued by the firm not because it was right nor even because the vice president in question liked it. It was pursued because it was the way things had *always* been done in the company and because in the past inefficiencies of this sort were tolerable to management in a situation where there were few competitors for the customer's dollar and little price pressure.

In this one instance, at least, it was possible to quantify the inimical effects of ritual and comfortability on the firm. Substituting a one-page "back of the envelope" ratio analysis of selling productivity (per staff assigned, and so on) for the firm's overly complicated and pseudo-democratic allocation system, and following a new system that offered more staff and dollars to higher-payback segments looked likely to afford the firm more than $100 million on the cost side alone, not counting increased revenues from the higher-growth segments and without threatening the firm's broad-base segment serving philosophy!

It is not only in large companies or ones facing rapid market change rates that errors of ritual make themselves felt. In a low-technology business serving a commodity market, management got used to a comfortable accounts receivable system that allowed its salespeople to make sales to customers in the spring with the expectation that those clients would be unable to pay for the goods until fall, when *they* were paid for their goods. The system was "comfortable" for everyone concerned: The sales force could sell goods for which the customers couldn't pay right then, the customer could take title to goods on which it "was understood" informally that some ninety days would be allowed for payment, and management moved inventory off its docks in a highly competitive environment.

As the 1981 recession turned into the 1982–1983 depression, however, management saw its outstanding accounts receivables go from 45 to 60 to 75 to 90 to 118 days, and almost lost the firm in Chapter 11 because a nonmarketing system, accounts receivable, was being misused by the sales force as a marketing tool. The firm became a bank, and as the economy worsened manufacturers with no banking skills were faced with an enormous number of "bad loans."

While other systems breed routinization of allocation, the marketing organization often breeds routinization of interaction in ways that can lead to poor-quality marketing. The product managers in one high-growth pharmaceuticals firm currently are up in arms because management pooled the firm's selling resources into a single sales force. Managers of lower-growth products or lower-margin ones feel they can't get the sales attention they need, while managers of higher-attention products sit smugly and grin at their colleagues' complaints. Sales management tries to satisfy everyone but is beset by a high number of recent recruits who need basic training, not fine-tuning.

The integrative mechanisms top management has put in place to make this organization work include a manager of "product line integration," who is charged with coordinating all product group requests for the sales force but is on a reporting par with the sales vice president and has no direct authority over either group. In this situation the brand managers believe they have no effective pathway to influence the sales force, sales management is besieged with requests from twenty or more product managers on which it cannot deliver, technical material is being delivered to the sales representatives by UPS truck, and the coordination function appears to all concerned to be blocking, not facilitating, those charged with maximizing returns on their product lines. While everyone understands the need to cut expenses by pooling selling, the systems that have been put in place to accomplish this function are both ritualistic and inadequate.

What *has* been done by way of routinizing marketing allocation and monitoring decisions often becomes inimical to what *needs* to be done in changed circumstances. We grow comfortable with what is already routinized, because we think we don't *have* to deal with that aspect of our already overworked marketing lives any more. When comfort is high, so are the odds that the functions the system was put in place to routinize will slowly go "off target" with serious consequences for the marketing effort.

Errors of Politicization

There is a naive belief among management that data, especially numerical data, are science-associated and therefore somehow "purer" than intuitions or qualitative statements. This naive belief, like most of its ilk, is pure bunk, for there is nothing so politicized in management as the collection and use of "quantitative" information.

Consider the humble sales call reporting system. It is safe to venture that nowhere in corporate America does management so freely discard, degrade, disable, and destroy such an inexpensive and often accurate source of feedback from its customers as it does when attempting to manage its own salespeople.

How is it that management can throw away the cheapest source of market intelligence available to it with such regularity? The answer lies in the politicization of the information sought and in sales and general management's repeated nonuse of that information. Call reports are either routinely relegated to the "circular file" or, what amounts to the same thing, are sent to the data-processing group for analysis. Where anything at all happens to them, the data often are employed punitively to "teach" salespeople who are perceived as not doing their jobs correctly. Or such reports are "cleaned" of potentially inflammatory data, a process called "weeding," before higher management gets a chance to see information that might reflect unfavorably on sales management.

The net effect is that management, through repeated ignoring, improper use, and general poor handling of sales force feedback comes to convince the sales force that it has no desire for customer feedback in the form of call reporting and is just imposing one more Mickey Mouse random harassment on salespeople to keep them from doing their real jobs, selling. Management in many companies doesn't want to hear what the sales force has to say, and it gets its wish!

At the Freuhauf Corporation, as in many others, sales expense checks are "held back" by management until call reports are turned in at the end of every month. When the reports are turned in, a primary use for them is "red-lining," which means punitive use by sales management looking for errant salespeople, not customer intelligence-gathering. As a result salespeople make their reports up at the end of every month half from fiction (to disguise the day taken on the golf course with a client) and half from memory. By its behavior management repeatedly has let it be known that it is not interested in intelligence from the customers via the sales force, only in meeting a ridiculous requirement that the motions of intelligence-gathering must be executed even if there is no utility in the act.

The politicization of systems and data is not limited to sales monitoring systems, however. Consider the case of division management in one equipment rental company which was under heavy pressure to increase share of market in a highly competitive situation. The executives came up with a clever pricing plan designed to recoup share through a projected 10 percent increment in volumes at a 13 percent decrement in margins, a hard enough set of facts for corporate management to swallow. What went conveniently unreported, however, was that the current fleet of equipment would be obsoleted several months earlier than management originally had planned (in a bad resale market) because of the increased volumes. Because the division's ability to conduct business in the future required good resale prices to fund the purchase of new equipment, management essentially hid the strong possibility of a later profit "hit" for a plan they thought they could sell to corporate management to get the heat off in the current fiscal year.

Data or information[6] in management, as in science, is politicized, tortured, bent, and occasionally broken in the service of vested interests in the marketing organization. Sometimes the politicization is not *meant* to have evil effect, as when sales force monitoring is done in a way that has injurious side effects on the customer feedback. Sometimes data are "bent" with a purpose, an axe to grind, or a reason, as when one manager must try to cover his tail with others in the corporation. It is folly to assume that just because a marketing system provides numerical or other "hard" data, these are good representations of the reality they are meant to portray.

Nowhere is this phenomenon more easily observed than in the operation of "marketing decision-support systems" in consumer marketing corporations. These systems, designed to aid decision-making, often wind up hindering it because they overly complexify the reality they are intended to represent and, worse, attempt to substitute mystification and mathematical algorithms for the judgment managers are paid to bring to the job. As a number of researchers have demonstrated,[7] research results and the output of decision support systems are susceptible to all the biases data normally fall prey to, with the additional problem that much of what is being done is esoteric, hard to understand, and therefore more susceptible than most data to politicization by the researchers or the managers in whose service the system is implemented.

Errors of Unavailability

If the data that do exist in corporations are routinely politicized and employed in the service of vested interests, even more surprising is the amount of simple data that don't exist at all. One might expect that in today's data-heavy companies managers could make projections based on detailed analyses, intricate competitive data, and clever segmentation. In all but two or three of the companies I investigated, however, marketing systems put in place to aid this decision-making simply didn't deliver on the kinds of data that management needed for informed decision-making.

Few managers in the companies I spent time with had any idea of profitability by segment, to name one statistic it is hard to do good marketing without. Fewer still had good numbers on profitability by item in the product line or service vended. Only once did I see a system in place that allowed profitability (or even margin) to be computed by individual line item on the order submitted by each account. Everywhere, as with one client in a supplies business, I was told by the president that such a system was in process, was being revamped, or was there but didn't quite work. In essence, management didn't have the information I asked about just then, but would have these essential data "Real Soon Now." The company in question was 182 years old!

Managers I came to know and work with put little faith in this promise. Rather they knew from experience that one of two things would happen when they made a request for, say, profitability by segment. If the manager was not a member of general management but two or three levels down in the organization, the answer that came back from the electronic data-processing (EDP) or finance people was "accounting doesn't give us the data that way." This answer was consistent across many companies and industries. Just imagine—a function designed to *account* for the profits made by marketing endeavors *won't* or *can't* provide that accounting in a useful way to those who earn the money!

If the request was not denied as impossible given the current status of the accounting system, EDP might reply that it would put a "rush priority" on the request and could perhaps have it available in fifteen months! No wonder there's a personal computer boom. Nobody can get the data he or she needs to do the most rudimentary analysis that would allow quality marketing.

If someone high up in general management made a similar request, no one would claim that "accounting doesn't do this" or that a year is necessary to get the data. Here, more often than not, the report will be on the executive's desk the next morning. The report will be *on* the desk, and *over* the desk, *all around* the desk; so much output will be provided that the manager would swear somebody in the bowels of the computer room is trying to send him a message never to ask for anything like this again! The president of one large optical company recently showed me a thirty-four-page report designed to interpret a promotion that was run for thirty of his more than five hundred retail stores. His request to me? Help his people learn to express the essence of what he needed to know about this request, if anything, on a single sheet of paper. The information as provided was unusable.

Though I overpaint a little here in the interest of making a point, the general thesis is accurate. Most marketers don't have more than the rudiments of the information they *need* to make sound decisions. If they have enough temerity to ask the system to provide these data, the request is either refused or fulfilled in such a way that they are discouraged from asking again. Management instead is treated to a plethora of data that are marginally useful at best, expressed in a fashion where it appears that those running the computer or generating the reports are getting paid by the digit, not the worth of the information provided.

When data are not unavailable because the marketing system can't or won't generate them, or when requests are not discouraged, the organization system itself often acts to keep information from those who need to know it. In a large computer company recently touted as one of the "excellent companies" by Thomas Peters,[8] for example, product managers in the bowels of the marketing organization (in one division at least) are *prohibited* from having any data relating to the costs, margins, or profitability of their product lines. While it is a commendable thing to keep data on a "need-to-know" basis, it is not so commendable to have those in charge of managing the returns on a line of goods ignorant of the basis on which they are measured!

A Comedy of Errors

If the foregoing sounds as much like preaching as it does research results, it is meant to. Marketing systems ordinarily do not provide what management needs to do the job, and what is given is wrong by virtue of ritualization, politicization, or oversupply and underanalysis. What is true for the numbers is also true for the marketing organization; again, ritual often supplants a simpler, more effective way of getting things done, fiefdoms and "empires" replace teams, and most of the people to whom a marketer needs access are inaccessible because they are in someone else's organization or otherwise unavailable. As one CEO has remarked, "The true job of the chief executive is to keep the bureaucracy away from the good people."

A SYSTEM THAT COULD

Frito-Lay rightly is held up by those who study excellence in management as an example of that phenomenon. I spent a good deal of time inside this company, both in its traditional "salty snack" business involving Fritos and Doritos and as the firm tried to export its salty snack franchise to the cookie business. The FLI sales management system can be used as a good clinical example of a marketing system that works.

One case study I give my students as an introduction to the FLI system (it is part of this research project) has none of the usual "decision dilemmas" involving grand strategy with which students are ordinarily confronted in the Harvard classroom. Rather, this case describes FLI and then presents a diary of one "day on the truck" with salesperson Jess Pagluica, whose territory is some 25 square miles in Waltham, Massachusetts. Yet the case poses a powerful puzzle for the students and holds a major lesson for management. I reiterate the main points here.

Frito-Lay (at the time of the case, in 1981) was a $1.5-billion company that vended more than twenty brands of salty snack foods to 300,000 accounts. Four *billion* units of product were moved yearly; some 180,000 sales calls were made per *day* by a 10,000-person force of "driver/salespeople" calling on all sizes of food, convenience, and other outlets from giant supermarket warehouses to D'Agostino's Deli in Waltham. Half of FLI's business is done in cash;

anyone with experience in cash business knows the potential *there* for problems.

FLI's system for sales control is a miracle of the attention to detail Tom Peters exhorts us to have in all endeavors. Each salesperson, no matter how experienced, must complete a ten-book programmed learning course, which covers everything from the Frito-Lay theme to likely consumer behavior to how to pack the delivery truck for maximum efficiency. Salespeople are *not allowed* to have their own route until they have served as substitutes for vacationing "regulars" for a year.

No matter what an outlet buys and no matter how busy the supermarket when the FLI salesperson calls, all stock bought by the account must be opened in the presence of the store manager and counted in front of him or her to ensure agreement on what is coming into the store. Since store managers do not have either the time or the personnel to do their own pricing or shelf maintenance, the FLI salesperson does this for the location, tidying the shelves, pricing the goods, and even doing some backroom stocking. Goods cannot be placed willy-nilly on the supermarket shelves but must be stocked according to what the company calls "national pattern," a display set-up which specifies that the Doritos go to the left of the Fritos, and that Jalapeña Dip is never stocked to the right of Onion Dip. Failure to follow these recommendations is a disciplinary offense.

The call allocation patterns have been thought through no less thoroughly. The salesperson receives a route book with a sheet for each day of the week to plan his/her calls; even the invoices are optical scan forms, and to avoid multiplication mistakes a complete table of extended prices for all of FLI's goods is printed on the back so that the salesperson can simply turn the invoice over to see how much eight cases of Fritos cost.

The puzzling paradox to the students in all of this is not the beauty of the FLI system, the attention to detail, or even the complexity of being able to move 4 billion product units in an industry where the average shelf life of the goods is thirty-four days and a high-turnover outlet will require service twice daily. Rather, the paradox is how salespeople like Jess Pagluica behave in the field.

Despite the rigidity of the FLI system and, indeed, some potential Mickey Mouse requirements of the system, the FLI salesperson does things other companies can't get their salespeople to do.

Pagluica routinely took the time to "flex" each *bag* of Fritos or whatever he was putting on the shelf, smoothing out the wrinkles so that the display would look better. He routinely removed "cord-wooded" displays that the store's staff might have set up since his last call, and restocked every last bag and product according to "national pattern." He religiously counted every package of goods coming into the store, was scrupulous in crediting the customer for damaged goods, and in general was almost frighteningly *zealous* about what he was doing. A visitor from another planet might have thought that the display was an altar, and FLI his religion. Most puzzling of all, Pagluica was a union man!

When the students (or anyone else) examine the FLI system in detail, they come up with a number of reasons why the system works so well. Of course the commissions Jess Pagluica is paid have a lot to do with his willingness to "flex" the bags, and the training he has received allows him to understand that a neater display is likely to get more sales from the shopper than a sloppy one. There are good opportunities for advancement in the FLI system; the company is paying Jess's way through night school, and he has high aspirations to become a FLI regional manager in time. The system of multiplication tables on the backs of invoices, the optical scan invoices themselves, and account call patterns make good sense, and Jess understands how using these can help make him more money and FLI move more goods.

But none of this, the students assert, *really* explains why Jess runs. Jess runs, one comes to learn from listening to him, because *he believes in Frito-Lay as a company, as a vendor of high-quality snack products, and as a good place to work.* He knows, accepts, and, best, believes the marketing theme of the firm that "we have two seconds to reach the customer with our fine line of high quality snack foods," and he *wants* customers, both trade and end user, to want Frito-Lay products. He understands in his belly that he is the link that makes or destroys the company's interaction with the customers. He *does* have a religion, but it is the religion that Peters has called "everyone is a marketer in a well-run company." He is, in short, Frito's best advertisement.

Frito-Lay shows a number of things about marketing system design, especially as it impacts the sales force. First, the company is in a relatively low-change situation regarding its selling: While the snack foods business has shown impressive growth over the years, it has a predictable trend in end use and distribution. In other words, systematization of the sales function is *possible* in this company because of the predictable trade and end use buying patterns.[9]

Second, there is no doubt that a great deal of careful execution and thought went into the creation of the system itself. The interrelationships of training, compensation, and call patterns, for example, show an enormous sensitivity to the needs of the customer and the needs of the sales representatives. The "national pattern" rule for packing the display was based not on ritual or comfort but on an enormous amount of color and placement research about retail buying. The optical scan invoices with their multiplication tables on the back show that even tiny details like multiplication errors have been considered and planned against. In short, the evolution of FLI's "store-door" system over the years has produced a finely tuned and detail-oriented system that *works* for the company, the customers, and the sales representatives.

But when all this is said and done, it explains nothing about the *zeal* that Jess Pagluica and the 10,000 other FLI driver/salespeople bring to their jobs. *That* is much better explained by the policies that Bill Korn (executive vice president), John Cranor (vice president of marketing), and Jack DeMarco (vice president of sales) have inculcated in the marketing organization under the direction of president Wayne Calloway. "Bonoma's Law" of marketing systems is this: *Without clear marketing theme, vision, and other policies from top management, even the cleverest marketing systems aren't worthwhile.* Policies, of course, are the subject of the next chapter.

CHAPTER SIX

Marketing Policies

People arrive at a factory and perform a totally meaningless task from eight to five without question because the structure demands that it be that way. There's no villain, no "mean guy" who wants them to live meaningless lives, it's just that the structure . . . demands it and no one is willing to take on the formidable task of changing the structure just because it is meaningless.

—Pirsig, *Zen and the Art of Motorcycle Maintenance*

INTRODUCTION

Pirsig's quote is instructive because it shows a deep understanding about the relationship of systems (the "factory") and policies ("the structure"). He goes on in this passage to say that if we tear down the offending factory but don't alter the policies that produced it, those policies will just cause another suboptimal one to be built. I continue with the Frito-Lay example we started at the conclusion of the last chapter.

When we left Jess Pagluica, a driver/salesperson for Frito-Lay, he was working diligently and even suspiciously *zealously* "flexing" bags of Fritos. I claimed in Chapter 5 on systems that it was not just the careful attention to detail in the Frito-Lay sales management system that kept Jess working the way he did. I claimed further that it was neither the carrot of commissions nor the threat of discipline from the district manager that motivated him. Rather I argued that top management in Frito-Lay had a direct and continual hand in getting Jess to work for that company as he had never worked for previous employers.

I call everything that management says and does to affect the way marketing practices in the corporation get done "marketing policies." Let's look at some signs of the sorts of marketing policies inculcated by top management at Frito-Lay.[1]

The first time I met Bill Korn, executive vice president of Frito-Lay, I had just gotten off an early morning three-hour plane ride and was in no mood for guessing games. Korn's first question to me as I entered the office where the president, Wayne Calloway; the vice president of marketing, John Cranor; and the vice president of sales, Jack DeMarco; were gathered was, "What don't you see?"

I looked around and somehow managed to stumble on the fact that Korn's office had no filing cabinets of any sort. "Aha!" he said, as he quickly reached into his pocket and gave me the briefest glimpse of two 3 x 5 index cards. "That's because I run the entire business from these!" Of course, he wouldn't show me what was on the cards, but as it turned out they held variance reports from each of FLI's thirty-eight plants and revenue reports from its twenty-eight sales districts. Right or wrong about the particulars, Mr. Korn had driven his understanding of the dynamics of this billion-dollar business to a powerful simplicity. "The essence of Frito-Lay," he pointed out, "is control and consistency."

Mr. Calloway, the president, agreed somewhat grudgingly. "That's true, I guess, but it's no accident that I've put all my vice presidents' offices within easy reach of my own. This business depends on communication, that's how we live and die—rapid change, high flexibility."

Mr. Cranor, the marketing vice president, was of yet another opinion: "We only have two seconds to reach the average shopper with our display of Frito-Lay high-quality snack foods. That means consistent displays in all areas of the country, and attention not only to the big supermarket customer but to the little delicatessen owner as well. We maintain a constant stream of innovation, like our Tostitos corn chips, but both the trade and the end user know that Frito-Lay means quality goods."

Jack DeMarco, sales vice president, had been quiet while the others talked. Finally it was his turn: "No, no, no. All that stuff's fine, but the guts of this business is execution and sales control. I have a 10,000-person army out there, and you'd better believe they know how to move the goods."

Several things, evident from this brief conference, became clearer as I spent time with many others in this company. First, as partly evidenced by their strong and somewhat divergent opinions, all these men were strong leaders who had formed their own clear understandings of what the company was about by staying up nights puzzling over the nature of the business. Their subordinates held this understanding as well, because these men preached it at every opportunity.

Second, their opinions were held passionately, not as if they were talking about some business they were given care of but as if they were talking about their lives. Third, their understandings of the business were all remarkably simple. They were uniformly customer-oriented and example-filled with "minicases" of their own experiences in the field that were obviously recent. Fourth, their opinions were, to a great degree, complementary. Everyone endorsed Cranor's "two-second" theme, for instance, though any particular individual thought some other aspect of his own job just as crucial. One got the feeling that if these men were talking about different parts of the elephant, they had a very good idea of what the animal looked like.

Fifth, there was clearly a culture of "daring to be great" (in the words of the 1930s Electrolux peddlers) in Frito-Lay. The visitor got the distinct feeling of healthy competition, excitement, innovation, and overall a "we can do it" atmosphere. This was most clearly displayed in a conversation I had with one of Cranor's subordinates at a later time, when I asked why the company was about to build a plant which studies showed was twice as large as Frito-Lay's sales probably would support. As this gentleman replied in a deep Texas drawl, "We don't see much sense in chinning ourselves on the curb around here."

Finally, the entire organization reverberated to the beat set by these men, repeated "stories" about what "Bill" or "Jack" was up to now, and, generally, looked to them and up to them for guidance and direction. Frito-Lay, in short, was a well-run company which knew who it was and where it was going in marketing.

It had all the components: heroes, "stories," and a clear vision and theme.

Top management often is credited with things it does not deserve in annual reports, and not credited for much it does. One of the most powerful things management can do is to set a clear "tone" for the organization via its policies and through its own behavior.

POLICY GUIDELINES

Marketing policy guidelines are the broad rules of conduct that affect marketing practices. Policies are unlike systems in that they are not techniques and often have a more general scope than systems. Policies share with systems an "overview" function, however, in that the specification of both systems and policy guidelines is intended to direct what goes on in marketing practice. Policies may or may not be codified; often they are written nowhere, yet they direct behavior powerfully.

The critical difference between marketing policies and marketing systems is that the former *prescribe* behavior, while the latter *describe* it. That is, while marketing systems such as the decision support system are meant to serve as descriptions of reality, marketing policies usually contain "should" statements that specify what things "ought" to be done and how. Exhibit 6-1 gives some examples of marketing policies, from the broad and general ones like marketing theme that form the outline of this chapter to some very specific norms found in firms I studied.

Some policies are more important than others to getting the marketing job done. While it is true that what goes on vis-à-vis recruiting, compensation, and the like is critically important to the quality of marketing practice, it is equally true that such policies may be corporate-wide and therefore partially or totally outside of the marketer's control. Other policies, such as the four listed at the top of Exhibit 6-1, *are* within his or her control and were found by me to be most important to execution efficiency.

The Implementation Frame

If marketing practice is composed of subfunctions that are combined into marketing programs that are implemented with the aid

Exhibit 6–1. Examples of Marketing Policies

LEVEL	POLICY GUIDELINE	COMMENTS
High	Marketing theme ⎫ *Identity policies* Marketing culture ⎬ Marketing strategy ⎫ Marketing leadership ⎭ *Direction policies*	⎫ Part of "policies frame" ⎭
	Recruiting policies	
	Compensation policies	
Low	"Commissioned salespeople must be self-supporting in six months." "No demonstration rides without sales manager's approval." "No memoranda to be written longer than one page."	

of marketing systems, then it is convenient to think of marketing policies as a "frame" around all else that is done in marketing. Exhibit 6–2 illustrates this relationship between the components of marketing action. The four critical marketing policies of theme, culture, strategy, and leadership form a "frame" that sets the tone and tenor for all else that is done when marketing practice is considered.

It aids understanding to group these four "frame variables," or critical marketing implementation policies, into two categories. I call the first category *policies of identity* and the second *policies of direction*. The former, comprising marketing theme and culture, generally tells members of the marketing organization and the firm *who the company is and what it does* as regards marketing. These two policy variables give the corporation its marketing identity.

The latter, marketing strategy and marketing leadership, are *policies of direction*. They tell the firm, its management, and its workers *where the company is going* vis-à-vis marketing actions, programs, and systems, and provide a general direction to all that is done in the marketing arena.

These two simple-sounding policy sets, those saying what the firm is and those saying what it does, form the most critical of the policies that management needs to implement well in getting the

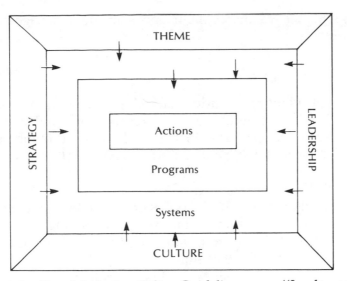

THEME

STRATEGY

Actions

Programs

Systems

LEADERSHIP

CULTURE

Exhibit 6–2. Four Marketing Policy Guidelines as an "Implementation Frame"

marketing job done. In my sample of firms it was rare to find a firm with a clear sense of identity as regards the marketing function. It was less rare to find a firm with a clear sense of direction if strategy alone is considered, but strategy plus strong leadership was not often present. Like the other structural components of execution, marketing policies were problematic for many companies.

When I say that Frito-Lay had a clear sense of who it was *and* what it did in marketing, I am paying that firm's management the ultimate compliment, for it and only one other company in my twenty-two firm sample could be correctly categorized as having attended with due diligence to these "simple" frameworks that allow good marketing practice to occur.

This chapter argues that in most companies unclear identity (most frequently) or unclear direction (less frequently, but still problematic) acts to inhibit the effective execution of marketing actions, because there is no clear "frame" surrounding all else that is done in marketing. This bugbear, unlike some others in the book, can be laid directly at the door of general management and top marketing management. Where identity is unclear and direction is unsound, there has been a failure of top management to manage the marketing function.

The next two sections look at each of the four frame policies in turn, giving case examples of what goes on when management sets marketing policies.

POLICIES OF IDENTITY

Policies of identity include marketing theme and marketing culture. While some might call these terms "soft" and ambiguous, these "soft" policies are "harder" than most numbers if by "hard" is meant having a direct effect on the bottom line.

Marketing Theme

Marketing theme is a fuzzy but significant term that refers to management's shared understanding of marketing purpose. The clearest example I can use to illustrate theme is drawn not from management but from academia.

At the Harvard Business School faculty with a particular disciplinary identification, like marketing, report to an individual called an "area chair," a senior colleague who takes on administrative and leadership functions for an interest area. When I joined the school some years ago, Professor Theodore Levitt was chairman of the marketing area. Levitt, to those who know him, is a brilliant individual who is one of the true intellectuals at the school. He is as likely to "chat" with a colleague about some obscure point of nineteenth-century German economics as about football. (Some might say regardless of the other's interests!)

It was Levitt's habit to manage the area, and new faculty in it, by "walking around." Once a quarter or so he would appear in my office, usually uninvited, and simply plop himself down to chat. I always found this annoying, because at the Business School we seldom "chat," at least without an appointment and an agenda. Ted would go on in a seemingly random fashion for ten or twenty minutes while I grew more and more impatient to get back to the work I was trying to get done. Of course, one doesn't throw the boss out but listens politely.

Just when the frustration was near its peak, Levitt would suddenly stop whatever bit of arcane thought he was currently sharing and look directly at me. His question: "What have you done today that's important to important people in important companies?" Then, not waiting for an answer, he would simply say, "Have a good day," and leave.

The effect, of course, was stunning. There I was in the office writing a memo to Buildings and Grounds about some light bulbs, or else trying to milk one more publishable article out of an old set of thoughts, and I was brought up short. With one stroke Levitt reminded me of *who we were* at the school, at least in the marketing faculty, and toward what ends we wanted continually to direct our attention. Ted's simple sentence was a powerful statement of our shared identity and a brilliant stroke of good management.

It is this strong sense of identity and purpose, expressed so clearly and concisely that you can *tell* it's internalized, that I found missing in most of the companies I spent time with.

In one company, for example, there was a clear "tearing" among top management about just who the firm *was* with respect to marketing. Some executives perceived themselves as heading a commodity-type vendor of supplies and equipment; they saw their only hope for the future as significant investment in "blue sky" R&D projects. Others believed that the company's key marketing identity was in its ability to differentiate commodity and other basic goods in a tough market. Still others held that what the company was uniquely good at was acquiring small competitors in the industry and allowing them to run themselves at a significantly higher profit level than before they were acquired.

These managers, of course, consistently functioned according to their different understandings in the sales, marketing, production, and R&D areas. The result was a confused and ineffective marketing effort, a sales force that thought headquarters gave it contradictory signals, a new product engineering group that felt torn three or four different ways by management's demands, a divisive trade, and exceptionally unhappy customers.

In the Benco Company, which we have come to know over several chapters, there was a very powerful issue of marketing theme that threatened the viability of a significant innovation. Benco, it may be recalled, was a $70-million producer of drainage pipe that had invented a triangular pipe called "Arch-flow." Archflow presented significant advantages to the company, middlemen, and the end user. Management was having great difficulty pricing the pipe, because its marketing theme drove all else that the firm did in sales and marketing toward a commodity, "price-per-pound" identity. Top management *thought* about the business in terms of pounds of plastic sold, not feet of pipe.

Benco's vice president of marketing quite rightly perceived that simply setting a high price on the pipe innovation would be a recipe for disaster in Benco. Top management did not know *how* to think about being a value-added marketer, the sales force did not know *how* to sell price-for-value-received products, and the simple declaration of such a program would not have worked. The question he asked at the end of our time together is most instructive: "The real problem is, how do I get this bunch of engineers and lawyers [Benco's top management were so trained] to think in terms of value-added instead of price-per-pound?" This is a difficult question, for marketing theme develops over time from the combination of all that top management does and doesn't do regarding marketing; once it has set, it has many of the characteristics of concrete.

It is tempting to dismiss the notion of marketing theme as a vague and insignificant "soft" idea. That would be ill-advised, for setting and maintaining marketing theme (with the other frame variables) is one of the most important jobs of top management. When Bennett Bidwell at Hertz took the important pricing plunge described in Chapter 3, it was as much a reassertion of Hertz's "We're Number 1" theme as it was a price move. It is usually believed that strategies drive acts; just as often it would be equally correct to say that values and philosophy drive management action, expressed as theme and acted out as culture.

As a test of your own executives' perceptions of marketing theme in *your* company, perform the following exercise. Write a *single sentence* in the margin of this book stating who you are in marketing. Ask your key people to do the same on a piece of paper and to give it to you.

The results usually are as instructive as they are shocking. What often comes back when I try this exercise with clients is a diversity of themes ranging from the vague platitudes that the company puts on its matchbooks to items suggesting a significant difference of opinion in management about just who the firm is as regards marketing. Often it is impossible for the managers themselves to believe that the statements could possibly be describing the same company!

More than any other "lever" they can pull, marketing theme is established, maintained, and changed by the things top management or marketing management *says* and *does* in daily interaction. Like coral on the sea bed, over time the bodies of past words and actions build up, solidify, and form a powerful wall directing the water of action that can either safely guide high seas away from the company's shores or else encourage a tidal wave that will engulf it. Once established, themes are difficult to change, though it can be done. But my research also makes it clear that changing marketing themes from dysfunctional to more functional ones wasn't the most common problem with which managers had to deal.

Rather, the most common problems regarding marketing theme were either (1) the absence of *any* shared sense of identity and commonality of purpose, or (2) the coexistence of *many* conflicting themes. Neither is conducive to good marketing practice. Neither will produce the kind of sales force behavior we see in Jess Pagluica of Frito-Lay or in the marketing people supervised by Bill Ryan at the Gillette Company's Personal Care Division. Rather, all the attention in the world to subfunctional excellence, programmatic brilliance, or systems design will come to little where there is no clear sense of identity or commonality of purpose. If there is a "great insight" from the study of marketing policies, this is it.

Marketing Culture

Marketing culture is a broader notion than marketing theme. Whereas themes often can be verbalized, culture is the underlying and usually unspoken "social webbing" of management. It subtly but powerfully channels managers' behavior into comfortable ruts. Culture can be observed clearly from such things as dress codes in the corporation, lunchroom conversations, and the way management decorates its walls.

To get a feeling for what I mean when I use the term culture, contrast the Frito-Lay manager's statement, "We don't see much sense in chinning ourselves on the curb around here," with the sign to be found at every AT&T installation that reads, "There is no job so urgent we cannot find a way to do it safely." These two mottoes show significantly different management cultures and correctly predict the significantly different ways that each management would come at, say, a new business opportunity.

Marketing culture at once is made too much of and too little of when it is written about by those who would explain management practices.[2] On the one hand there is a powerful force called culture that directs and shapes all that is done in management; marketing culture, like this force, operates as a "subculture" to shape marketing practices. On the other hand we make too much in this day and age of what I like to call "invisible gremlins" in the management process.

It is in many ways a relief for a general manager to hear that he or she has a "bad culture," for no one can be fired when the culture "goes bad." Culture, like some other topical interests in management, offers the seduction of a committee of the president. If there are five people who *could* have messed things up, nobody gets fired! So we approach culture gingerly, recognizing its power but fighting its seduction, because it can be all too easy to blame all the marketing organization's problems on such an "invisible gremlin," then to relegate the so-called identified problem to some consultants or to some squishy organizational behavior types.

A good way to think about marketing culture is as a powerful "invisible shaper" of practice, but one *created by top management and for which top management is responsible.* That way *somebody* gets fired if there's a "bad culture." That way the correct linkages among management actions and words, other marketing policies and the resulting atmosphere in which work is conducted become clear.

There are two views of culture I find useful when thinking about what goes on in the marketing function. The first is that of Vijay Sathe of the Harvard Business School, who refers to "important shared understandings" when he talks about corporate culture. This view is quite congenial with my emphasis on culture as one of the important *identity* policies of marketing practice; it relates theme (a narrower set of understandings) with culture (a broader one) nicely. Sathe identifies three components of this understanding: shared objects or things, shared sayings or talk, and shared doings or action. He argues that the objects to which management relates together, like Porsches in the parking lot, reveal as much about what management will do when faced with a tough execution problem as does the corporate plan. I would argue the Porsches reveal more.

The Deal and Kennedy analysis of corporate culture is consistent with Sathe's view of culture and more specific in identifying the components of culture that can be applied to marketing from their set of observations. They identify *values, heroes, rites, and rituals* as key elements of culture, and my field observations indicate these can be found clearly as elements of marketing culture as well as the broader management culture.

Consider Dan Siewert, President of Cole National Corporation's Optical Division (CNCOD). CNCOD runs more than five hundred optical departments leased from Sears and other retail chains and provides spectacles, contact lenses, and other optical services to shoppers. Siewert's performance since coming to the Optical Division can only be considered stunning: Sales in the "traditional" leased department business are up significantly, and the division is opening a new chain of stand-alone eyewear "supermarkets" as a new business direction.

Just one visit to Siewert's office[3] makes the marketing culture of the division, as well as a number of other things about its operation, clear. The walls are filled with Vince Lombardi speeches, sayings, and memorabilia, including the famous quote about winning not being everything, just the only thing. On Dan's desk is a brass sign that says "No Excuses." On the obverse is another that says "No Surprises."

In addition to Siewert himself, the district sales managers are the "heroes" of the division; it is about them that people talk and about sales increases and "small wins" in the field. The story is told repeatedly, for example, about the regional manager who did not have enough advertising money for both production costs and talent costs to make a local "spot" commercial, so dressed herself up as a television set and handled the talent problem herself. She reported a 37 percent sales gain!

As to rituals, the president (not an assistant or subordinate) reviews sales numbers with the district managers monthly; weekly reviews are held with direct supervisors, and *daily* sales statistics are collected. As to rituals, the summer marketing meeting was held to inaugurate a "Stop Slop" program, which was intended to reduce the division's proportion of spoiled, damaged, or returned goods from an already low number to half that amount.

The sense a visitor gets from this organization is that it is driven by, toward, and for some simple "shared understandings" that include a focus on the customer, on sales, on detail, and on other strong values. The managers in the Optical Division at Cole *manage* and are strongly value-oriented.

My sense from the field work is that it is not so terribly important just *what* values are held high in the marketing function, providing they in some sense talk to the "simple" and "common sensical" reference points of marketing, like the customer and quality. And it is not so much *who* the heroes are that matter. Rather the important thing is that the heroes exemplify cultural values in the same way that the rites and rituals reinforce them.

When cultures go ''bad,'' they appear to do so from diffusion rather than inappropriate values. The usual state of affairs, rather than dysfunctional or ''weird'' cultures, is an *absence* of any strong culture, a kind of ''free-floating'' we-don't-know-who-we-are sense that, like the absence of thematic identity, has no power to tell anyone in the firm, from management to the receptionist, *who* they are vis-à-vis marketing.

The effect of having no clear identity is so traumatic and debilitating that an entire subset of Hollywood and television movies play out the sad personal consequences of such an ''amnesia'' problem. When there is cultural amnesia in the corporation, or when strong subcultures (e.g. engineering versus sales) in the company conflict, the firm's internal message to its own people will be weak or cacophonous. Where that is the case the company cannot help but present a confused and confounded image to customers and distributors.

DIRECTION POLICIES

Direction policies concern marketing strategy and marketing leadership. If identity policies tell the firm, its personnel, and its customers ''who the company is'' when it comes to marketing, direction policies inform about ''where the firm is going.''

Marketing Strategy

This book is not about marketing strategy. Indeed, the reason a book on implementation is needed is the historic overemphasis on strategic concerns, and the underemphasis on getting the marketing job done well. The literature fills us with the promise of great ideas, but often the company can't deliver.

Nonetheless, marketing strategy does form one of the four legs of policy guidelines, and that which management does in the matter of formulating sound strategies will have important effects on how the marketing job gets done. But this repositioning of strategy as *only one* of four key policy guidelines is intended to reemphasize that we must stop thinking about strategy as the *deus ex machina* that will descend from the sky and save us from inattention to key aspects of marketing execution.

If, as the books tell us, strategy is the alpha and the omega of marketing, then it is high time we started working hard on beta, gamma, sigma, delta, and epsilon. Strategy is not the be-all and end-all of marketing—it is no more than a set of goals, a "wish list" if you will, of what management *would like to happen* when marketing gets executed. It is execution that is the key to the ability to deliver on strategies, just as it is the quality of the sergeants and the strength of the supply lines that have as much to do with an army's ability to carry out an invasion as the general's clever plan.

Marketing Leadership

References to the quality of leadership in marketing and in management have gone out of fashion, almost as if they are in bad taste. We prefer in these modern days to think in terms of "task forces," "committees," and other social units larger than the individual, because then we don't have to point fingers or make sometimes hard judgments about the quality of the individuals making up the marketing team. Indeed, the entire art of performance appraisal has been degraded and depraved in most institutions: Reputedly, to get less than an "excellent" rating in some governmental units requires a degree of moral turpitude that carries an eight-to-twenty-year sentence in Joliet State Prison!

Despite our desire to avert our eyes as if confronted with some embarrassing sight at a dinner party, it is undoubtedly true that some marketers are able leaders and some are not. The former inspire subordinates and bosses with their eagerness to get out into the field; they are clever at designing simple and effective monitoring methods to "shore up" shortcomings in the system's structure, and their understanding of customer and trade dynamics is powerful.

Others, sadly, are much less effective as leaders, immersing themselves in incomprehensible complexities about the market place, unwilling to leave their leather chairs and vast expanses of mahogany for the uncertainties of the field, and inspirational only as models of what their juniors hope not to become.

My observations are that the quality of marketing leadership has far-reaching effects on the quality of marketing practices. Indeed, of the business units I observed, not once was high-quality marketing execution associated with a low-quality leader, whether that person was leading something as low-level as a pricing implementation or whether he or she was chairman of the board.

I shall have more to say about the kinds of managers that make good implementers, and hence good leaders, in Chapter 10, but the following is a "quick list" of some of the attributes I observed in high-quality leaders of the marketing effort:

- Better leaders were more willing than many others to tolerate "bad followers." That is to say, those who were associated with really good execution of marketing practices ran shops that allowed, even encouraged, diversity, divergence of opinion, even outright and near-violent disagreement about contemplated moves. The good leaders tolerated a fair amount of this creative diversity, knowing that the shared sense of understanding, vision, and theme held by all the members of the organization acted as a "glue" to hold things together. A simple statement of this rule is: "Good leaders, poor followers, strong theme."

The analogy may be made to a family having a "difference of opinion" about the site of its annual vacation. Husband may prefer the shore; wife the mountains; and kids not to go at all because they wish to be near their friends. In better marriages, such "discussions" may be heated or not, but there is never any question about the fact that the *family* will take a vacation, and together, no matter who wins out.

- Better marketing implementers are willing to allow subordinates to substitute their own skills for shortcomings in the marketing structure.

A story told about a manager at United Parcel Service is worth remembering. On December 24 a regional manager at a UPS depot learned that a large shipment of Christmas presents had been misdirected to the wrong part of the country. There was no one to call at headquarters; everyone had gone home for the holiday. On his own authority, this manager diverted two of the company's 727s and rented a fast freight to get the shipment of Christmas packages to their destination. I have no idea how much it costs to rent a freight train, but we can be fairly certain that the manager exceeded his authority extensively in this situation!

The interesting thing about the story is what *didn't* happen on December 26. The manager wasn't fired! Indeed, he was congratulated by his superiors on his excellent judgment and rewarded. This man's bosses can take as much credit for having a culture in which an employee can dare to make decisions as the employee him/herself gets for saving the day.

- In no case is marketing leadership to be judged adequate where there is no clarity of theme, strength of culture and vision, or willingness to manage by example as well as word.

There simply can be no compromise here. Top managers and top marketers who do not or cannot instill in their units a clear marketing theme, work for a common vision that allows a powerful and customer-oriented culture to emerge, and *act* in such a manner that these things become ingrained in their organizations cannot be certified as good marketing leaders.

Marketing has a number of unique facets, as we discussed in Chapter 1. For one, it involves customers. A top executive out of touch with those customers, *including* the distributors, can have no credibility in setting a marketing theme. Marketing also involves *everybody* in the company. The executive who is unwilling to lead by example, by his or her deeds, cannot lead.

CONCLUSION

Marketing implementation is affected at all its structural levels through the policy guidelines laid down by top management. Two special classes of policies affect the *practice* of the marketing job: policies of identity, which include marketing theme and culture, and policies of direction, which include marketing strategy and leadership.

Interestingly, these four "frame variables" seem to have much more to do with how the top marketing men or women and the top managers in general *act*, rather than with how they *say* they act. Where the top man is customer-oriented, field-savvy, and willing to listen to (and act on) distributor gripes, where he possesses a powerful and clear vision of what the organization is and what it does in marketing, the rest will follow. Where he or she does not or will not, there is ultimately little any consulting company or "quick medicine" can do to change what will happen, or rather won't happen, in the marketing function. Want to know how to make Jess Pagluica work? It's easy—show him!

CHAPTER SEVEN

Bridging the Gap

Maybe it's just the usual late afternoon letdown, but after all I've said about all these things today I just have a feeling that I've somehow talked around the point. Some could ask, ''Well, if I get around all those gumption traps, then will I have the thing licked?''

The answer, of course, is no, you still haven't got anything licked. You've got to live right too. It's the way that you live that predisposes you to avoid the traps and see the right facts.

Pirsig, *Zen and the Art of Motorcycle Maintenance*

I'VE MADE MUCH in previous chapters of shortcomings in the structures firms put in place to aid marketing practice. Whether low-level actions, programs, systems, or policies, structural aspects of marketing practice often are problematical and get in the way of execution excellence.

Clearly, some structural components work as we'd like them to: Hertz's ability to roll radical pricing moves through a far-flung system in a couple of months and Frito-Lay's running of the store-door sales force are examples. But my field work indicates that in the vast majority of instances, marketing structures become constraining and even inimical to good marketing execution.

Much of the time, then, it is necessary for the managers doing the marketing job to "bridge the gap" between structural shortfalls and good practices with their own execution skills. How that happens, as well as the relationship between marketing implementation structure and the managers who execute the strategies, is the subject of this chapter, which is itself a bridge between the analysis of marketing structure completed in the preceding chapters and the analysis of implementation skills to come.

THE MOTORCYCLE AND THE MECHANIC

One has to wonder how good marketing gets done at all in corporations if the structures for marketing practices are as regularly flawed and encumbered as I claim. Understanding how good marketing *does* occur despite flawed structures and learning something about improving the structures themselves is helped by understanding something about motorcycles and mechanics.[1]

It is convenient to see marketing structures as the "motorcycle" of marketing, composed of an engine, frame, drivetrain, and other subassemblies that have been well engineered to take the driver wherever he or she wants to go. But unless the motorcycle *runs*, nobody gets anywhere. Often it is the skill of the mechanic that determines whether the machine can be kept in good running condition, kept "patched up" despite increasing age and debilitation, to get to the destination anyway.

The remainder of this section summarizes some characteristics of successful marketing structures and suggests a way to assess them. The next section turns to some facets of the managers doing the job by way of introduction to the chapters that follow.

The Motorcycle: Marketing Structures

I have been specific about what goes wrong and (less frequently) what goes right in marketing structures in the earlier chapters. Here I'd like to summarize some generalizations learned there as a way of closing out our discussion of the "motorcycle" and as a prelude to turning toward the "mechanic."

From all that has gone before, several points present themselves to the observer of marketing structures. One important generalization about marketing structures is that they as often get in the way of good practice as they aid it, for a number of reasons that have been discussed in previous chapters. These include (1) management error, (2) creeping change that occurs as current reality slips away from old constructions of it, and (3) systems dominance over information needs. No matter how clever its actions, programs, systems, and policies structures, every firm will suffer from some of this debilitation. It's like the unavoidable calcification of bones or hardening of arteries that occurs as a side effect of life.

However, in those companies where marketing structure more often facilitated good practices than impeded them, several general patterns regularly appeared.

First, there was "soundness at the top and at the bottom, *not* flashiness in the middle" in these companies. That is, management worked hard at its blocking and tackling (actions) and also at knowing who it was (identity policies). In other companies management seemed not preoccupied with low-level blocking and tackling nor committed to identity clarity, but rather concerned with designing and redesigning clever programs it could not make work.

Second, in the well-structured firms there seemed to be a rule of "program pickiness with allocation extravagance." This phenomenon, also discussed in an earlier chapter, occurs when management is careful about its programmatic bets and knows how to say no to even attractive opportunities that would diffuse its mission. But once a "bet" is placed, the structure encourages backing that program or direction to the hilt with a useful extravagance of people, time, and money.

Finally, in the firms where structures worked invariably could be found clear themes, strong cultures, and powerful leaders. Without clear policies of identity and direction, little of worth is going to get done in the marketing function and, quite possibly, in the firm.

Without a doubt, however, the most important generalization about marketing structure is a reconfirmation of "simple" common sense. It suggests that the *people are more crucial than structures* in most corporations, because often the structures don't work. It is the managers and their skills (or lack of them) that will most often foster or impede quality marketing practice.

A mechanic, to use Robert Pirsig's terms, is a great deal more relevant to the daily operation of the motorcycle than the design engineers who made it. If you must choose between spending your money on a racing bike and a bad mechanic or on some machine a little less flashy that comes with a fix-it genius, it is usually wiser to go for the latter. Over time both motorcycles will become dirty, come up with loose chains and bald tires, and in general become less capable at doing what they were designed to do as they get older and are used in conditions for which they were not made. Continued performance depends on the abilities of the mechanic to keep the machine running.

Assessing Structural Adequacy. It is to be expected that top management or top marketing management occasionally may wish to get a perspective on the *overall* adequacy of its marketing structures. The quickest way I know to get a handle on the adequacy or to pinpoint bottlenecks in marketing structure is to conduct a "marketing audit."[2] In this technique an individual or group of insiders *or* outsiders asks the basic question, "How are we doing in marketing?" It is important that the question be posed just this broadly so that the scope of inquiry is wide enough to admit all sorts of questions and answers.

Usually an "audit" (or better, marketing opportunity analysis) involves simultaneous examination of several data streams. The first, of course, is a look at the numbers and the kinds of "back of the envelope" analyses of the business that we shall describe in Chapter 9 on monitoring. Relevant numbers streams are focused on, but so are the "simple divisions" that often are not done in companies. What, for example, is the dollar revenue generated for each manager, support person, and secretary in the marketing group? Does this "feel reasonable," both overall and in light of what the executives know about practices in other companies or industries?

The second audit aspect involves both internal and external interviews with managers, customers, and distributors. These are paramount, for customers and especially distributors have enough axes to grind to be straightforward (if biased) in their evaluations. It is not as important to take a statistical sampling of the customers as it is to generate a clinical sense of "deep knowing." Often I simply talk to the company's top three accounts, bottom three accounts, and three ex-customers, in addition to a distributor sample. It is also most important to talk with the sales force at length for these are the company's "close-to-the-customer" employees. They often represent both a disaffected and a highly informative group.

The third and most important part of a marketing audit is what I call a "structure analysis." This piece of the investigation looks specifically at the firm's actions, programs, systems, and policies to detect dysfunction and assess effectiveness.

Of these three pieces of a marketing audit, the most central and least often done is the third. If a simple and clear theme cannot be explained to outsiders by top marketers or general management, one might be suspicious that there is none. Alternatively, if several themes are voiced and they conflict, signs of trouble exist. And if the quality of marketing leadership is not high, it is almost impossible for good execution to follow.

The only reason to consult outsiders for such an intimate and sometimes uncomfortable analysis is if honesty is in short supply to inform the tough judgments that must be made in this sort of evaluation. Then, and only then, it might be worthwhile to pay outsiders for their "objectivity." Otherwise no one can bring the kind of in-depth industry knowledge to the business that a firm's own management has available. The foregoing chapters give a detailed checklist for what might be looked at structurally in a marketing audit.

The Mechanic: Subverting the Structure Toward Quality

Having thoroughly examined the motorcycle, we turn our attention fully on the marketing manager or "mechanic" in the next few chapters. The thesis of the book bears repeating. While marketing structures are important to the analysis of marketing practice, "rogue" or inadequate structures often cause marketing practices to go awry. Whether because of management by assumption, a phenomenon that occurs at the actions level, because of a weak theme or poor leadership at the top, or because of any other reasons, marketing practice seldom lives up to the plans set by marketing strategy. The poor manager finds himself stuck in the middle, charged with executing plans that the organization may not have the structural wherewithal to facilitate.

Or is he so stuck? The model of marketing implementation proposed in Chapter 2 suggests that marketing managers often can "patch up" shortcomings in the execution structure by exercise of personal implementation skills. They can, in a phrase, *subvert the organization toward quality.* Examining what skills best help managers perform such subversion is the purpose of the remainder of the book.

Exhibit 7–1 shows an outline of four execution skills essential to good marketing practice. They are interacting, allocating, monitor-

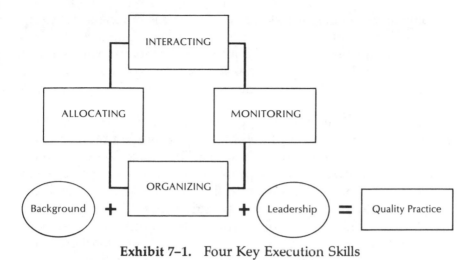

Exhibit 7-1. Four Key Execution Skills

ing, and organizing. Also shown as circles are two other variables that are perhaps less straightforwardly but no less importantly associated with getting the marketing job done. The figure shows these skills as interconnected because they *are* interconnected; they tend to exist or be absent in the manager as a piece. Exhibit 7-2 offers brief definitions of the four execution skills discussed below.

It is important to recognize that skills are not systems, and often the application of personal execution skills by managers runs counter to systems the firm has in place. The marketing organization, for example, is a system partially intended to regularize interactions among managers. Interact*ing* skill, though, pertains to a personal and informal application of talents at managing one's own and others' behavior that may run counter to the reporting hierarchy as formalized in the organization.

Exhibit 7-2. Definitions of the Four Key Skills

Interacting: Managing own and others' behaviors. Implies power, exchange, empathy, "street smarts," and "hustle."
Allocating: Apportioning time, people, and money across the tasks to be completed.
Monitoring: "Back of the envelope" and other watching skills that promote clarity and simplicity of understanding.
Organizing: Networking informally. Creative re-creation of temporary groups.

Similarly, a manager's skill at monitor*ing* is not the same thing as the operation of the firm's monitoring *system*. The former refers to "back of the envelope" calculations and other informal control devices, the latter to formalized intelligence and reporting systems. All the skills end in the *-ing* form to keep this distinction in focus.

Interacting. The marketing job by its nature is a matter of influencing others inside and outside the corporation regularly. Inside there is a continual parade of peers over which the marketer may have no power to impose preferences; instead he may have to strike horse trades, as when a brand manager asks the sales director to give "his" product more attention than it may otherwise merit in a pooled selling effort. Similar interactions may occur with R&D, purchasing, and manufacturing. Usually the marketer cannot *tell* any of these individuals what to do but rather is placed in a ticklish personal persuasion setting where the informal rules of social exchanges, favors, and "free lunches" can make the difference between marketing success and failure.

Outside the corporation the marketer deals with two distinct constituencies. The first is a plethora of "marketing partners," including advertising agencies, research suppliers, consultants, manufacturer's representatives, and the like, each with an agenda and an axe to grind. The classic manufacturer–distributor conflict described in an earlier chapter, for example, shows that the marketer often is put in a position of "balancing" the demands of the corporation against the very real needs of the customer when the two are distinct if not irreconcilably opposed.

The second constituency with which the marketer *should* regularly deal and about which he/she must remain continually aware is the end user. In fact, the marketer's job can correctly be categorized as one of a "boundary role person." That is, the marketer stands at and "owns" the boundary where firm capabilities meet customer needs and is responsible for adapting the one to the other. While customer "interactions" are not interactions in the usual sense of daily contact and employment of persuasive skills in conversation, the marketer needs to be aware of his key constituencies' preferences.

Allocating. The good implementer parcels everyone's time, including his or her own, across the myriad marketing jobs needing to be done. Not only time is parceled, but people, assignments, and dollars too, often in the face of a formal budgeting system that seems committed to overallocating resources to programs that cannot deliver marginal returns and underallocating them to higher-risk projects that might. Allocat*ing*, in the words of one executive, is the fine art of shifting small bits of discretionary money and "pieces" of people from "here and there" to make marketing work despite the formal allocation system.

Interacting and allocating are taken up together in Chapter 8, the first of two chapters on execution skills.

Monitoring. Trying to monitor the marketing effort through the formal systems made available to the manager in most corporations has been likened by one executive to having on one's desk a control panel of the complexity of those found on a 727 jet airliner. The control panel, however, has been vandalized repeatedly. It has broken dials, rusted levers, and numerous patches in the wiring harness. Some dials seem to read "OK" no matter what setting their associated levers are pulled to. Others fluctuate wildly, so that it is impossible to get a clear reading, and still others refuse to budge from their pegs. The really frightening moment, this manager points out, comes when the manager looks behind the control panel to see a tangle of wires meant to run out into the field, many dangling unconnected and still others apparently wired right back to his own chair!

The fine art of being able to drive one's own understanding of the business and the market place to such a finely honed point that one can manage the entire business on index cards is taken up in Chapter 9. We look there at monitor*ing* as an intrapersonal skill of the manager, which can be invoked to reconstruct degraded corporate information and control systems.

Organizing. The fourth skill is organizing, which others have termed networking. Good implementers have an almost uncanny ability to create afresh an informal organization, or network, to match each different problem with which they are confronted. They seem to "know somebody" in every part of the organization, and outside too, who by virtue of mutual respect, attraction, or some other tie, can and will become part of a *de facto* group to help with each different problem confronting the manager and the organization. These managers seem able to reconstruct or "re-create" an informal organization to suit the marketing job that needs to be done at any given point in time. They customize their informal organization to facilitate good execution. Sometimes their informal organization and the formal one through which they are instructed to act bear little in common.

We take up this customization of informal organization for execution efficiency, organizing, along with monitoring, in Chapter 9.

Other Variables Related to Execution Efficacy. The two circles on Exhibit 7–1 represent two factors less directly implicated in, but no less important to, subverting the organization toward quality practice.

In addition to my case work, I have researched the general question of whether some managers find implementation concerns more congenial while some are more comfortable with strategy. An alternative, of course, is that any manager can be adept at both types of managerial behavior. To see which account was appropriate, I set about giving top managers and top marketers in a number of companies a battery of psychological tests.

My beginning results suggest that there are "types" of individuals, or at least problem-solving styles, better suited to execution than to strategy pursuits. This research is taken up in Chapter 10. The preliminary results are interesting because they are counterintuitive, at least considering my initial ideas on the subject.

Chapter 10 also returns to the topic of marketing leadership as an outcome of the background variables that predispose managers to good execution.

Chapter 11, the last in the book and set in a section of its own, comes full circle to the most important question of all: What is quality in marketing practice, and how can it be recognized as well as assessed?

CONCLUSION

If marketing structure is the "motorcycle" of getting somewhere, then the managers' personal execution skills are the "mechanic" of execution efficacy. Often for reasons beyond the marketer's control, the structures put in place to make marketing practice easier make it more difficult, and the marketer is left high and dry with weak actions-level responsiveness; a bloated playbook of programs that are either empty promises or else represent the consequences of bunny marketing; systems that are ritualized, degraded, and useless; or policies of identity and direction that are vague or conflicting. Some characteristics of good marketing structure are identifiable and affectable by managers, but the usual state of affairs will be that marketing structures will not contribute to, and may even inhibit, quality marketing practice.

It is the manager's personal execution skills of interacting, allocating, monitoring, and organizing that can help "subvert toward quality" faulty organization structures and even organizations. Quality in marketing practices is a direct result. Interacting and allocating are taken up in Chapter 8; monitoring and organizing in Chapter 9; background variables and leadership in Chapter 10.

To assess marketing performance and practice adequacy fully, it is not enough to analyze the marketing structure, to "audit" only it to determine what is going on in the marketing function. The managers themselves and their personal execution skills are the fourth key component to assessing the adequacy of marketing practice. It is to this assessment that we turn in the next three chapters, leaving the question of whether it is managerially "better" to act on the structure or the people for the last chapter of the book.

CHAPTER EIGHT

Interacting and Allocating Skills

It must be considered that there is nothing more difficult to carry out, nor more doubtful of success, nor more dangerous to handle, than to initiate a new order of things.

—Niccolò Machiavelli, *The Prince*

ONE OF THE EARLIEST cases I prepared for this research project contained an unintended controlled experiment showing how the exercise of personal execution skills in one instance rescued, and in another harmed, a marketing program. What is interesting about this experiment is that these different outcomes occurred with the same cast of players, the same product line, in the same division, managed by the same top management in the course of little more than a year! The story of Nancy Christie at Gillette's Personal Care Division is instructive, for it shows how the exercise of interacting and allocating skills can make the difference between execution successes and problems.

Nancy Christie, new products manager at the Personal Care Division (PCD) of Gillette, found herself with a marketing problem and a political problem. Executives from PCD's advertising agency, Advertising to Women, were insisting on including a "conditioning" claim in the national advertising campaign to be launched shortly for Christie's newest product, Silkience Shampoo. Christie strongly believed that the conditioning ads would cannibalize sales of her latest product introduction, Silkience Conditioner, which had been highly successful in the market place.

Because both the brand and the agency were working against very tight deadlines and program delays, there was no time for gathering "objective" data on how much cannibalization would indeed occur, but the agency was confident it would be minimal —Christie was worried they were wrong.

Problematically for Nancy Christie, ATW had been intimately involved in the success of the conditioner product, and because of its successes there had the division vice president's ear on the shampoo launch. Indeed, the vice president had announced in a meeting that he thought Christie ought to trust the agency's judgment about the conditioning claim and wanted the ads run as recommended. Christie rightly was concerned that her relationship with the advertising agency had gotten out of control during the shampoo project and that the agency, rather than she, was effectively making the important decisions on the brand's line of goods.

Christie's Silkience Conditioner product had come from nowhere to account for 15 percent of the hair care group's and almost 8 percent of division profits in the two years that Nancy had managed new products. She had become a star in the organization. Everybody knew, though, that a good portion of her success should be credited to the advertising agency personnel. Close collaboration of Christie's team with agency people had brought about market success neither group alone could achieve.

For example, while Christie had invented the conditioner's "reason to buy" (the special properties of formulation that caused Silkience to condition damaged hair differentially more than it did healthy hair), ATW had been responsible for (1) the product's name, (2) its powerful "science of silkening your hair" slogan, and (3) clever advertising using computer-simulation techniques to illustrate the difficult-to-demonstrate notion of a differential-acting conditioner.

Much of the creativity in advertising had come as a result of involvement of the agency's president, Lois Geraci Ernst, a strong-willed and outspoken manager. Ms. Ernst had founded her agency on the premise that only women could advertise for women, because "men may have taken off a lot of bras, but they've never put one on."

The conditioner project had gone like clockwork. The agency executed flawlessly, developed creative strategies and new promotion techniques, and generally worked in such a way that Christie's reputation was enhanced while her goals were achieved for the product launch.

The second launch, that of the shampoo, by contrast, had been a comedy of errors between the agency and division personnel, and as far as Christie was concerned it was fast turning into a Saturday night horror movie. How is it possible for the same teams on both sides of the agency/client street to turn in such different performances within a very short time span with an identical marketing structure?

Some obvious answers are given by even a cursory look at the way the two collaborations were conducted. In the first, the conditioner project, PCD did not know ATW well; neither party was comfortable with the other. Members from both organizations, led by Christie, spent much time exploring each other's values, both toward work generally and as regarded the conditioner project in particular. Meetings between the brand and the agency groups were regular and frequent over the project's two-year development horizon. Testing and checks on ATW's work by Christie and her team were frequent[1] and almost compulsive, with feedback and readout occurring every month. There was no question that Ms. Christie and her brand group retained responsibility for the relationship and provided leadership for it. Christie was the dominant personality in the group.

The shampoo project, by contrast, was managed quite differently by both parties. First, agency and brand were not strangers, having worked together before and having what looked like a major success with the conditioner under their belts. Each was highly credible with the other. Meetings between brand and agency on the shampoo project were less frequent because brand (and agency) was under an exceptionally tight twelve-month deadline to introduce the shampoo as the first "flanker brand" in the Silkience line. Responsibility for the shampoo campaign was left largely in the agency's hands, and only infrequent checking was done by Christie's brand group during the development period. Because of the agency's previous success with the conditioner launch, Ms. Ernst found it increasingly easy to "go around" Ms. Christie to the PCD vice president when a conflict arose. It was clear that Ms. Ernst "owned" the relationship, supplied the leadership, and was the dominant personality in the shampoo program.

The immediate consequence of Christie's loose application of her interacting and allocating skills in this second agency collaboration was that Ms. Ernst took her "case" for a conditioning claim to the division vice president when the conflict erupted. Christie had few immediate alternatives except to swallow hard and vow that things would be different next time.

The interacting and allocating patterns Ms. Christie displayed in the shampoo program contributed toward attenuating[2] PCD's market share in the shampoo launch, and conversely her group's better behavior in the conditioner program had much to do with *that* product's success. There were no *structural* constraints here of the kind that mucked up marketing programs in earlier chapters;[3] it was Ms. Christie's exercise of personal execution skills that made the first program work and made the second one a problem.

This chapter is about *interacting* and *allocating*, two of the four personal execution skills important to fostering marketing quality. What interacting skills can the marketer bring to bear in order to "bridge the gaps" in execution structure and evoke quality action? The next section of the chapter takes up interacting. When the question is one of allocating time, people, and money across the myriad marketing jobs to be done, what skills are associated with quality practice? The third section of the chapter looks at allocating. The conclusion relates these to monitoring and organizing, skills to be discussed in the next chapter.

INTERACTING

Interacting skills are the abilities the marketer brings to the job for managing behavior. My observations[4] suggest that it is possible to categorize interacting skills into two major classes: those concerned with the management of *intra*personal events, or the manager's management of him/herself, and those concerned with the management of *inter*personal events, or the manager's management of others.

The marketing manager who would "bridge the gap" in execution structure shortfalls has to manage his own behavior and that of others in two critical contexts: in situations *internal* to the firm and in those occurring *external* to the company's confines. The former category concerns the application of behavior management skills with peers, co-workers and other firm functions, such as production. The latter category pertains to how well the marketer manages the parade of outsiders with which he or she must deal regularly: the ad agencies, distributors, and even consultants.

Exhibit 8–1 shows these two interaction contexts crossed by the type of behavior (own or others') being managed. What set of skills runs across the contexts to evoke quality marketing implementation?

The variables I cite below, though they are informed by science whenever appropriate, will not be found on the "top ten" or even "top hundred" list of those researched by psychologists or organizational behavior scholars. That is because traditional analyses of interaction have not found it easy to concentrate on the complex pattern of behaviors observed in the real world and because I have made a concerted effort to keep my analysis trained directly on the behavior of operating managers as they work in that world.

Managing One's Own Behavior

Three critical components to managing one's own behavior recur across the cases and managers I've studied. The first relates to the forces driving managers toward action, their "hot buttons." The second relates to the manager's understanding of what drives

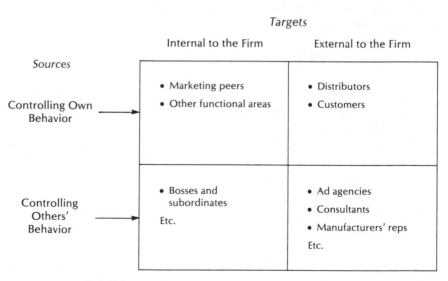

Exhibit 8–1. Interacting Sources and Targets

others. And the third concerns the manager's understanding of, and ability to manipulate, how people relate—what has been called "bubbapsychology,"[5] or the informal psychology of how the social world works.

Hunger, Guts, Motivation, and Fire in the Belly

John Wayne, Gunga Din, the U.S. Marines, and a number of my managers—what the heroes and the military share in fiction the good managers have in reality: They're *hungry*. Not literally hungry, of course, though that doesn't hurt either. Rather, they're hungry in the same way Shakespeare's Caesar saw Cassius: He "hath a lean and hungry look."

What the old Marine movies and John Wayne used to call "guts," what Professor Theodore Levitt calls a "fire in the belly," what the corporate trainers call motivation is what good marketing implementers have in high supply. Just so we're square on terms, what I mean by "hungry" is useful aggressiveness and high motivation to succeed.

Dan Siewert, written about in Chapter 6, is hungry. Joe Lawler, president of Boston Whaler, is also hungry. Victor Kiam, president of The Remington Company, was so hungry that he bought this failing division from its large parent, turned it around in less than three years, and paid down a twenty-year debt in four years! Equally hungry were a host of the other managers I studied who exhibited a consistent willingness to make up shortcomings in the execution structure with their own abilities in order to get the job done. Remember the manager at United Parcel Service who diverted the two 727s and rented the fast freight train in order to get the Christmas presents where they belonged. He was *hungry*.

The "hungry" managers *would not accept* failures in the structure as either reasons for or contributors toward program failure. As one CEO whose division quite literally was in life-threatening trouble recently said to me, "It *has* to succeed, and it *will* succeed." The rule seems pretty simple: Hungry managers get the job done, at least in marketing, and "fat" ones don't.

The existence of a "fire in the belly" is well documented in the psychological literature. Psychologist David McClelland and his colleagues,[6] for example, have written a number of books about the "need for achievement" and its relationship to behavior. Their evidence is solid that individuals differ regularly in how much of the motive to achieve they display and that differences in the achievement motive affect behavior powerfully.

One early method used to check on the effects of achievement motivation was to ask people to play a dart or other target game while standing at various distances from the target (like 3, 6, 9, 12, and 15 feet), and to estimate how many "hits" out of ten they were likely to get. Over a number of experiments using this method, a peculiar finding kept recurring. First, all participants who were asked to stand at different distances from the target showed the expected effects on their estimates of how well they would do. When they stood very close, estimates of success were quite high, and when they stood very far, quite low.

Participants high in the motive to achieve showed a distinctly different pattern of estimates at intermediate distances; they estimated a much higher success rate than did other participants when placed at the middle range, and they were right! They were, as long as the task allowed it, willing to bias their estimates upward and to deliver on their promises. There are internal motives to achieve success, and those high in this drive are behaviorally "overconfident" when facing the vast majority of intermediate-risk tasks.

Also, it has long been known in the social psychology literature that recruits for a group will value that group more if the premembership hazing is more severe than if it is lenient. In a famous experiment, females (in a time when things were different) were asked to read in front of a male experimenter either an innocuous or a quite sexually explicit passage into a tape recorder on the pretext that this audition was a precondition for joining a discussion group. Those who read the embarrassing passage wanted to join the discussion group more than those who read the innocuous one. Similarly, military reservists who agreed to eat grasshoppers on request of a gruff and unlikable doctor doing an experiment reported liking the grasshoppers more often than those who agreed at the request of a likable and attractive physician. This phenomenon, in which individuals evaluate as more worthy those things which come with more effort or those that they do with only little justification, is called "effort justification."

From data such as the achievement experiments, it is an easy conclusion that people in general *and* managers differ in the amount of "useful aggressiveness and high motivation" they bring to the job. Second, powerful findings from the "effort justification'' experiments suggest that motivation or ''hunger'' is manipulable and has predictable effects on behavior.

Sources of Hunger

Where do you get ''hungry'' managers? How (if at all) can managers be made hungry? Useful aggressiveness and high motivation seem to be provoked largely from two sources: background and current environment conditions. The first source, background, is more permanent and probably cannot be modified easily. The other, social environment, is less permanent but possible to arrange managerially.

Regarding background, some marvelous sociological research shows that the reason so many immigrants to this country (some used to be called ''DPs'') in the 30s, 40s, and 50s became successful entrepreneurs was that the alternative to succeeding was too horrible to contemplate! Having nothing, arriving at Ellis Island not speaking the language in which an official-looking inspector was asking questions, and remembering constantly the alternatives in the ''old country'' had a remarkable way of making these people long-term hungry.

This background effect reappears in attenuated form for many of the good implementers in my sample, who often came up ''the hard way'' and were ''climbing above their station.'' Similar effects are possible whenever even a watered set of ''immigrant conditions'' obtain, whether these are as relatively short-lived as switching careers to an industry where the manager is initially suspected of not having the credentials to do the job to more deep-rooted causes, like poverty in childhood.

Now, it is not considered good personnel policy to recommend recruiting freshly landed immigrants for marketing jobs or good training policy to starve people into action. Making people eat grasshoppers also is out of the question for most corporate training departments. It is fortunate, therefore, that environmental conditions can have powerful effects on motivation in the manager.

Perhaps the most important precondition for developing ''hunger'' is a *belief that effort, performance, and reward are related.* This low-level requirement is *not* present in very many corporations or marketing departments. Informal ''lunchroom'' conversations with marketers or any one else in most companies would convince the observer that effort often is punished, performance leads only to demands for more performance, and rewards are dispensed either in some poor mimicry of socialism or else randomly. In point of fact, most marketers don't seem to believe there *is* much of a connection between what they do and what they get, and they're probably right.

Julian Rotter,[7] a social psychologist, has found evidence that different generalized belief sets about effort and consequences exist and that such beliefs vary among people. He distinguishes "internal and external locus of control orientation" or, more simply, internally and externally controlled individuals. Internals believe that their own efforts determine their fate, that "there are no accidents and no excuses" and that they personally are responsible for what happens to them. Externals believe that luck, fate, and other "external" sources of control have large impacts on their lives and that, as a consequence, there is not much they can do to make things turn out right.

From our standpoint, a most valuable finding of the studies conducted is that behaviors characteristic of each orientation, though highly correlated with background variables, are affected by others as well as by training. For instance, it has been found that when commitments ("I can get this done for you, boss!") are made publicly rather than privately, there is much less tendency to "back off" from them, an outcome bearing the earmarks of control. We know also that very bad internal administrative decisions often are taken because of a kind of flocking in staff groups to a position of conformity with the dominant opinion being offered, even if it is wrong. Internal and external control behaviors, in short, are powerfully affected by the social context in which they occur.

The second precondition for provoking hunger is an *atmosphere in which goals are clear and the individual can matter in their attainment*. This is a precondition that was not met in many of the marketing groups I observed, at least if by "matter" is meant to be able to have an impact on the organization. Rather, the trend seemed to be toward encouraging group behavior, lack of accountability, and (in the larger companies) a kind of anonymity as a result of size that makes clever execution frustrating because it is the managerial equivalent of trying to push a glacier. What happened to quality in our society has a lot to do with what happened to the ethic of individual responsibility—they both vanished about the same time.

The primary force encouraging an "atmosphere" where managers could develop was the presence of good implementers who *made* the atmosphere happen for their direct reports. It did not matter if the corporation as a whole encouraged such an atmosphere, but only if the individual's immediate bosses were the kind of good interactors who encouraged it. Good interaction, quite simply, breeds good interaction. Interestingly, good managers in not-so-good companies often had remarkably able units, abler than any assessment of the environment in which they worked would lead an observer to predict. In essence, they "insulated" themselves and their staffs from the mediocrity prevailing in the company as a whole and did their jobs anyway.

The third and fourth preconditions of hunger are, respectively, *other hungry people,* and *leaders who tolerate, encourage, and reward hunger* in subordinates. There is nothing so conducive to getting hungry yourself as learning that hungry others are "helping" you with your job, as when the plant manager learns that the marketer is spending as much time on the line as he is. Indeed, much of the impetus for the highly touted "managing by walking around" philosophy comes from the effects of a highly motivated general manager's poking his/her nose into, and mucking with, others' areas of responsibility.

Without good leaders (see Chapters 6 and 10) to set the tone of tolerance for "poor followers," the hungry marketer will either be driven out by the incompetents or else threaten the less able so much that nothing will get done.

In summary, there are two sources of hunger, one intimate and personalistic, the other environmental. Of these sources, the former is permanent but rarer and essentially untrainable. It is easy to point to studies about immigrant zealousness but hard to test for it in the job interview.

The second source of hunger can be developed in subordinates by a good interactor. The good interactor tends to establish an atmosphere, conditions for rewards, and environmental contingencies that encourage more good interaction in a beneficial cycle, so that the whole department or group becomes able "hustlers." One good strategy for increasing hustle, then, is to "seed" marketing groups with one highly placed hustler.

Knowledge of Others: The Unholy Triad

The example of Nancy Christie shows clearly that the manager who controls only his or her own behavior will fail for want of controlling the actions of the numerous others with whom he or she must deal. Whether interacting with the production group, with finance people on budgets, or with any of the numerous outsiders like customers and trade that define the uniqueness of the marketer's job, interaction skills presume a good knowledge of what drives others and what makes them tick. The best implementers have this "second sense"; the others do not.

The "second sense" is made up of (1) a single behavioral constant in the good implementer's behavior and (2) regularly asking three questions about every interaction engaged. The constant is that good implementers are *avid observers* of others' behavior. I have seen this trait regularly displayed by the good implementers in the sample—whether in a shopping mall or at work, a curiosity about and great interest in the behaviors of others are always present.

But just watching will not tell any marketer why customers are doing what they are doing, why the trade is behaving as it is, or even why a co-worker is acting in a particular manner. Watching is enhanced by asking three simple questions about the behaviors and actors themselves:

1. What do they want?
2. How do they see things?
3. How powerful are they?

This "unholy triad" was the analytic frame used by many of the managers whom I would call good implementers. They were vitally interested in the motivations, the perceptions, and the power relationships occurring in the world around them. Their interest seemed to come first out of the natural curiosity I described above, but second from a very real belief that if they understood the dynamics of what was driving the other party, they could control these to the advantage of both, the betterment of the business, and, most centrally, the accomplishment of the task at hand.

It did not matter whether the manager in question was a first-line sales manager or the head of a billion-dollar division. Regularly, those whom I would call especially able at substituting their own skills for shortcomings in the execution structure were quite good "amateur psychologists" in that they were active observers of others and quite sensitive theorists about what was going on in each situation in which they found themselves involved.

The net result, of course, is that these individuals seemed especially adept at figuring out what the finance person or distributor wanted, how he or she saw things, and where the power lay in the interaction. Joint tasks, with this understanding, became possible even in conflictful settings where a less sensitive or active observer might have made crucial mistakes that would short-circuit execution.

Such other-directed interaction skills *are* teachable, but not in the way many of us go about trying to do it.[8] A key requirement for teaching interaction skills is that curiosity must be bred and developed by watching—regular watching.

For example, regarding the development of customer-watching skills, I routinely recommend to marketers that *everyone* in the marketing department have one "selling day" per quarter, in *direct interaction* with customers (not with regional managers or branch people, but on sales calls). "Customer days" should be held regularly as well, when end users and distributors (separately) are invited to gather, share their concerns, and *be listened to* by management. On these days managers should try to limit themselves insofar as possible to pure question-asking of the customers or distributors, not to defending the product line or explaining how the customer is wrong. The goal should be to understand where he or she is "coming from." Such days with the marketer's prime constituency, provided they are undertaken *by top management* and not just dictated from on high as requirements for others, have remarkable effects in breeding the curiosity that I indicated above was so important.

When curiosity exists for one marketing constituency, the customer, it will not be long before intrafirm interactions show the same "heavy communication" effects of (1) trying to take another's point of view and (2) learning what his or her "hot buttons" are. When that happens, the inevitable conflicts that arise in the management of marketing can be resolved in favor of effective execution no matter how poor the formal structure.

This approach, it should be pointed out, is quite different from making people who would rather be in their offices sit in training seminars hearing guests of dubious relevance talk about "team building" and "empathy." Get them out in the field! Limit everyone to questions! Most important, *go yourself!*

The Bubbapsychology of Relationships

The final characteristic of effective interactors was an implicit understanding of the nature of relationships as characterized by exchange, tit-for-tat, trading of utility for utility, and other "social market value'' characteristics. No matter how expressed, whether as ''there ain't no free lunch'' or ''you give and you get,'' it was implicitly understood *and acted upon* by the good interactors that compromise, logrolling,[9] and the principles of exchange are what dominate management life.

This ''grandmother psychology'' of exchanges served the good interactors in solid stead in their intra- and extrafirm relationships. Those managers were quick to recognize that sales force management might allocate more time to well-supported products than poorly supported ones, and even that a liked product manager has more leverage with the reps than one regarded neutrally. They did not regard the notion that they should provide something ''in exchange for'' another's cooperation as either morally reprehensible or evil, but rather as a sound principle of management action. In essence, they used their analysis of others' motivations to figure out what was important in the relationship, then tried to provide it in the interest of getting the job done.

Others less skilled at interaction were quicker to use phrases describing how the other party *should* behave (''You ought to go along with this price increase. We need it!'') instead of making a descriptive analysis of how the other *did* behave and then trying to work with it.

The critical difference was whether the manager started from an assumption that managing customers, distributors, peers, or whomever required willingness to make deals and to structure mutually profitable exchanges, or whether the base assumption was that the other party ''owed'' it to the manager (by virtue of clarity of position, company responsibility, or whatever) to go along with proposed actions. Those who were sensitive to exchanges, who treated their own peers like customers, got things done. Those who were not didn't understand either customers or peers and had great trouble executing even the simplest marketing actions.

Summary: Interacting Skills

What good interacting skills come down to is a set of simple characteristics that can be fostered in managers. The first characteristic is hunger, having high personal motivation. The second is having a curiosity about and a willingness to analyze the behavior of others, both inside and outside the corporation. The third is having a realistic understanding of how the social world works. Where these are present, so are interacting skills; where they are not, one can only hope for soundness of structure, because the ability to "patch" weak structures is limited.

You should note that I do *not* cite as a characteristic of good interactors the "bias toward action" that others think is a key criterion of excellent management.[10] That is because I think that calling bias toward action a characteristic of good management mistakes symptoms for causes. Good implementers *do* have a bias toward action; but it is as *a result of* their "fire in the belly," understanding of others, and poor followership that they display that characteristic. Action tendencies without an understanding of others' positions, moreover, produces catastrophe. It is far better to work on the skills that make for high motivation and understanding of others than to encourage action, any action, without these crucial prerequisites.

ALLOCATING

I recently attended a meeting with a divisional president who had gotten himself into the proverbial marketing soup. By virtue of his persuasive powers and solid results, he persuaded corporate to part with several million dollars for a three-city rollout of a new concept in retail stores. Penetration in the first test site was complete, but early sales returns indicated a performance rate about one-half what both the president and his corporate superiors had hoped for. Corporate management, in its inimitable way, was urging retrenching on expenses (particularly in advertising) as a way to make the less than adequate numbers at least more presentable on the bottom line.

My friend, of course, wanted no part of this. He was convinced that because of the window of market opportunity, there was no way he could lose *enough* money in the current year to position himself correctly for the fat margins and high share he saw available. He thought as well that the best way to increase store sales in the test site was to double advertising. The corporate plan had been submitted and approved. It promised neither doubling nor halving of advertising. What should our president do?

Well, I think you might counsel him as he did himself: Go for it! He reasoned as follows. First, his largest problem was not the lower-than-expected store sales; he thought those were explained quite nicely by the increased competitive advertising that had been

going on in response to his high-profile market entry. His most immediate problem, he felt, was corporate itself. If he failed to produce numbers as quickly as necessary, the capital available for
more stores might "dry up" at corporate, causing him to miss a
market window he thought was no more than two years wide. If he
missed the window, in turn, he would wind up with twenty stores,
no national image, and an "also-ran" (in his opinion) diversification effort. In this case he had no wish to be president.

On the other hand, if he went all-out now and just took the
beating corporate was sure to give him, there was a good chance he
could "punch up" the stores' sales to keep the capital coming, the
building continuing, and the future of the division sound. Most
important, he was convinced, though the numbers did not yet
demonstrate it, that he had a winner on his hands, and come hell or
high water he intended to bet his money on what he perceived was
a sure win for the corporation despite what he perceived as a case
of cold feet in his superiors.

This example has all the elements of a good case, because we do
not know how it will come out. Yet it teaches much about allocating skill. First, at least in the division president's view, the
allocating system (planning and budgeting) is getting in the way of
"right action." Second, a tough decision must be made whether to
(1) look bad by listening to corporate and thus (in the manager's
mind) short-circuit the potential of the rollout, or (2) look bad by
sticking to his guns and allocating monies[11] that were not approved
while trying to deliver on a promise.

The manager in question, to my mind (I can almost see the con-
trollers blanching!), made a good decision in proceeding with
"allocation extravagance" despite the problems. He believed his
idea was a several-hundred-million-dollar one for the company
and was not going to begrudge the attempt several hundred thousand dollars and fail for want of decking resources against an unex-
pected problem.

In large measure, there is not so much known from other
disciplines about allocating as there is about interacting. I am
therefore reduced to repeating and expanding on some points I
have made earlier about (1) avoiding global mediocrity and (2)
showing program pickiness with allocation extravagance as evi-
dences of good allocating skills. First, however, it is worth a short
digression to talk about what *exactly* the marketer allocates in the
day-to-day routine.

The Routines of Allocation

There are only three commodities available to the marketer for allocating: his/her own time, others' time, and "loose money." By "loose money" I mean either the approved or unapproved reallocation of resources from one category to another as day-to-day requirements demand and skill permits.

Without a doubt the most important commodity allocated by marketers is their own time, though this is not generally perceived. What the top marketer or general manager pays attention to, so will others. If he or she goes down into the plant to make sure that towing hooks do not pull out of their sockets, quality control will be emphasized. If he or she constantly computes "back of the envelope" ratios, pores over customer research data, and visits stores, so will others do these things and attend to them.

Thus, while it is generally thought that time allocation on the part of the manager is a simple matter of dealing with one task or another, the *real* effects of how the top marketing manager allocates his or her time are in the effects *by example* on the remainder of the group. One easy test of this phenomenon is to start staying an hour later than your usual departure time or start arriving an hour earlier. Then watch the parking lot!

The guidance given to others in how they allocate *their* time also has powerful effects. What is the reaction of the marketer to requests to spend a day in the field to gather customer data? Is it thought to be a "useful day" for subordinates routinely to spend significant time in planning or other administrative meetings, or are they encouraged continually back to problems, projects, and deadlines? Is the time of others a valuable resource to be spent carefully or a slavelike "on-call" status that permits interminable interruption, reallocation, and then blame for nondelivery at the whim of the manager?

Finally, how does the manager deal with "loose dollars"? Every organization has a budgeting process, but every budgeting process can be and is subverted in the interests of getting the marketing job done. These subversions, parenthetically, are not always in the direction of increasing expenditures either, but often concern decreases in what was planned because funds are not needed or are needed more urgently elsewhere. What we are discussing here is not the allocation *system* but rather the *allocatings* that go on within system constraints.

In talking about our three allocating tasks below, I divide them into the management of existing marketing subfunctions and programs, which really is concerned with the avoidance of global mediocrity, and new venture allocating, which means the way programs are "bet on."

Avoiding Global Mediocrity—Managing Existing Events

If there is one thing formalized systems tend to encourage, it is equality of allocation across existing subfunctions and programs. If there is one thing the manager with good allocating skills does, it is to subvert this parody of democracy toward what might be called subfunctional and programmatic "allocation portfolio management." That is to say, the most able implementers in my sample were religious about feeding the skinny kids, keeping the fat ones on diets, and letting their best people have a crack at the "impossible" situations that just *had* to work.

The tricks used to avoid global mediocrity in spite of the encouragements of the formal budgeting system were multiple. In some firms it was done with the informal allocation of monetary resources, "shoebox marketing." But in others, where the budgeting and planning systems didn't allow that kind of flexibility, reallocating was done with people and time.

The head of production engineering in one firm, for instance, was asked to spend the next business quarter on special assignment to the commercial products division in order to bolster this fledgling group's sales efforts (which involved a high component of custom design), and also to reduce the power concentration between design and production engineering, which management thought had become a roadblock to the firm's ability to listen to its dealers and customers in the design process. No formal reorganization or even rewriting of job descriptions was made; indeed, the general manager (there was no marketing department in this $35-million firm) simply got concurrence from the parties involved and went ahead with the "temporary assignments."

Whether the tactical allocating fix involved money, time, or people, however, some common behavioral rules were observed from the good implementers. These rules seemed to categorize a three-stage allocating model:

1. Good implementers looked closely at their business to

isolate the marketing subfunction or subfunctions that provided their "distinctive competitive advantage," in the terms of the consultants. Usually this function was obvious, as with advertising at Gillette or the store-door distribution system at Frito-Lay. These critical subfunctions in the first cut received the "extra" time and monetary allocations they needed to keep them at premier status.

2. A hard look was taken at the more mature, relatively risk-free programs that were the mainstays of the company's business in order to see if perhaps certain younger individuals couldn't be reassigned to other projects, if certain monies couldn't be saved through systematization of activity or other "behavioral automation," and thus if some costs couldn't come out of the program.

3. The resulting "loose resources" in terms of young "up and comers," "shoebox money," and the like were decked against a small array of high-risk programs or activities that management wanted to encourage developmentally.

This allocating flow from premier function assurance to mature program thinning to developmental program feeding, diagrammed on Exhibit 8–2, seemed to mark a relatively general pattern for managements able at marketing execution. It must be emphasized that this *allocating* often was carried out *between* planning and budgeting periods, as well as fostered *within* allocation mechanisms. The dominant trait of the good allocators, as with the good implementers, was a continual attempt to subvert the organization toward quality in marketing practices by everyday "management latitudes" with money, time, and people.

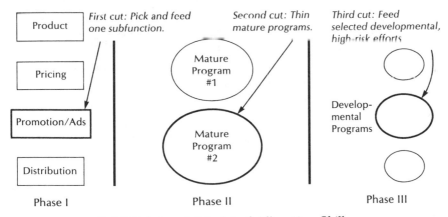

Exhibit 8–2. A Model of Allocating Skill

Program Pickiness: New Program Development

Exhibit 8–2's model leaves how new marketing programs are picked unclear, and it is here that our second behavioral rule of allocating comes to the fore. It has been mentioned previously that one distinguishing characteristic of good marketing implementers is that they seem to display "program pickiness with allocation extravagance." That is, it is not so easy to get a glimmer of a new idea endorsed by these men and women, but once they decide to back the horse they will back it to the full extent their own commitment and wallet allows.

There are two components of this second allocating rule: the pickiness and the allocation. Regarding the first, we are talking about the ability to say no to opportunities for programs, acquisitions, or whatever, because they are not right for the business, the management, or the abilities found in the marketing group. The ability to say no is *not* present in many of the managers with whom I have worked; they instead seem to have learned the "bias toward action" rule without learning as well the need to discriminate between good opportunities and bad.

There is nothing wrong and everything right with being an opportunist. But the good implementer knows that resources are limited and is careful about what he takes on both because it may prevent a better opportunity from being engaged and because his management group is good at some things and not at others.[12]

The second component is allocating extravagance. I pick "extravagance" as a provocative word, for my better implementers were indeed extravagant with the few new marketing programs in which they had decided to believe. The best people, the most "shoebox" dollars, and, most important, the greatest bulk of their time were allocated to nurturing these few endeavors, even when things did not look very good for their future.

I have seen more "about to fail" marketing programs pulled back from the brink of disaster and made into successes by marketing or general management allocation extravagance and persistence than most of the managers with whom I've been associated would like to recall. If the predominant allocating sin in program pickiness is the failure to say no, the predominant one once management has chosen its horses for betting is the failure to keep saying yes, to "keep the faith" during a project's growth and development.

Often, as in the case of the incremental advertising allocating problem described at the beginning of this section, formal allocation systems or corporate oversight gets in the way of managerial persistence. Here the good implementers kept allocating time, money, and people anyway and *made* the programs work. There is something to knowing when to say no and when to say yes. That's what the good allocators showed.

CONCLUSION

It is easy to get the false impression that any of these four marketing skills can be talked about or fostered in isolation from any of the others. That is an impression I had when I started this research, an impression of which the data rudely disabused me.

To allocate effectively *requires* good monitoring skills, for how is the continuing stream of allocating decisions to be modified by feedback without this capability? Similarly, effective interaction presupposes a group of "relevant others" with whom to interact, and this in turn presumes good organizing skills, which is how such a group gets assembled.

Interacting, allocating, monitoring, and organizing come of a piece, and it is rare to see a manager who is a good allocator who is not also good at monitoring the guts of the business. This fact has two implications. The first is that marketing implementation skills *do* come of a piece more often than not, rather than as abilities to be trained in isolation from each other. There are interesting consequences for training from this insight, which we shall take up in Chapter 9 as we discuss the remaining two execution skills, monitoring and organizing.

The second implication is that it may be possible to talk about managers whose career preferences and general abilities sets predispose them more toward implementation than strategy formulation, a topic we'll take up in Chapter 10.

CHAPTER NINE

Monitoring and Organizing

We say that a formal control is one that's driven by a complicated rule book. An informal one is driven by, maybe, soft "symbolic behavior." Exactly wrong. . . . The soft stuff is that rule book. Nobody reads the blasted things anyway! As one savvy senior officer said to me, "You ought to call it what it is, an 'excuse book,' not a rule book. The only time anyone ever reads the 400-page procedure manuals is after somebody screws up."

— Thomas J. Peters, "Moving Toward Excellence"

RECENTLY I WAS ASKED to sit in on an advertising agency research readout to management in a consumer goods firm. The croissants were warm, the show multimedia, and the presentation a provocative one on the agency's segmentation conclusions from some focus groups it had conducted. The agency had isolated four "psychographic profiles" that its research director implied represented viable industry segments. Each profile was supported by slide portraits of a "typical user" of the product, a snappy lifestyle biography of each person in the photo, and an impressive array of detail about each person profiled. The agency was asking for an incremental amount of money for advertising programs and more research money.

After asking only a couple of questions, it was possible to establish that (1) the photos shown were staged, not pictures of real consumers; (2) the life-style biographies were based on "informed speculation" in addition to the clinical data from the focus groups; and (3) the research personnel were mainly trying to stimulate management's thinking about its market rather than to report empirical results on which they felt confident to base significant marketing actions.

None of these things were unusual practice by the agency. It is common in preliminary psychographic research to compile a semi-speculative biography of typical segment representatives and even to hire actors to pose for "naturalistic" photos. But had management not thought to have someone around familiar with the ins and outs of qualitative research, a different set of conclusions could have been reached by management about the findings. No one from the agency, for instance, volunteered that the photos were "staged" until they were questioned directly on the matter!

Monitoring marketing research, like anything else in marketing, requires an intimacy with the tasks at hand that allows converting *data* offered by the environment into *information* useful to management, even when the systems in place to provide that information do not do so in the manner best suited for decision-making. Generally speaking, there are far too much data and not nearly enough information available—the manager good at monitoring is the one who can make the translations.

Return to Gillette

In the previous chapter I suggested that Nancy Christie's problems at Gillette's Personal Care Division implicated failures in *monitoring* skills as much as they did interacting and allocating ones. Christie, you'll remember, managed a first collaboration with her advertising agency well but a second one poorly. A new product introduction was threatened by the resulting conflict.

When managers look at the Christie dilemma, they are quick to point out that whatever else Ms. Christie did differently between the two projects, she chose to *monitor* the agency's activities far differently (and worse) in the second collaboration from the first. What happened, the managers point out, is the understandable but not excusable sloppiness that comes from growing acquaintance and trust.

In the first project they did together, brand management continually monitored everything the agency did, from expenditures to intermediate work to test commercials. Because they didn't know *what* to check on, brand management checked on everything, overmanaged the monitoring, but wound up with a highly successful project and a good product introduction.

In the second project Christie brought a history of prior success to the job that included a growing feeling of trust in the agency's judgments. Consequently Christie monitored the agency with neither the formality of measures (monthly progress reports, weekly meetings, and so on) nor the "tightness" of control she showed in the first collaboration.

The problem was not that Christie monitored *less* in the second project; any manager would have done that, given the good history from the first project and the growing trust in the relationship. Rather, what Christie failed to do was to transform her "tight and formal" monitoring demands in the first project into "tight and informal" ones in the second. She became sloppy as well as informal, and thus risked her project by not relaxing formality while insisting on the key measures previous experience had taught her were essential to project success.

Having gotten into trouble, Ms. Christie further was experiencing significant *organizing* problems with the shampoo launch as well. Her execution network for getting the shampoo out paid good attention to the R&D, sales, production, and other links in the division, which she had developed carefully to ensure smooth execution on tight deadlines. She even had managed her immediate boss carefully and knew she could count on him to provide support in the event of glitches. What she did not carefully organize was ATW's ability (and willingness) to go around her to division general management, an omission that threatened what she believed was the soundest course of action to take on the advertising campaign for the shampoo introduction.

This chapter is about monitoring and organizing skills. The former refers to the managerial ability to drive one's understanding of events relevant to the business to a powerful simplicity, providing oneself and others timely information that the formal reporting system may not be able to provide. The latter concerns "social networking," the ability to create informal cross-functional groups that can get the marketing job done regardless of constraints existing in the formal organizational system. The second section of the chapter takes up monitoring, the third organizing, and the conclusion summarizes the four personal execution skills and their relationship to marketing execution structures.

MONITORING

Monitoring skill is an *understanding of relationships and events* essential to executing marketing strategies, plans, and programs. What must be understood, of course, varies according to one's position in the organization and also with the marketing task at hand. The product manager with a specific mandate for a single product line has one set of needs; the new marketing vice president contemplating a clean desk and innumerable questions about the health of his or her new marketing unit has quite another.

Yet there are regularities that appear in the tasks of monitoring, the principles of good versus not-so-good application of monitoring skills, and even in the personal and company preconditions that foster creative monitoring of the marketing effort. It is to these that we shall turn, then circle back to the general or top manager's needs for looking at the marketing function.

What Marketing Monitors

Regardless of a manager's narrow or wide scope of marketing responsibility, there are four essential monitoring tasks every marketer tries to satisfy. They concern monitoring *people* engaged in the marketing effort, *markets and products* concerned, *time*, and *money*. Exhibit 9-1 shows these four tasks (plus some subtasks implicated in the management of markets and products), the utility of monitoring systems data ordinarily provided to the manager, and the consequent need to supplant systemic data with clever understandings provided by the exertion of monitoring skills.

The manager *needs* good monitoring skills because of the pervasive inadequacy of monitoring systems, which was commented on in Chapter 2 and again in Chapter 7. Over time, systems put in place to serve managers wind up driving them, because information needs are dynamic while systems are static. Especially sensitive to this problem are marketing control systems, which often get "bundled" with financial accounting ones or else have such a high need for *ad hoc* or changing requests that the systems simply cannot keep up with the needs.

The items listed on Exhibit 9-1 can be aggregated into two groups. The first, which includes both people and time monitoring, is in large measure an attempt to get a look at how human effort is paying back against tasks and projects. Here the marketer is interested in monitoring not only others' progress but his own

Exhibit 9–1. Monitoring Tasks

TASKS	SAMPLE QUESTIONS	ABILITY OF SYSTEM TO PROVIDE
1. People	How are marketing peers and subordinates doing on various projects?	Low
2. Markets/Products • Data overview needs • Information on customers and trade	How are we doing against competition, across segments and product lines? How are particular programs being accepted? How do customers and distributors feel about ____?	Variable, but generally surprisingly low
3. Time	How are our time allocations paying off by segment, program, products?	Low
4. Money	How are our dollar allocations paying off?	Moderate

against marketing goals. "Interest" is the key word in this sentence, as we shall see below.

The managers best at monitoring time and people (including themselves) that I observed showed several characteristics not observed in other managers. The first and most important was honest, genuine *interest* in and detailed *knowledge about* what their peers and subordinates were doing on a day-by-day basis.

When I was introduced to one of his subordinates by an especially able manager, for example, I invariably got a thirty-second thumbnail biography of the person that was so remarkably detailed that it had to have come from interest rather than memorization (including, often, undergraduate majors in college!). I also was treated to another thirty seconds on what the subordinate was working on *right now,* why it was important, what the key problems in the task were, and what was being done about them. A sample introduction would go like this (all done, generally, in less than a minute):

> You'll need to spend some time with John Jones here to understand how we do agent distribution. John's one of my key people. He came to us from Honeywell Information Systems, where he previously managed a $20-million spare parts group. Before that, he majored in chemical engineering at Yale, then went on to get a Harvard MBA. We forgive him the former, but not the latter!
>
> Seriously, John tells me our most pressing problem with the agents is that, while they're good at making the small-unit sale, they just aren't responding to or following up on all the leads we keep sending over to them. John's taking a look at what we can do in the way of training agents better, and also at other distributor support programs that we can put in to try to fix this problem.
>
> Oh, by the way, John. One of the things I was reflecting on last night from our dinner with Avco Supply was what we could do for Charlie, and maybe the other agents, by way of better incentives to help us partner with them. Are you looking at that area too? Maybe you could discuss it with Susan at the next staff meeting if you think the issue's got merit.

The obvious interest, detailed knowledge, and "deep background" on the subordinate are evident from the vice president's introduction. The VP knows *what* Jones is up to, *how far* he's gotten with it, and *what's to do* on Jones's agenda next. His intimate knowledge of Jones as a person had a lot to do with Jones's assignment to this job despite a background that may not be relevant to it.

Equally important, he takes the opportunity of any good manager to redirect attention to the critical component of the job (the distributors), reaffirms his own commitment to Jones's project by having thought about some issues raised from an off-site dinner *with the customer,* and nudges Jones toward "owning" these issues too. He also suggests to Jones a networking (see the organizing section below) opportunity for working with Susan on the incentive angle.

The interesting thing about all of this isn't what the vice president is doing; it's good, but mundane. The interesting thing is *how does he know?* After all, he has five direct and fifty-five indirect reports, and Jones is one of the indirects.

Clearly, the vice president isn't drawing his information from the MBO system or even from the weekly reports he makes his people write. Rather, he knows because he couples one of Tom Peters's principles with one of my own. He *manages by walking around* (Peters), and most of that walking around is devoted to *listening* (Bonoma). If there is one characteristic of managers good at monitoring time and people, it is their willingness to ask, and then to *hear.* The dinner with the supplier and the entire text of the quote point to the fact that this manager and his subordinate talk, and the manager has *heard* some things. That's how to monitor people and time.

When it comes, however, to the effects of managing one's own time for impact on others, Peters's[1] dictum that what the boss pays attention to *gets* attention is worth underscoring. Much of management is the manipulation of symbols, and the top marketer's calendar is one of the most powerful symbols available. If he or she goes down to the plant to monitor the towing hooks, quality control will get emphasized in the marketing group. It is hard to overstate this powerful and potentially positive linkage between monitoring and allocating, as I noted in the last chapter.

As time and people monitoring go together, so do the monitoring of markets/products and money. The latter is inextricably intertwined with the former, as many of the monitoring details we should like to know about our competitors, customers, and products are money-oriented. What was sales volume last week in the three new stores we opened in Minneapolis? What was the average revenue per transaction? How do those data get cut by male and female shoppers?

Interestingly, the rules for monitoring money and products/markets are more extensive than, but similar to, those for monitoring people and time. That is, commitment/interest, walking around, and *listening* are key requirements for these monitoring tasks as well. For instance, it can be stated as one incontrovertible truth of marketing[2] that no manager can do the marketing job well without *getting out into the field* with the customers and the trade.

I used to think that quarterly field visits would do it; my good implementers convinced me that at least monthly visits are required; for firms with no clear theme or vision and otherwise in trouble, I recommend that the chief executive and all his staff *take over* a branch sales office for a week. Regardless of how it is done, listening is a critical component of monitoring products/markets as well as money. One good way to do this is to get out of the leather chairs and into the field. As one manager puts it, "You can't learn anything about marketing in the office."

There are other marketing skills that good managers bring to the job as well, and they can be grouped under the term "back of the envelope" skills. By dint of experience, knowledge, and just sheer sweat, the manager good at monitoring marketing endeavors has driven his or her understanding of the requirements of good monitoring to a powerful and elegant simplicity. Over time and with hard experience, he or she has learned some "shortcuts" to the marketing effort's "vital signs," which are religiously tracked. Those vital signs may bear little or no relationship to what the measuring system offers; rather, they are the marketer's way of taking the marketing effort's pulse out in the field to see how things are going.

At Frito-Lay, for instance, Bill Korn religiously got reports every Monday on sales by zones (there were 128!) and manufacturing variances (38 plants); it was all he needed, he said, to run the business, and waiting for the control system to produce the data would have meant always managing a week behind. At Cole National Corporation, as well as at Benco, Incorporated, close attention is paid to the national weather service forecasts by market area. Indeed, in both companies these forecasts are delivered to the top marketer daily. Why? Though they are in very different businesses, eyewear retailing and drainage pipe, both managements believe the weather is an excellent "pulse" measure for, respectively, retail shopping statistics or drainage sales. At Benco, for instance, dry weather is not desirable, as it means farmers may well try to "squeeze by" the current planting season without draining their fields. At still another firm top management believes that if it tracks the base price of copper and also the cents it spends in rebates per dollar of sales, it can get a marvelous readout on how well it will do each month in selling an agricultural fungicide!

All of these informal monitoring "tricks" are just that; *currently useful generalizations* a manager believes he knows about the relationship of some variables in the environment to some certain variables (sales, share) in which he is interested. Some of these get formulated into systems; most don't because they're too "touchy-feely," quick-changing, or downright weird to formalize.

Nonetheless, the manager good at monitoring has at his fingertips several such generalizations with which—he or she feels—the pulse of the business can be tracked. Whether or not the variables identified are causally related to the effects measured in a scientific sense is immaterial; the point is, the manager has driven his or her understanding of the business to such a fine point that he or she has isolated the two or three really useful measures about the products, company, and industry and religiously tracks these as a test of progress and a barometer of change.

The four tasks of the manager who would apply monitoring skills to the marketing job are monitoring people, markets and products, time, and money. The list of behavioral rules that seems to differentiate those managers good at monitoring from those who are not is a relatively mundane one, including:

- *Interest* in and *commitment* to the people and tasks
- *Walking around,* inside the marketing group and out in the field
- A *propensity to listen* rather than to talk, give directives, or "make important decisions"
- A real *willingness to noodle* about the business, to discover its pulse, and to create *back of the envelope* measures to track it

While mundane, this list is neither easy to live by nor simple to learn. Most of the managers I worked with simply did not do much monitoring, and many didn't have much of an idea about what was going on "out there" beyond what the monitoring system could cough up. Since this ordinarily is very little, it is astounding that *anything* relevant to the market place gets done in most marketing groups!

Monitoring Processes

When monitoring is used to bridge the gap in systems' shortcomings, however, it is not just because managers good at monitoring seem to follow a list like the one above. Rather there is a "template" or model of good monitoring that seems to be applied regularly by the managers I've studied. I've reproduced that template in Exhibit 9–2.

The monitoring model in the chart suggests that managers good at monitoring go through a series of process stages in the construction of their "back of the envelope" ratios to keep track of people, time, markets/products, and dollars. The five steps form a loop through which good monitoring managers regularly cycle.

Though the assertion would be debatable in the view of most managers, one of the most powerful constructs the manager brings to monitoring tasks is a *theory* of how the marketing problem of interest works. I say "highly debatable" because the managers I have studied would not agree that they fool with *anything* as esoteric as theory. Yet they are some of the best theoreticians I've come across, within science or without. By "theory" I mean a collection of presumed causes that lead to presumed effects about the customers, trade, or company, the three legs of the marketing

Theory	A strong set of beliefs about the relationship of manipulables to results, and about their meaning;
Powerful simplicity	expressed in just a few powerful statements, not mired in awesome complexities;
No trivia	where no detail of the identified measures or variables is too unimportant to be concerned with, and no measuring task too menial for personal attention;
Regularity	engaged with great regularity, almost compulsiveness;
Feedforward	from which learning is regularly taken to inform both the actions being engaged and the understandings in the theory.

Exhibit 9–2. A Model of Good Monitoring: Principles

tripod. Marketers good at monitoring have quite articulate theories about why the people in their organizations, the products, the markets, and the customers work the way they do, and they constantly test these against reality by application.

At the Atlantic Aviation Corporation, for example, senior vice president Mack Graham has a well-articulated theory of when a company chief executive is "ripe" for a business jet sale. First, the firm in question must already own turboprop or better aircraft equipment. This is because such a prospect already has "bitten the bullet" on a flight department and the other expensive accoutrements of corporate flying and is already convinced of the basic benefits of private versus commercial flight. Second, Graham's people routinely plot circles around a prospect's operating installations and go after those prospects whose radius of regular travel entails more than two hours in the air using a propeller plane. This qualifying variable comes from Graham's "two-hour posterior" theory: CEOs can't sit in one place for more than two hours without going crazy, so look for the poor devils who are doing it and solve their problem by getting them to the site faster with a jet. Mack would argue that he's no theoretician, just a pilot who also happens to know some things about selling jets. But his two-hour posterior theory is a sophisticated analysis of buyer behavior that helps Atlantic target its sales efforts to good effect with corporate prospects.

Another example of theory in monitoring processes concerns the highly placed executive of an industrial company who wished to talk *only* with ex-customers and nonusers in order to get an idea of how his marketing effort was going. Indeed, he would go out of his way to follow up with calls, letters, and even visits when the monthly "lost business" report came through (it was sent directly to his office). Why? "We make a good piece of hardware," he said, "but really, it's nothing that has any unique competitive advantage vis-à-vis the customers, regardless of what my engineers tell me. That means we can't compete on product. We're about the same on price and availability as everybody else in this business, which only leaves sales and postsale service as distinctive competencies for us. I religiously talk to the no-sale prospects out there to see what it is we could do better in the selling process. I religiously talk to the accounts we lose to see what it is we could do better in the service process. If we do those things right, we win."

The theory, obviously, both *directs* where the marketer applies his monitoring skills and *informs* the principles that the manager thinks are true about the customers and the market. Right or wrong about the base of the business, this marketer has driven his understanding toward a powerfully profound theory of buyer behavior. Better, he does not sit in his office propounding it, but gets out in the field to test whether it is right. The theory tells him where to look; the data, whether the theory has any meaning.

If managers are insulted to learn they are theorists, they will be outraged to learn I consider them powerfully simple as well. Not simple-minded, though. The generalizations that good implementers reach about the business drive *through* the irrelevancy of the marketer with the 2-foot-thick printout on his desk who says, "Now I understand it. It's a 47-variable multiple regression model!" No, the kind of generalizations the good monitoring managers come up with are the sort that are *simple*, not because they understate market or customer complexities but rather because the manager has done the detail work and put in the long hours of homework from which true understanding is bred. As a result such managers' monitoring needs often are quite simple, though quite puzzling to the EDP department.

"Find out for me how often CEOs' wives travel on the jets with them, and whether these women aren't embarrassed by only having a curtain partitioning the 'head' from the main cabin." This example of a monitoring request led to the redesign of the Israeli-built Westwind II business jet so the craft had room for a full stand-up lavatory at the rear instead of the curtained between-pilot-and-passengers arrangement in common usage. It has led to the sale of many planes as well.

In addition to being parsimonious[3] theorists, managers good at monitoring did not admit the existence of trivia concerning their businesses and the monitoring tasks they had identified as crucial. There was no monitoring task so lowly it would not be done by the manager personally, assuming it was one critically related to the manager's theory of how the business worked and, consequently, to his/her "back of the envelope" monitoring needs. Managers good at monitoring were exceptionally willing to go selling, to "run the ratios," even to make calls to customers *on their time, personally*, because no matter how trivial the task, it was not trivial to them.

There is some interesting independent confirmation of this finding, that the managers good at monitoring don't ignore the "routine trivia" of the job, from research done by John B. Miner.[4] Miner devised a series of tests that he felt measured the "motivation to manage" and validated the tests with successful managers. His thesis is that he finds a regular and recurrent decline in the components of "motivation to manage" in college students and junior managers, and that we should all worry that there just aren't going to be enough good, tough top executives to go around for the next generation.

Whether or not one credits his conclusions about a managerial shortage, Miner's research is instructive. One of his six key components for the "motivation to manage" is "sense of responsibility in carrying out the numerous routine duties associated with managerial work." It is useful to quote him at length:

> The managerial job requires getting the work out and keeping on top of routine demands. The things that have to be done must actually be done. They range from constructing budget estimates to working on committees, to talking on the telephone, to filling out employee rating forms and salary-change recommendations. There are administrative requirements of this kind in all managerial work. . . . To meet these requirements a manager must at least be willing to face this type of routine. [p. 7]

My results on monitoring confirm the Miner findings with an important twist. My managers would hang "No Trivia" signs and work their personal tails to the bone learning even a small thing about a customer or their business, *as long as* the tasks were *relevant* detail work important to their understanding of practice problems. Random Mickey Mouse harassments from the system, while complied with, were approached with none of the zeal Miner implies a good manager has for junk work.

Along with powerful theory, simplicity of generalization, and a "no trivia" rule, the manager good at monitoring shows another process characteristic: regularity of the watching. Whatever it is he or she watches as a vital sign of the marketing effort, it is watched the way a hawk watches a crippled sparrow—steadily, closely, yearningly. The profit plan may be due, there may be a disaster in the Houston plant regarding returned units, and one of the kids may be sick at home, but what are the sales by region? There is no substitute for regularity.

Finally, the information (*not* data) from the monitoring process was regularly "fed forward" by the manager to improve (1) the theory and (2) the cleverness of the monitoring methods used. When a new generalization emerged or a new observation imposed itself as an enduring one, these facts were fed back in to improve the theoretical process.

More Processes and Preconditions

There were four more observations or characteristics or processes associated with managers good at monitoring that fitted into no process model but rather seemed to pervade it. These characteristics were so general I have come to believe they are *preconditions* to good monitoring and will discuss them here. In a way they are all either causes or consequences of the operation of the Exhibit 9–2 model, however.

The first—clear theme and vision—is the *sine qua non* of all marketing practice but also of monitoring. It is amazing how many managers who have not clarified for themselves what they are about in marketing have grave difficulties with monitoring. Like their more able counterparts, they complain about system inadequacy. Also like them, they try to invent monitoring schemes to get around the system's shortfalls. Their inventions routinely come to naught, however, for it is not clear what they should form a theory *about*, what should be monitored, and what the returned data mean. There are frequent joint failures of theme-to-theory and of data-to-information translations where there is no clarity of vision.

The "no trivia" rule discussed above is reflected more generally in managers who are good at monitoring in a "homework and details" ethic. There is a story, perhaps apocryphal, about Ray Kroc of McDonald's finding a fly (dead) near the food preparation area of one of his many thousand franchises. As the story goes, the franchisee didn't have a franchise any more. Kroc's "homework," like that of many good marketers, was visiting the outlets religiously, regularly, everywhere he went, until near his death. Kroc's "details" often were as small as a fly.

Coupled with the "powerful simplicity" process is a personal characteristic on the part of the manager that can only be called "driving through to insight." When I was a psychology doctoral student, it was considered both good training and good hazing to make us learn advanced statistics and experimental design. Not being one of the most mathematically able people I have ever run into, at least with calculus, I struggled mightily night after night with the strange notations, incomprehensible proofs, and weird logical notions ("lemmas") involved in this endeavor.

After midnight on one of those Florida evenings when you wonder if God maybe didn't misplace hell in the Southeastern United States, I was doing my usual "pounding of the books," getting my usual nowhere. Suddenly, without warning or any special preparation, something "snapped," and the subject I had been learning about for a year became transparent to me. There was no longer any need for the book—I *saw* what they were talking about, and it was inordinately simple and obvious. I even wondered why anyone had troubled to write such simplicity down.[5]

Call it insight or just the results of repetitive "noodling," but the best managers deal with monitoring the same way: They puzzle, sweat, even *plead* with the data to make sense to them, and sometimes it becomes blindingly clear. They can "throw away the book," make clearer sense of the market on the back of an envelope than a $1,500 research report can in a hundred pages, and, as my colleague Ted Levitt would say, *know some things* about the market. This insight was present in the best managers I observed.

Finally, the theoretical notions we discussed above imply an experimental bent in the manager. He or she is not so stultified by experience that the possibility of trying out new ways is abandoned. Rather, there is a "I don't know about this, but let's see what happens" attitude, which (when coupled with rough and ready measures bred of understanding) can produce marvelous results!

I have summarized these final characteristics in Exhibit 9–3.

Exhibit 9–3. Monitoring Processes and Preconditions

Clear theme and vision	Without clarity of theme, monitoring will be poorly directed and largely unhelpful
Homework/details ethic	"God is in the details"
Driving through to insight	The clarity that can come from so much pondering that what was complex looks simple
An experimentation bent	The willingness to try "strange" or "weird" measures of what is going on

Summary and Extension: Monitoring by Top Management

As one of my pokings into the dynamics of monitoring, I collected four separate instances of "marketing auditing" during the case research process. I collected these data because the marketing audit represents a special and important application of marketing monitoring skills that arises when general management wishes to get an overall look at the operation of everything its marketers do. Chapter 7 briefly introduced the marketing audit as a structural analysis tool. Here, I'll elaborate on some of its process characteristics.

This is not the place for a full excursus on the marketing audit, but much more attention should be given to this interesting monitoring tool. In a marketing audit, management wishes to do a one-time monitoring of *everything* that is going on in the marketing function, either because it suspects dysfunction, to familiarize itself with marketing practices, or for some other reason.

The audits I looked at varied from an internally generated and numbers-free memorandum written by a company chairman to his cousin, the vice president of marketing (who had requested the audit) to a very careful and complete $125,000+ evaluation done by a consulting company for another firm. It is interesting to contrast these two situations to see what generalizations present themselves.

In the insider, subjective, qualitative audit the chairman writes his cousin a thirteen-page memo that at times is *ad hominem* (the memo has been characterized by one of my students as "sewer gas"). Indeed, the chairman refers to one of the operating units as being "as headless as Anne Boleyn" and in general rampages over what he doesn't like that is being done in marketing. He also goes to great lengths to comment on, encourage, and reinforce some things he does like, such as the new marketing organization that has been put in place. Overall the memorandum is powerful, and the conclusions (managers think) offer good advice to the VP for the future.

In the expensive outsider audit, the consultants develop a clever auditing model, interview almost everybody imaginable, and analyze the numbers in more ways than a Wharton MBA. Yet one gets the feeling that management is more taken up with the consultants' repetitive requests to do the next "stage" of the study than it is with their findings. In the period covered by the case the outsider, "objective," quantitative process pursued by the consultants seems to have had no powerful impact on the organization.

Interestingly, when I ask managers who have analyzed both situations to tell me which the "better" audit is, they almost invariably choose the "sewer gas" one! The differences they cite as prompting their choice, mostly, seem to be the ones of (1) caring, (2) listening (which doesn't always happen in interviews!), and (3) theorizing to simple generalizations.

The most interesting thing I have learned about marketing auditing is that *the monitoring principles that apply above apply equally well in the auditing situation*. It does not matter whether marketing audits are internally or externally generated, whether they cost several hundred thousand dollars or just a couple of CEO days, or whether they are "objectively" oriented to the number streams or just a "subjective" commentary on how things seem to be working. Management may make different choices on each of these parameters, depending on its needs, and still have a "valid" audit.

Rather, what seems to be the differentiating factor in a quality audit is simply the application of the monitoring factors cited above to the task. Does the consultant (or insider) formulate a theory of the marketing group? Does he/she *get into the field* to see what is going on? Is there an experimental bent and also a "feedforward mechanism" in the evaluation? The critical notions are listening, getting into the field, and all the others cited above. That's how to do a good marketing audit, just as it's how to run a good marketing group.

ORGANIZING

John Edwards, the poor devil who got the siding and roofing division at Alcan Aluminum, was marked for either stardom or doom. He had to be, for his bosses had given him an impossible situation.

Edwards managed a $70-million division within a $1.2-billion subsidiary of a $5.2-billion worldwide aluminum miner, refiner, and producer. The parent corporation, Alcan Aluminum Ltd., unabashedly thought of itself as an "aluminum pump." With its cheap Canadian hydroelectric power, management of the parent corporation knew that the trick for long-term earnings was to keep the smelters running flat out. This, of course, created needs to *do* something with the ingots, and Alcan's subsidiaries were charged with adding value to them in the production process.

From where Edwards sat, though, it didn't look like much value was being added. Aluminum siding, Edwards's primary business, was fast falling prey to the incursion of vinyl siding. Vinyl siding was cheaper to make, easier to install, and offered already tightly squeezed distributors and installers margins up to twice what was available if aluminum was chosen as the siding material. Straight-line projections indicated that the aluminum siding business would be gone in the early 1990s.

Edwards had twice been to division management and once to Montreal at the parent company to request monies for a vinyl siding line. Only a year before he had been given some $3 million for a restricted production capacity in vinyl, which allowed him to produce a narrow line of goods. Along with the cash, however, had come an admonition from corporate to ''sell the vinyl only defensively to increase aluminum sales.''

The problem is, nobody *believes* Alcan is serious about vinyl! The distributors are threatening to switch their aluminum purchases from Alcan unless a viable vinyl capacity is proffered; the sales force is in near revolt, for it has only limited vinyl capacity to offer its accounts (it could sell all it could get), but unlimited aluminum (which the accounts don't really want). Other managers' morale is low, for they see the parent pushing them to sell aluminum against a market tide swinging to vinyl.

Edwards has many other problems, like figuring out the meaning of ''defensive marketing,'' but one of the critical issues facing him is how to organize to do the impossible!

Networking to Do the Job

Many times a marketer will be given assignments for which the formal organization chart is either irrelevant or inimical to good execution. Our eternal tendency to ''box'' management functions so that production doesn't talk to R&D, R&D's bailiwick is immune from marketers, and sales is unrelated to everyone else gives rise to reporting chains that are empty of accountability, at cross purposes, and a parody of what cross-functional integration should look like.

Even within the marketing function these isolationist tendencies occur, so that in many companies the notion that marketing has anything to do with sales, and vice versa, is profoundly foreign. Pity the poor product manager who is charged with ''all elements of the product line which impact or affect profitability'' in such circumstances.

As a consequence, a daily need of the good marketer is what I call organizing, or networking with others. The others include people in the marketing function, outside marketing but in the firm, and outside the firm. Networking is engaged in to get the marketing job done despite territorial boundaries, "local" interests, and protectionist managers in formal organizations. Unfortunately, the formal organization often produces islands of isolation from the rest of the company or else matrixed confusions, rather than quality execution.

The task of networking is not the same as that involved in interacting. Networking involves group and organizational skills; interacting is more one-on-one management. Two principles were applied by those managers especially competent at networking: re-creation/reconstruction and what I've come to call "the exchange bank."

Re-creation/Reconstruction

Marketers capable of getting the marketing job done seemed especially facile at getting around organization system roadblocks and at creating mini-, task-based informal organizations that were created, executed against the job, then melted away until needed again. Invariably these "organizings" were temporary; invariably they were task-oriented and often cross-functional.

The able organizers were capable of creating multiple temporary, task-based, and usually unnamed "subversive organizations" within the formal system to get the marketing jobs done regardless of system roadblocks or formal task-based constraints. In an important way, these informal task-based organizations were *reconstructed* continually on an as-needed basis, and different organizations were constructed for different tasks needing completion.

For instance, when one product manager in a telecommunications company needed a pricing tariff (his company's proxy for setting price) changed, he called three acquaintances. The first, a relatively low-placed colleague in customer service, could provide information on the complaint rate about prices at the current price. A second colleague in sales was able to give good intelligence on potential customer reaction and distributor feedback about the proposal. A third colleague, this one in the pricing department, was able to do most of the legwork on what a formal request *might* look like if submitted through regular channels.

In this manner the manager in question acted to (1) collect a group without formal responsibility or charge, (2) enlist its members' help in certain actions that would "pre-grease" his tariff submission through the normal organizational channels, and (3) get data to disarm possible opposition both within related functional areas and among his own general management, who certainly would ask other functional managers about customer or other effects from the proposed price hike.

When the same manager felt that advertising effectiveness was lower than it should be in generating leads, he called a *different* person in the sales department to check on lead follow-up there, made sure he had dinner with a group of distributors (thereby gaining information about their lead experiences), talked to three customers about why they had bought the service, enlisted the cooperation of the research director for current studies on leads, and talked to someone in the promotion department about experiences on advertising placement and lead generation.

When it came time to make proposals formally on the ads for the coming marketing plan, the organization was already "pre-sold" to a degree on a more formal evaluation of advertising effectiveness, and a new lead follow-up program was proposed by the marketing vice president as an "original idea" he had from "just thinking about things."

There is good evidence from the management literature that the most effective groups in formal organizations are the ones that are temporarily created for a task-based purpose, whose main goal is to dissolve themselves as soon as possible (which, of course, requires solving the problem at hand!). What good organizers have learned is that this principle of *re-creation/reconstruction* can be applied profitably to getting the marketing job done as well, and that one does not have to be a general manager or vice president to engage in such organizings regularly.

The Exchange Bank

In the early 1970s the social psychologist Stanley Hollander devised an interesting theory of leadership and provided some data to suggest it was valid. It was Hollander's notion that what determines who leads is who follows. Hollander argued that followers have certain expectations of their leaders, which had better not be violated very often if the leader expects to remain at the head of the group. His theory formalized this notion: It was Hollander's belief that the leader earned, by virtue of loyal service and good follower-ship him/herself, a certain latitude to do things not approved by, difficult for, or unpleasant to the followers. He called these chits for latitude "idiosyncrasy credits." All leaders, Hollander noted, had to be very careful not to overdraw their "credits," or they would quickly find themselves no longer leading.

The marketer who is a good organizer employs the same kinds of notions in his/her management of others. Individuals in other functional groups ordinarily *don't* do something without getting something in return, and the astute organizer is careful to build up a variety of "credits" with a large number of people in the formal organization who can be "called in" when information, help, or collaboration is needed.

One manager may get help with a vexing problem even though our marketer is too busy to give it; perhaps there will be a time down the road when the help will be recalled. Another may get time or personal advice. The good organizer, like the mouse in the fable, removes thorns both because of citizenship and also because you can never tell when you're going to need a lion who owes you a favor!

The essence of organizing is the continual re-creation of temporary, undeclared, formally "illegal" task groups in the service of good practice. The able organizer creates the raw material of these groups by being a corporate citizen who in the past has given much to a variety of individuals who can be called on to help in various ways to produce excellent results regardless of the shoddy state of systems.

CONCLUSION

One powerful question running through both this chapter and the last is to what degree the four implementation skills are trainable. Put another way, are there "born implementers" who are much more comfortable with execution than with strategy formulation, or are the strategic and implementation skills two sides of the same managerial coin, so that we might expect the most able manager to be equally adept at doing *and* planning? That is the subject of the next chapter, which will offer more discussion on the topic of marketing leadership.

CHAPTER TEN

Strategists and Implementers: Are They Different?

To the untrained eye ego-climbing and selfless climbing may appear to be identical. Both kinds of climbers place one foot in front of the other. Both breathe in and out at the same rate. Both stop when tired. Both go forward when rested. But what a difference! The ego-climber is like an instrument that's out of adjustment. He puts his foot down an instant too soon or too late. He's likely to miss a beautiful passage of sunlight through the trees. He goes on when the sloppiness of his step shows he's tired. He rests at odd times. He looks up the trail trying to see what's ahead even when he knows what's ahead because he just looked a second before. . . . What he's looking for, what he wants, is all around him, but he doesn't want that because it is all around him. Every step's an effort, both physically and spiritually, because he imagines his goal to be external and distant.

—Pirsig, *Zen and the Art of Motorcycle Maintenance*

AT A LUNCHEON the chief executive of a major corporation had put up with my sermonizing about there being too much strategy and too little attention to practice in marketing management. He showed the poor judgment of appearing very interested in what I was saying and, worse, of thinking the problems he had were similar to what I was describing. *That* lapse cost him thirty more minutes of listening to the implementation model. Finally running out of breath, I managed to ask him if he thought that some of the implementation variables we were discussing, such as "hunger" and "hustle," were trainable.

His response, interestingly, was that he thought he could neither train managers to be "hungry" nor select especially hungry managers out of a group of interviewees. He was of the opinion that almost all the other marketing implementation skills I had mentioned could be trained, mostly by example of senior management, but just didn't think that motivation was trainable.

If he is right, if there are some abilities involved in marketing implementation that defy behavior modification by training or example, then *somehow* we had better learn to select the "right" managers beforehand, because we're not going to make them over once we've got them. On the other hand, to the degree to which marketing (and management) implementation skills *are* trainable, then to that degree can hope be held out for improving marketing practice at companies where, for one reason or another, systems fixes are not quickly possible.[1] Put another way, where marketing implementation is concerned, are its leaders born or made?

I cannot answer the training question with scientific evidence, for I have none. But I do have four years' experience in the MBA and executive classroom which suggests marketing implementation skills can be trained, and we shall address ourselves to that experience below.

Common sense and cultural stereotype, however, argue that some managers are better, more comfortable, and more able at implementing strategies than are others. What factors produce a "good implementer?" Are some managers better at implementing strategy, and others better at conceiving it? If there are any personal or other executive correlates of implementation ability, do these vary by stage in the career life cycle? Or is the "best" manager, as the textbooks say, the one best suited to doing *both* strategy formulation and implementation, a kind of "six-gun Pete" (or Polly) who can ride, rope, and read Hannibal for Indian-fighting strategy too? These are the questions that this chapter addresses; the "Conclusion" returns to the trainability and the marketing leadership questions more broadly.

STEREOTYPE OF THE GOOD IMPLEMENTER

You've seen the action movies. So have I. It doesn't matter *which* action movies you've seen; they're all the same. The grizzled sergeant, the Indian scout, even the beat cop (never a manager —who'd want to watch *that*?) saves the day, gets the platoon up the hill, catches the bad guy every night on the UHF channels. What is this man or woman like? You know—everybody knows. He, or rarely but increasingly she, is a loner, a "high bias toward action" person, sometimes a rule-breaker, always inordinately macho and set apart from his fellows. Thinking further, we would probably add to the description risk-taker, not rich, and perhaps even not as bright as some others. But definitely highly motivated, highly value-oriented, and highly (in the movies, at least) successful. Nobody taught him or her to be these things, either, unless you consider watching your mother killed by hostile savages or seeing your partner attacked by crazed New Yorkers "teaching."

The stereotype of the good implementer in management is not nearly as clear, but still it stands in relatively sharp relief. I've made it a habit to ask many managers and students alike whether there are some managers who are "better cut out" for implementation. When they agree to this, and everyone *does* agree that some managers are born strategists and some born implementers, it is fun to ask what such "born implementers" are like. The following represents a composite of their responses.

Like his or her movie counterpart, the good implementer has a high bias toward action, is a moderate risk-taker, and is maybe even a little bit of a rule-breaker as well. He/she is one of those likely to offer aphorisms like, "Not sure if it's allowed? Well, *do it,* then apologize afterward."

But there's more, and the stereotype of the good implementer starts to move away from the movie screen and toward enough precision to be testable. A majority of the students and the managers whom I've informally surveyed on this subject would agree that good implementers have the following characteristics as well:

- They are primarily goal-oriented. That is to say, if we were to make simple discriminations, and all stereotypes *are* simple discriminations, we would think good implementers endorse that "the end justifies the means."

- They are highly internally controlled. We introduced the notion of internal locus of control in Chapter 8. It means that
  good implementers believe that there are no accidents, that
  everybody is responsible for his/her own fate, and that much
  in managerial life (and personal life too) is under the actor's
  control.
- They are highly intolerant of noncompliance. This bit of
  technical jargon says that there are two kinds of people in the
  world. The first sort suffer someone else's disregard of their
  requests with relative aplomb and little persistence. The second kind are likely to take action given the noncompliance of
  others. Good implementers fall into the latter category. Better
  not cut in front of them in a line or ignore a memo they've
  sent!
- Most of all, good implementers are thought to be what is
  called "high Type A" individuals. Several years ago the
  physicians Rosenman and Friedman[2] found out that there
  was an "itchy," "bias toward action," "never late," "can't
  wait" personality pattern that was associated with their pa-
  tients' experience of serious illness, like heart attacks. The
  stereotypic implementer should place on the Type A behavior
  scale.

The managerial stereotype of the "good implementer," in
short, starts with the *assumption* that some managers are better implementers than others because of personality patterns, not training. It goes on to prescribe what some of these personality traits
might be. In the stereotypic view, the implementer is said to be a
"go get 'em," action-oriented (probably young) Turk who undoubtedly confounds his elders and gets the job done in spite of
their old-fogey backwardness, sick systems, and terminal tendencies toward planning.

Some Science That Supports the Stereotype

The strategist/implementer question is a new form of the old line
versus staff roles. There is good evidence from the study of
managers in line as opposed to staff positions that there are powerful differences in orientation and in behavior between these
groups.[3] Staff professionals are more likely to have a professional
group as their primary loyalty (e.g. other engineers or purchasing
agents), while line managers (e.g. sales management) are likely to

cite as their primary loyalty the company for which they work. Line people are most likely to associate with other line people *in the same company*, staffers with other staffers in a broader social net that transcends company boundaries.

There are other differences as well. For instance, when the job interests of research and development engineers were compared with those of their supervisors, the engineers were found to be low in "interest in other people" and in "wanting to get people to do things." The line supervisors, in contrast, were high in both these interests.

Again, we know from psychological research that there are strong differences in *cognitive style* among individuals, and this evidence tends to support a line–staff or strategy–implementer distinction. For instance, some work done with managers suggests that some prefer to learn by *actively doing,* while others learn best by *passively thinking.* Certainly this kind of learning style difference is highly suggestive of the possible validity of a strategist–implementer distinction.

Given the powerful presence of a clear stereotype distinguishing strategists from implementers and at least some scientific work that indicates the distinction is plausible, it seemed reasonable to look further into the strategist versus implementer dichotomy. A question I asked with the help of two doctoral students[4] is just how much water this "standard" stereotype held. While what I will show you is preliminary, it contains some surprising findings on the question of whether marketing implementers are "different" from marketing strategists.

STRATEGISTS VERSUS IMPLEMENTERS

The Research

The Harvard Business School is fortunate in having many of the country's leading managers pass through its doors each year. In one of our many executive education programs, top marketing and general managers come to the school for a two-week period to focus on general marketing problems. We presumed on the patience of executives attending this marketing program in order to gain some insight into the strategist–implementer question.

The study participants were, respectively, forty-eight and fifty-three (over two different years) marketing directors, vice presidents, and general managers with marketing responsibilities in both U.S. and foreign firms. Over 90 percent were males. On average, the operating units for which the executives had marketing and, often, general management responsibilities generated about $100 million in revenues annually; both consumer and industrial goods firms were represented.

The general format of what we asked the executives to do was (1) to complete some background and psychological scales and (2) to give us a written report on a case study assigned as a normal part of their curriculum.

In addition to background information about salary, number of direct reports, and how they rated themselves as a marketing strategist and marketing implementer, the executives were asked to complete a battery of psychological instruments relevant to the stereotypes of the good implementer described above. The instruments were four in number:

- A scale that measured the extent to which the manager could be characterized by the Type A, coronary-prone activity syndrome. This activity pattern involves excessive achievement-orientation, competitiveness, and speed and impatience. It has been found to be predictive of the incidence of a variety of stress-related illnesses.

- A scale that measured "machiavellianism." Machiavellianism is a psychological construct which relates to persons' general strategies for dealing with others. In particular, it inquires into the extent to which managers feel that others are manipulable in interpersonal relationships, and whether the manager would endorse that "the ends justify the means" in a number of scenarios involving others.

- A scale that measured how much the executive was internally, as opposed to externally, oriented. That is, this scale tried to measure whether the manager was primarily one who believed that all that happens to him or her was produced through his or her own efforts, or whether the main component of events that occur was "luck" or "fate."

- A scale that I developed with Professor Dennis Slevin of the University of Pittsburgh, which we call "intolerance for non-compliance."[5] Essentially this scale measures how little or how much noncompliance from others in a social situation is necessary for the executive to intervene. In one sample item, for instance, someone "cuts the line" in front of the manager while he is waiting to make a banking transaction. In another his/her children watch forbidden TV programs. In a third purchasing people disregard a memorandum about minimum stocking levels. What the executive reports he/she would do is used as an indicator of how the manager reacts to little or much provocation from others, and how he/she reacts in settings (like getting cut off on the freeway) where it won't do any good.

Though all the scales were disguised[6] and their purposes not obvious during the study, I was looking for confirmations or disconfirmations of the stereotypes inquired into above. For example, the "typical" stereotype of the good implementer might portray this individual as highly Type A, highly machiavellian, highly internally controlled, and highly intolerant of noncompliance. Consistent with the "street stereotype," we checked whether good implementers were highly manipulative, multiple-action, and "never late" people (Type A behavior); believed that they and not the environment controlled their fate; and were unwilling to tolerate noncompliance from others in their drive to "get things done."

Strategists, those more comfortable with planning and less with action, might be thought to be low on all these variables. There is little reason for the strategist to be manipulative or even highly internally controlled, since the environment controls much about strategic outcomes. Similarly, the reduced needs for action in strategic pursuits might allow a lowered Type A reading and also more tolerance for noncompliance.

We allowed managers to characterize themselves as strategists and implementers. The questions about strategy and implementation ability were separate, so the manager was perfectly free to say he or she was a good strategist *and* implementer, neither, or any other possible combination. We then categorized those managers reporting they were especially good implementers but not strategists as "implementers," and those whose strategy scores significantly exceeded their implementation ones as "strategists."

In addition to these measures we asked each manager participating in the study to analyze a case from this research project (the two cases used were Benco, Incorporated [A] and Computer Devices, Incorporated), and to submit a short (three to five pages) written analysis of the case suggesting what the manager would do if he or she found him/herself faced with this situation. These written analyses were subjected to a technique called "content analysis" by my social psychologist colleagues, in which the number of words, what is said, and other measures are applied to the manager's written report to learn about the content.

For instance, we coded the written reports on a number of variables relevant to the implementation model presented at several points before in this book: How often was reference made to making structural changes, for example, versus the application of managerial execution skills? We also categorized the managers' action recommendations in many other ways, including number made (many or few), options versus actions ("You *could* do this" versus "You *should* do this"), decisiveness (did the manager come down clearly in favor of one specific action?), and a number of other variables.

We also applied some other content analytics to the written reports, like counting the number of words in each report and noting whether the report was prepared in pencil or pen, whether graphics exhibits were appended, how neatly it was prepared, and the number of times the word "not" was used. This latter measure, called "inhibition," is frequently associated with more general personality patterns like risk-taking and willingness to experiment in situations.

STUDY RESULTS

Strategists and Implementers

One of the simplest things to look at in the strategy–implementation dichotomy is whether participants who say they are good strategists also say they are good implementers, and *vice versa*. Finding such a relationship doesn't mean much, for if there's anything top managers are, it's fairly vocal about their own high abilities at almost *everything*. Not finding such an expected "halo" of "I'm good at it all, buddy," however, would be an indication that *something* is different about the strategists and the implementers that causes them to provide different estimations of their abilities in these job areas.

Though we had somewhat conflicting results across our two samples of top marketers, the overall findings indicate that whatever else strategic abilities and implementation ones are, they are different. In our first study the correlation between managers' ratings of themselves as strategists and as implementers was precisely zero! This means that knowing a manager's rating of him/herself as a strategist was completely unhelpful in predicting his or her self-rating as an implementer. In the second study there *was* the expected positive relationship between managers' ratings on strategic and implementation abilities, but it was weak.

Thus it appears plausible that strategy and implementation abilities (at least when measured by something as simple as *asking* managers to tell us how good they are at each set of endeavors) are not thought of by the managers themselves as the same thing, or even necessarily as abilities that inhere in the same person at the same time. They may be different skills, or at least differently called for at different points in the managers' careers.

The Stereotype of Macho Joe

Interestingly, *every common component of a stereotype of the ''good implementer'' was discomfirmed by our findings.* It was most emphatically *not* the case that managers good at implementation were higher on Type A behavior patterns than those who said they were better at strategy; it was also *not* the case that good implementers were more internally oriented, more machiavellian, or less tolerant of noncompliance than good strategists. Indeed, there was absolutely *no* relationship between any of these stereotypic variables and marketing implementation ability.

The only relationships we found on these personality measures had to do with the good strategists; interestingly, *they* were slightly more likely to be characterized as Type A individuals and intolerant of noncompliance! The storm trooper stereotype of the marketing implementer as ''Joe Charge-up-the-Hill'' simply holds no water.

But there were important differences between strategists and implementers nonetheless. As predicted by past line–staff research, persons rating themselves high on strategic skills said they were more loyal to their professions than were those who said they were good implementers; strategists also reported that they felt less loyal toward their companies. The good strategists also were much more likely to have staff jobs than those who thought they weren't very good strategists.

And there was a strong relationship between age and self-rated skill as an implementer. The more senior the manager in age, the more likely he or she was to claim to be better at implementation. The good strategists, but not the implementers, described themselves as much more analytic and more "big picture"–oriented than the implementers.

Thus the stereotype of the good marketing implementer appears to hold and not to hold at the same time. None of the traditional John Wayne–type variables appear to have much meaning in distinguishing good strategists from good implementers, but much of the previous psychological research on those finding themselves in line (implementation) versus staff (strategy) roles appears to be reconfirmed by our research. Just how, then, do strategists and implementers differ when it comes to behaving in a problem setting?

Implementers Versus Strategists: The Real Differences

It is only when the executives' written reports recommending *actions* for the companies they analyzed are examined that some things become clear about the more important behavioral differences between strategists and implementers. First let me explain the case analysis tasks in the two experiments, then show you the findings.

In Study I, the executives analyzed the Benco, Incorporated, case we have learned about in previous chapters. In this case management had discovered a significant innovation in the plastic drainage pipe business, Arch-flow pipe, and was concerned (1) with how to price it in the market vis-à-vis its other and competitive goods and also (2) with its own marketing culture, which did not seem to be one that supported value-added new product introductions. The marketing vice president was looking for pricing *and* cultural advice. You can find a more complete description of the Benco case in Chapter 1 and an abstract of it in the Research Appendix.

In Study II, executives were given the Computer Devices, Incorported, case to deal with. In this case, a small, $17-million firm has completed a sales blitz that produced disastrous nonresults for its new line of "smart" terminals and portable microcomputers. The company essentially is attempting to "migrate" its strategy, and thus its implementation and sales force strengths, from selling dumb terminals to intelligent ones, and is having great difficulty in doing so. Mr. Stofer, the marketing vice president, needs a new tactical plan to make the migration happen. Chapter 2 contains a more complete summary of the CDI case, as does the Research Appendix.

I have listed the differences between strategists and implementers from the written case analyses as Exhibits 10–1 and 10–2. Exhibit 10–1 gives the findings from the first study, which used the Benco case, and Exhibit 10–2 the second study, which employed CDI. The findings, though generated from very different case stimuli, are strikingly similar.

As Exhibit 10–1 shows, the most surprising finding from managers who analyzed the Benco case was that good strategists tended to *emphasize* corporate culture in both defining the main case problem and suggesting fixes for it, while good implementers tended to *ignore or minimize* corporate culture aspects in both problem definition and recommendations. This finding was surprising, because my field work and theory led me to believe culture was a very important, indeed central, aspect of quality marketing implementation.

Culture *is* an important factor in good marketing implementation, but apparently one to be addressed when the luxury of time and reflection permits rather than when there is some hot-burning fire that needs immediate extinguishing. The good implementers did not try to make long-term fixes when immediate actions were called for. Rather, they "went for the throat" on the immediate problem, deferring to the future actions on changing the sales-oriented culture to a more value-added one.

In the Benco case the primary problem was pricing the new pipe and finding ways to get the company's value-added marketing structure to work in a volume-oriented company. Interestingly, what the good implementers did was to figure out clever ways to (1) price the pipe and (2) allow a value-added tactical plan *even in a culture not suited for it*. The strategists, in contrast, refused to price the pipe and instead were taken up with the cultural aspects of the case. They wanted to hold seminars, to work on "marketing theme" as the main immediate action implication, and thus to defer the pipe-pricing problem and introduction until environmental variables were more propitious. Implementers found a way to get the immediate job (pricing) done and only then circled back on the larger problem.

Exhibit 10–1 shows other interesting strategist–implementer differences as well. The implementers proposed many different

Exhibit 10–1. Results from Study I: Strategists Versus Implementers

GOOD STRATEGISTS	GOOD IMPLEMENTERS
Emphasized culture in their problem definitions	Ignored culture in problem definitions
Emphasized culture in their action plans	Ignored culture in action plans
Did not give an exact price for the pipe	Gave an exact price for the pipe
Suggested fewer action alternatives	Suggested many action alternatives
Were highly inhibited (many "nots")	Showed low inhibition
Were younger and less experienced	Were older and more experienced
Were not as contingency-oriented	Were highly contingency-oriented

Exhibit 10–2. Results from Study II: Strategists Versus Implementers

GOOD STRATEGISTS	GOOD IMPLEMENTERS
Emphasized doing more research on the problem	Emphasized incentives and other specifics
Emphasized the "big picture"	Emphasized increased product knowledge on the sales force's part
Suggested few action alternatives	Suggested many action alternatives
Were younger and less experienced managers	Were older and more experienced managers

alternatives to fix Benco's problems; the strategists tended to spend their time in analysis, coming up with few action alternatives. The implementers were quite positive (very few negatives) in their reports; the strategists' verbiage was filled with ''can't,'' ''don't,'' and ''not'' statements.

The implementers invariably were highly contingency-oriented; the strategists were absolutists. For the former, many statements of the type ''if this doesn't work out, try that'' was seen in the analysis; for the latter, there appeared to be a real striving toward a ''right'' answer which admitted of no ''ifs'' or ''thens.'' Finally, a preponderance of the managers assessing themselves as good implementers were older in years and more experienced (in years of management) than were their more strategic colleagues.

Exhibit 10-2 supports and extends this picture of the implementer with a very different case stimulus, Computer Devices, Incorporated. The good implementers suggested that the critical problems in the failed blitz were related to (1) insufficient incentives for the salespeople to make the extra effort to sell the new terminals over the ''dumb'' ones they knew well how to vend, and (2) insufficient product knowledge about the new, ''smart'' equipment. The implementers again suggested many different action alternatives to ''fix'' these tactical problems and again were older and more experienced than their strategic peers.

Those managers rating themselves as especially able strategists, by contrast, wanted to do more research on the problem before making a decision about its probable causes. They again tended to emphasize the ''big picture'' in their case analyses, suggesting that perhaps the product or the market segmentation was at fault in producing CDI's difficulties and wondering whether the whole strategy ought to be rethought as a consequence. The action alter natives they proffered to fix the problems were few in number. Again, overall the strategists were younger and less experienced at management than their colleagues who rated themselves high on marketing implementation ability.

Implications of the Findings

It is easy to make too much of the findings reported above, generated on a total of 101 managers who all have reached relatively senior positions in relatively large operating units. We simply don't know what would happen if a less selective or less senior sample were subjected to this set of procedures. But, generalizing only a little from these preliminary research findings, the following points appear to be substantiated pending further study:

1. There are *no* stereotypical personality correlates that differentiate good implementers from good strategists. This argues strongly that whatever else implementers are, they probably are made, not born. The "storm trooper" stereotype of high internal control, Type A behavior, machiavellianism, and intolerance for noncompliance is not supported in the data that managers shared with us. Our data do not comment on the question of whether motivation to implement is trainable, however, so that question remains unresolved.

2. The fact that implementers tend to be older and more experienced than their more strategically oriented peers suggests that the complex set of implementation skills talked about in the last two chapters are not quickly acquired and perhaps suggests that the *need* for such skills is not as easily perceived at the front end of one's career as it is at a later stage. Indeed, if this speculation were true, it would argue that common folklore about general managers is quite wrong. Instead of starting with implementation and working their way up to strategic concerns, it appears that managers (at least marketing ones) start with strategic concerns and abilities and *work their way up to implementation.* Along with some complementary findings in the literature,[7] this suggests that implementation may be a primary concern of the top or general manager and that the common view of "life at the top" as a succession of armchair strategy sessions may be inaccurate.

3. The more specific results suggest:

- *Implementers tend to focus on the fixable.* That is, they don't try to muck with culture when there's some pipe to get out the door. This finding does not suggest that the implementers are insensitive to the cultural problems in Benco or the possible strategic ones in CDI; rather, they respond to the parameters of the situation and try to provide "Band-Aid" action to get the job done and keep the company going until the longer-term issues can be tackled. The strategists, conversely, go for the "big picture" but never get the pipe out the door.
- *Implementers tend to focus on multiple contingencies.* They formulate a variety of action alternatives and suggest the order in which to try them. They seem wedded to no approach but

whatever works and are not too proud to try a variety of things, with the implication that the last one was wrong. This willingness to be wrong was not seen in the strategists, judging from their action recommendations.

- *Implementers tend toward exact and specific action. Specific* pipe prices were proposed, and *specific* incentives proffered in the CDI problem. There was no vagueness, no waffling, no "well, sort of set the price somewhat high." Rather, the implementers went right at the problem: "24 cents."
- *Multiple, contingent, specific actions are not inhibited, but positively and robustly offered.* Instead of filling their analyses with reasons "why not," the good marketing implementer analyzes for reasons "why" (low inhibition) his or her action alternatives could work. This is done, as noted above not in the spirit of being wedded to some "right" action but rather as a realistic assessment of probabilities of success.

Boiling these points down to a sentence, the gist of the research completed to date suggests there is no such thing as a "born" implementer, but rather a set of trainable skills about problem analysis and action recommendations that can be learned by many managers to help them improve their practices. The learnable skill set seems to involve focusing on the fixable, going directly for specific actions to fix current problems, being willing to experiment with multiple contingencies (along with the willingness to be wrong when they don't work), and displaying a robust positiveness about the action proposals.

This research presents a positive and encouraging account for those companies and those managers who assess themselves as having problems with marketing practices. It suggests that (1) there *are* some "zero-level" orientations that predispose implementation abilities, and (2) these will generally be acquired later rather than earlier in any management career. It suggests further, though, that one may want to work with the managers one has to see if some help in learning this "implementation template" can't help to short-circuit the ordinarily long process from strategic adequacy to implementation soundness in individual managers.

To the extent that this "implementation template" *is* trainable, it is interesting to ask what tools could be used to sharpen these abilities in managers or to instill them where they are not present.

The next section turns to some anecdotal evidence of what works and what doesn't in training marketing implementation skills, derived from my classroom and other training experiences.

HOW TO TRAIN FOR IMPLEMENTATION ABILITY

For a long time now I have threatened to use "stop and shoot" films in lieu of final examinations in the classroom. The general format of these films, used mostly in police training, arms a police trainee with an unloaded pistol and faces him or her toward a screen on which vignettes are shown. In one, for example, an alleged perpetrator is seen on a suburban front lawn holding a gun to a woman's head as the officers drive by in response to a "trouble call." Seeing the police car, the hostage-taker runs toward a hedge and begins firing at the officers. Two small children are at play on riding toys in the yard. The trainees must decide whether or not to shoot, balancing in a few instants (1) applicable law, (2) observation skills, (3) the safety of uninvolved bystanders, (4) their own safety, (6) the consequences if they shoot, and (5) the consequences if they don't.

I have reflected often that this approach contains many of the elements necessary to train marketing implementation successfully (using brand management or selling or pricing scenarios instead of perpetrators, of course).

First and foremost, the exercises are *experiential* but *simulated*. Like case study, "stops and shoots" are active learning, not passive. They involve the participants in a kind of role-play, which is not less real or engaging for that fact, any more than a video game is unengaging because the aliens aren't real. But at the same time the simulation of the experience simultaneously allows (1) the relevant components of the situation to be distilled out by the creator, so that much learning can occur in a little time without the significant "dead spots" of real-time experiences; (2) the safety of doing things "off line," so that careers and business units' futures don't need to be put at risk for the sake of learning; and (3) the advantages of letting learners experience an especially broad series of situations compared to the ones available on the job, which often are narrow.

In management a number of "stop and shoot" alternatives already exist for the training of marketing implementation. Case study is certainly one such method, and I've used it successfully to teach implementation skills in the classroom for four years to both MBA students and managers. The thirty-eight cases cited at the back of this book have been especially prepared to help in the training of marketing implementation and appear to work to inculcate in students and sharpen in managers the critical implementation tendencies brought out by the research above.

But it is not necessary to be wedded to case teaching methodology in order to set up implementation simulations that breed the quick, contingent, multiple-action tendencies cited above. For a number of years, for instance, Merrill Lynch is said to have used an "in-box/out-box" simulation to test and train stock brokers. In this simulation, the trainee or broker is brought to a training site where he/she finds an in-box filled with stock orders to execute, "telephone messages" relaying problems with clients, and other normal aspects of the broker's job. Experienced brokers call the trainee on the telephone while he or she is trying to cope with the in-box mess, and raise still other problems with which the trainee must deal. The result of the process is either a job recruit whose aptitudes at this kind of work are quickly assessed or else a trainee whose skills can be sharpened by ruminating on the results of the simulation, watching a videotape of his/her performance, or discussing his/her behavior with the observers.

Regardless of the type of experiential simulation selected, it is my experience that such exercises must (1) be regular, (2) be repetitive, and (3) above all, *engage* management in the implementation skills to be learned. It is not such a tough matter to figure out the critical practice elements of a brand manager's job (or even a vice president's) using the implementation model given in Chapter 2 as a guide, especially if we are willing to follow our implementation rules and spend some time with the "customer," the manager in the job to be analyzed. The tough task for any training endeavor is meeting the three conditions of regularity, repetition, and engagement I have just cited.

It is interesting to contrast these three requirements for training *practice* skills with most of what occurs under the rubric of marketing training. Speaking only for some sessions that I have been involved in, it is seldom that such exercises are regular. They are more likely to be engaged as a kind of quasi-entertainment at the annual sales conference ("motivational speakers" and the like) than they are to be a vital part of the job. This pattern, of course, gives managers the (correct) idea that if only they keep their heads down, they'll get through the meeting and be able to get on with more important things.

Where the exercises are regular, topics are hardly ever repetitive. Rather, training seems to show an almost terminally topical interest in what's "hot" this year rather than in what skills management needs to get the marketing job done well. As in doing good marketing implementation, the training of good implementation skills requires clear vision and theme inculcated by repetition of a few basics rather than a hodgepodge of topical diversions.

Even when training is regular *and* repetitive, it very, very rarely is engaging. Managers are more often treated to a series of "experts" propounding on the nature of truth as the experts see it, as opposed to being *engaged* in a learning process with a coach (preferably another manager). This is the saddest part of all: Instead of using good job-time to coach better practice, we all too often duck to the resorts and the croissants to bore people with the managerial equivalent of English Composition I. Like English Comp students, the participants are quick to see the irrelevance of the theory to the needs of practice, and to "turn off."

It is probably not from formal training symposia that marketing practice is best trained, but rather from the day-to-day coaching provided by senior management, who must be *exemplars* at the skills they wish to inculcate in their subordinates. As previous chapters have argued for marketing implementation itself, training good practice in peers and subordinates also hinges on top marketing management—if the organization is to take up the staff of better practices. I shall return to the exemplar notion briefly in the final chapter of the book.

CONCLUSION AND EXTENSION: MARKETING LEADERS

My beginning researches into the personal determinants of marketing implementation abilities suggest two things. The first is that good and bad implementers are not picked from the management ranks the same way one can pick Clint Eastwood out of a UHF crowd of "bad actors"; they just don't stick out that way in terms of personality patterns or identity. But even though there is no fixed personality pattern characterizing the good implementer, there is a recurring set of skills.

Speaking most generally, these are the analytic biases and predispositions my top marketers and general managers brought to their case analyses: a thrust toward the fixable, a bias for action, contingency, and specificity, among others. The research was clear in suggesting that, begging the question of motivation, the "implementation template" of the senior managers in the studies was (1) identifiable and therefore (2) trainable. It was also powerful in its implication that this implementation template is a complex developmental task for the manager, appearing better as experience and age increased. Therefore, whatever training might be done to encourage the development of a template for good practice in younger managers would be well-engaged activity, for it can help short-circuit an otherwise long developmental process.

Training for better marketing practice needs several critical elements: experiential nature, regular occurrence, and repetitive concern. "Normal" training is not likely to achieve these ends, but top management example and day-to-day coaching *can* produce visible changes in subordinates' ability to get the marketing job done, which can have profound effects on practices.

The marketing leadership question I promised to return to in this chapter thus admits of an easy answer. The best marketing leader is that senior manager who most clearly embodies the characteristics of the good implementer uncovered in this chapter and who regularly, repetitively, and engagingly *coaches* his or her subordinates to help *them* learn these habits as well. In my view of the world the leader "just happens to be the guy out in front" and thus is in no way born "special." What he or she is, however, is a powerful role model for subordinates. Those who pick up this responsibility are good leaders; those who do not are not.

The next chapter takes up the nature of "quality marketing practices" and what this phrase means in measurable terms.

CHAPTER ELEVEN

Marketing Quality

Quality . . . you know what it is, yet you don't know what it is. But that's self-contradictory. But some things are better than others, that is, they have more quality. But when you try to say what the quality is, apart from the things that have it, it all goes poof! There's nothing to talk about. But if you can't say what Quality is, how do you know what it is, or how do you know that it even exists?

—Pirsig, *Zen and the Art of Motorcycle Maintenance*

IT'S EASY TO MAKE pronouncements about excellence in management and marketing practices. All the books do it. It's much harder to be specific about two critical aspects of such pronouncements. The first is *what* quality in marketing activities *is*. The second is how you know you've attained it.

This chapter addresses both issues, for without a clear understanding of them we conclude the book in the precarious position of having recommended a model of marketing practices and a set of managerial execution skills that, if useful, are less than persuasive because they don't address the critical issue of *what good practice is.* Failing to think carefully about the nature of good practices is inviting disaster, much in the same way as taking cures without knowing how to recognize good health.

The first section of the chapter examines some innovative work from disciplines as diverse as philosophy and behavioral engineering to help set the parameters of quality in practice and to form a backdrop for a more specific discussion of what marketing quality is and is not. Marketing quality is taken up in the second section. The third section of this chapter explores the definition arrived at in some detail in terms of two primary components of marketing quality, effectiveness and efficiency. It proposes some benchmarks and implications for your own assessment of quality in marketing practices and some ways to improve it.

MARKETING QUALITY

I don't use the term "productivity" in connection with marketing activities, because that term carries an inordinate amount of baggage, and inquiry into it has caused nothing but trouble for scientists and managers alike.[1] I prefer the broader term "marketing quality," because the sum and substance of what we have been discussing in this book is *increasing quality in marketing practices*. Being able to do this requires an examination of the general notion of quality. Then we can turn to the specific question of quality in marketing practices. Fortunately some solid, provocative, and unusual thinking has been done by others that can point us in good directions.

Excursus on Quality

Those who have read this far may feel already somewhat too familiar with my interest in Robert Pirsig's *Zen and the Art of Motorcycle Maintenance*. If you can bear with the reference one last time, however, it will be worthwhile, for Pirsig has thought further into the causes and consequences of quality than most of those who have gone before.

Peace of Mind. Pirsig's inquiry[2] into the nature of quality was provoked by observations from everyday life. He noticed that one group of his friends approached life, work, and projects from a scientific, experimental, rational point of view. They enjoyed household plumbing chores, motorcycle maintenance, and current technology because it seemed appropriate to experiment with the logical order others had brought to the world by those inventions.

It was *fun* to muck with the plumbing or the chain on a motorcycle, because the world was seen as a set of causes and effects. Through the application of the scientific method even complex and "sticky" problems could be brought to heel. These friends were highly rational thinkers, enamored of science and its deductive methods, and concerned with "objective" reality. They wanted less to do with the subjective, qualitative, "soft" aspects of reality and tended to discount these as "feelings" or romanticism.

Pirsig's other friends, equally able and equally bright, could only be called "technophobes." They avoided even *knowing about* the motorcycles they owned, were grossly unconcerned with maintenance, and certainly didn't care to fix their own plumbing. Rather, they perceived beauty in a "hereness and nowness" relation to the world, immersing themselves in the romantic, subjective, and hence "nonrational" aspects of life (sight, sound, experience) rather than being bound by what they thought was the trivia of existence. *They* were not experimenters; they were *livers* who thought there was something wrong with folks who were always analyzing, dissecting, and changing reality in order to deal with it.

For the first group, beauty and goodness were analysis and science-like manipulation; for the second, just "feeling good" or "being with it" constituted the preferred method of interacting with the world.

Pirsig remarks on this great cleavage not only in his friends' lifestyles but across all of philosophy as well. He notes that two distinct kinds of quality have existed in philosophical thought from the time of Aristotle. The "greater," more "worthy," "useful" sort of quality always has been thought of as the rational. It is that which the Western (but not Eastern) philosophers singled out as the basis for all reason, science, and hence progress.

The other, the "romantic," "squishy," "feelings" quality one gets from being romantically *involved* in what is going on, "digging it," routinely is held suspect and thought unworthy by the great Western philosophers. After all, "rational" quality can be tested, probed with experimental methods, and used to develop "truth." "Romantic" quality is *subjective,* and therefore undocumentable. What is undocumentable, say the philosophers, is worthless to him who would be *correctly* informed about the world and is the stuff of witch doctors and fairy tales.

Pirsig's accomplishment was to integrate these two kinds of "goodness" into a single overarching notion of quality, a notion he thought of as logically prior to either subset. He suggested that feelings *and* evidence are just opposite and equally valid sides of the same quality coin. The "out there" and the "in here" are not separate at all: In Pirsig's words, "they grow toward quality or fall away from quality together." And when this real quality is present in living, the rational and subjective work together in a kind of harmony where one shapes the other.

Quality, for Pirsig, is *peace of mind.* It occurs only when the scientific/technical and the romantic/subjective views meet in such a way that the *observer is at one, and at peace with that which is being observed.* The junction of the two kinds of quality happens only when manipulations being made on the world (whether these are in creative writing or in marketing practices) produce and reinforce the inner feelings of peacefulness that the craftsman has as he molds the work. When this happens, according to Pirsig, it is correct to speak of Quality as "occurring" with a capital "Q." What psychologists call "integration," being so involved in experience that you don't even know you're involved, what the sports psychologists try to develop as "inner tennis," is something like what Pirsig means by this notion of Quality.

Some of what Pirsig said on this rapprochement between technical/objective and romantic/squishy quality as peace of mind is expressable in his own words. The passage in question refers to quality control procedures in the factory:

> Peace of mind isn't at all superficial to technical work. It's the whole thing. That which produces it is good work and that which destroys it is bad work. The specs, the measuring instruments, the quality control, the final check-out, these are all *means* toward the end of satisfying the peace of mind of those responsible for the work. What really counts in the end is that peace of mind and nothing else. [p. 288]

The first reaction of many managers to this definition (and that of students as well, I might add) is shock and disbelief. Quality is *peace of mind?* Quality is "just" *feeling good* about the marketing actions you're taking or the marketing practices you're involved with? But that's *exactly* what quality is, regardless of whether you reflect on marketing, management, fixing a motorcycle, or painting a masterpiece.

Quality is no more and no less than the perception that what we're doing to manipulate, change, observe, interact with, muck about in, or otherwise *relate* to the world makes us peaceful about the interaction between us and events. It is a process of moving from discomfort with events, things, observations, or people before we've acted, toward comfort after we've acted. To achieve comfort may require applying a set of calipers to a part to determine if it is in tolerance or redesigning a marketing organization to promote better accountability and interaction.

Regardless of whether the topic is marketing or music, Pirsig would say that we move from being "uncomfortably involved" with what is going on to more comfort with events, people, and things by our acts. As we do this, we move toward Quality. In this view Quality is bred of caring, not just technical skill, and is the brother of involvement. It is the guts of the thing. It is the difference between the mechanic who botches the valve job and the one who saves the machine; it is also the difference between the excellent marketing implementers we observed in previous chapters and other managers.

"But, but . . .," the students say, "how do you know that what makes you feel peaceful is good? What is it you look at? The behavior of the *people* in the marketing group? The *outcomes* of their acts? What?"

They're right, of course. Just saying that quality means peace of mind, the oneness of the craftsman with the block of wood as he or she shapes it into a table leg, doesn't tell us very much about either the craftsman or the block of wood. If the craftsman is supposed to be making chairs, not tables, all the Quality in the world isn't going to help. It is here that a second important notion about Quality, one proposed by the engineer Thomas Gilbert, becomes important.

. . . *And Performance.*   Gilbert is an engineer and consultant who writes on how to help managers increase their competence in action.[3] Stripped to the bone, Gilbert's thesis is that (1) we spend too much time looking for quality *behavior* when what we want is quality *performance*, and (2) we often mistake effort for performance. Gilbert claims that even complicated performances, like those of the marketing manager, can be measured if only by looking at the best existing exemplar of the performance in question.

There is much that is interesting in this view of quality performance. Gilbert rejects the viewpoint that structures for routinizing behavior have much to do with quality performance. He tells the story of a subcontractor "mining" an old rifle range for lead bullets who hired a group of college students as "fill-in" help to augment the permanent crew. The college kids showed up without decent work clothes, carrying radios and newspapers, and did not show the "right" demeanor for employees. As they were assigned to work teams, they ignored the complex work "system" the employer had developed, turned up their radios, and even threw down the shovels they were given in favor of scraping the sand into the sieves with their bare hands. Nothing the supervisor could do would get them to change their behavior, so they were all terminated at the end of the day. The trouble was that when their output was measured they had mined three times as much lead as the "regular" crew!

Gilbert also rejects the notion that high effort is related to quality performance. Protestant ethic or no, it is *not* the person who works hardest for a given level of performance that is the most able, but rather the one who works *least*. Worthy performance, Gilbert suggests, is associated with doing the most difficult thing best with the least effort.[4]

Finally, Gilbert rejects the idea that performance, even in complex, qualitative, or hard-to-understand tasks, is impossible to measure. Want to know how to measure a gargoyle carver, Gilbert asks? It doesn't matter that there are maybe five people in the world who can still carve these fancy stone figures for museums and cathedrals. Go watch each, then pick the one who seems to produce the best performance (most, most complicated, closest to design specs—it's your decision). Then see what elements of his/her performance you can isolate to help improve others.

Taking Pirsig and Gilbert together leads to an interesting definition of quality. Pirsig has it that quality is peace of mind, a notion of a "oneness" with the work. Gilbert adds, "Right, but that peace of mind must lead to performance." He says we must watch to isolate the critical elements of the performance in which we are interested and then encourage it along with a "right-thinking" attitude.

That's what we need to do, all right! That feels good! What we *want* is *quality in performance* for marketing practice, Pirsig tells us that isn't achieved without a certain peaceful mindset that implies a oneness with the work; Gilbert tells us output, not behavior, is measurable. Maybe we can work with this. To see if we can, we need to ask what the keys are to good performance in marketing practices and what the components of such performance might be.

QUALITY IN MARKETING PRACTICES

What Marketing Quality Isn't . . .

The interesting thing about most past attempts[5] to talk about quality in marketing is that they almost all mistake ultimate market place performance for quality practice, with nothing much assumed to be happening in between. Some observers write as if the managers at headquarters think up a strategy and, just like that, results occur or fail to occur. All too often it is asserted that quality in marketing is measurable directly as market share, sales revenues, financial performance over long periods of time, low complaint ratios, or some other quantitative measure of customer responsiveness to marketing efforts, with nothing in between to explain how the firm got from strategy to results.

Such a direct and immediate linkage between strategy and output simply doesn't hold; implementation intervenes. Even then, my observations indicate, more often than not the "rigorous" measures aren't well related to the quality of management's marketing practices. Whatever else it is, quality in marketing practice is *not* measurable simply by looking at share numbers or sales figures and taking evidence of good practice from acceptable results.

This provocative assertion is easily documentable. Sales and share of market do not track *current* quality of marketing practices for a number of good reasons:

- First, financial and market results *lag* current marketing practices, often by years. It takes a long time to build up responsiveness to good marketing execution, and sometimes an almost equally long time to destroy the faith and goodwill the customer has invested in the firm with bad practices caused by inefficient systems or unskilled managers.
- Second, sales, share, and other quantitative measures of market place success are only tenuously related to the quality of marketing execution. The quality of marketing strategy, competitive reactions to various moves, pure luck, and a hundred other factors have as much influence on "making the

numbers'' as does quality in practice. It is hard to isolate marketing implementation or, for that matter, marketing efforts overall from the hundreds of other market place factors that enter into the determination of results.

- Finally, even consistently good long-term financial or market share performance cannot be *causally* asserted as the effect of the quality of the marketing strategy or the marketing practices engaged. It's true that the continued good performance of an IBM or a P&G *should* lead us to look at those organizations as possible sites of excellence in practice. It's also true that some of those high-share, good-performing companies would not score very well on the list of marketing implementation criteria we developed in the previous chapters.

This line of argument says that the observer interested in quality marketing can't just look at 10-Ks, market share data, sales revenue growth, or *any* simple set of quantitative measures to unearth quality execution. There's just too much going on out there to make such observations reliable.

. . . And What It Is: Coping Behavior

But the real reason share, sales revenue, and the like won't wash to help identify quality practices is that good marketing practice doesn't mean that there will be fewer daily execution fires that need to be put out. Rather, my observations suggest that good ''implementation shops'' and poor ones experience the same frequency of execution problems. The differences are in how they handle them.

There is no guarantee that if you do everything right with marketing execution you still won't have incomplete strategies that need patching up, there won't be the same number of strategic shortfalls that need repairing, and marketing systems, no matter how clever, won't get old and mislead the effort. Rather, the management that is good at marketing implementation *copes better with execution fires.*

Whatever else it may be, quality in marketing practice can be defined as the presence of *coping skills* that allow the managers to deal with the plethora of execution crises that crop up daily and, if left untreated, lead the best-laid marketing strategies to failure.

Coping skill, a measure of output that meets Gilbert's ''performance'' yardstick, can be defined further. Chapter 1 argued that good marketing practices occurred at the triple interface of company, customers, and trade. Marketing practice encompasses all those actions and outcomes that implement the firm's marketing strategies for good effects on the end user, remembering that much of what goes on to execute marketing plans involves internal firm dynamics, marketing structures (programs, systems, and the like), and management's interactions with the distribution channel or trade.

Remembering this basic structure of marketing practices allows us to partition coping into two pieces. We are concerned with two kinds of marketing performances in the assessment of marketing quality: those relating to intracompany dynamics and those affecting the customers (and trade). Put another way, we are interested in *marketing efficiency*, the quality with which intracompany moves are made, and *marketing effectiveness*, the impact of those moves on consumers and distribution networks.

Implementation Precepts Reinterpreted as Quality

The preceding chapters in this book can be viewed as qualitative reports on some important internal and external coping skills displayed by managers practicing marketing. These managers often worked in marketing structures that were weak or dysfunctional. Low-level actions were done poorly, with little attention to detail, structural contradiction, and global mediocrity. Marketing programs were beset by empty promises syndromes or else just proliferated like bunnies. Systems either misinformed management about what it needed to know or, more commonly, just didn't inform about anything at all. And policies everywhere were characterized by vague marketing themes and weak cultures.

Yet the managers got the marketing job done, often through the exercise of personal execution skills. When we analyzed these exertions of personal execution skills a number of "implementation precepts" became clear. Among others, these included:

- *The "Soundness" Rule.* Soundness at the top (strong leaders, clear theme) and the bottom (well-implemented low-level actions), not flashiness in the middle (too many programs). This was an "internal" rule, concerning marketing efficiency.
- *The Clarity Rule.* Be sure of who you are and where you're going, another efficiency precept.
- *The Leadership Rule.* You can't practice marketing well with weak marketing leaders, which goes with—

- *The Poor Followers Rule.* Seek bad followers who will bend the rules a little in the service of quality execution. (These were still more efficiency precepts.)
- *The Partnership Rule.* The notion of "partnering" with other firm functions, with the end users, and especially with the trade is a lucid expression of marketing effectiveness.
- *The Pickiness Rule.* Be selective about allocations, then back them to the hilt. This rule involves both efficiency and effectiveness notions.

But if our inquiry into marketing effectiveness and efficiency is going to delve into quality marketing practices, we need to take a closer look at these recommendations. In particular, we need to reopen the structures versus skills question that has formed the backbone of the book.

Systems Versus Skills

The "implementation precepts" are valid and valuable but lead to an overgeneral conclusion that *structures invariably "go bad," and managers invariably must fix them.* This has been the descriptive premise of the book; for whatever reasons, marketing structures ordinarily are found wanting and marketing managers must use their skills to "bridge the gaps" in the execution structure. But are any other alternatives possible? Should the manager ever seek to build structure, even at the expense of skills? Can *that* ever bring peace of mind to the marketer?

It is this question that a closer analysis of marketing efficiency and effectiveness addresses. That analysis also breeds some interesting rules for increasing marketing quality.

MARKETING EFFECTIVENESS AND EFFICIENCY

Marketing Effectiveness

Marketing effectiveness, management's coping quality when dealing with customer or trade problems, is a thorny issue. What follows is admittedly exploratory thinking on my part. It goes beyond the clinical data, though you'll see it tracks our execution model nicely, fulfills the requirements for coping measures discussed above, and as a bonus has some interesting implications about the structure–skills issue.

Marketing effectiveness by definition refers to a comparison of achieved outputs with intended goals. In everyday life we call that comparison "satisfaction." I propose that satisfaction on the part of management is one of the main components of marketing effectiveness. The satisfaction component of marketing effectiveness is similar to Pirsig's "peace of mind."

If you throw a ball and it goes a great distance, this knowledge tells you nothing. Perhaps you were only trying to throw it to an individual with a catcher's mitt crouching behind home plate; "throwing great distances" with this set of goals means a wild pitch! The first component of thinking about marketing effectiveness is the comparison of what was achieved through certain practices versus what was intended.

A second component of marketing effectiveness is the effort expended to obtain the satisfaction in question. The management that devotes all its attention, time, and best people to producing the success of one program clearly hasn't done as much as a management that produces the same result while implementing three other programs too. The effort expended to get a result also must enter the effectiveness equation. Following Gilbert, the lower the effort to produce a given level of satisfaction, the higher the effectiveness.

Thus marketing effectiveness, the quality of management's implementation moves as these affect the customers and trade, can be defined as management's satisfaction with the results of its moves relative to the effort it expended to produce the results.

It is interesting to look into effort more closely. From our model of implementation and the observations we've already detailed, the amount of effort any management must expend to get desired results is a joint function of:

- The strength of its execution structures
- The skills of its managers
- How tough the competition makes it to do anything in the market

The stronger marketing's execution structures are, the lower the effort required to perform a given action, and the higher the effectiveness. That is a commonsense conclusion from our implementation model. The more management can routinize practice, *assuming that routinization produces desired results,* the lower the effort expended and the higher the marketing effectiveness.

Conversely, the more intervention (execution skills) required from management to "bridge the gap" and get the marketing job done despite inadequate structure, the higher the effort required to produce a given effect, and therefore the lower the marketing effectiveness. The exercise of personal execution skills tends to be effortful, time-consuming, and plain hard work. That reduces effectiveness.

And the tougher the competition, the higher the effort needed on the part of management and the lower the marketing effectiveness. This is because competitive reaction can blunt even the best-executed program in the field.

Thus marketing effectiveness is a joint function of (1) satisfaction with what is achieved and (2) the effort expended to achieve it. Satisfaction, in turn, depends not only on shares, sales, or revenues results, but just as much on what management *expected* would happen from its coping actions to produce the numbers.

Effort, on the other hand, is made up of three pieces. Structural adequacy means that systems and other "marketing routines" can be used for much of the people-work that would otherwise have to be expended to get the marketing job done, reducing effort. On the other hand, structural inadequacy means that marketers have to be highly skilled to bridge the gaps in the execution structure to get results, which means more effort, which in turn means lower marketing effectiveness. And the degree of competition in the market is related to marketing effectiveness directly as well, for competitors' possible reactions to management's marketing moves mute the results achieved.

Implications of Satisfaction and Effort

This set of observations about marketing effectiveness produces a powerful set of implications for understanding, improving, and manipulating effectiveness in marketing practices:

1. Marketing effectiveness increases directly with results and inversely with expectations.

The management that *either* achieves the most *or* expects the least is the one that is most effective. The first management must go a long way to achieve "peace" with reality; the second, only a little way. Market place results cannot be divorced from management expectations, and any meaningful program to evaluate or improve effectiveness must (1) account for different management expectations for a program or action and (2) change those expectations.

No one needs to tell anyone but the greenest rookie that one of the ways an astute manager gets to be judged effective in most corporations involves "sandbagging" the goal-setting process. Having promised little, he delivers much and thereby looks effective.

The other side of the expectations–results coin holds true as well. When managers at Frito-Lay first rolled out GrandMa's cookies, they had set themselves a goal of $120 million in sales in three years. Because of supermarket resistance, however, "only" a $50-million business was achieved. The interesting thing about this performance, which almost anywhere else would have been considered a roaring success, is that management considered it a failure! Satisfaction is a *joint* function of results and expectations.

There is a way we can make the expectations phenomenon work for us. If we *manage* the power of expectations in a careful way, we can act to increase marketing effectiveness. By getting managers to expect more of themselves we improve results, for they will drag up their output to match their expectations in order to feel satisfied.

2. The need for sophisticated marketing execution skills increases the effort needed to get results, which decreases effectiveness. Higher structural adequacy reduces effort and increases effectiveness.

Now we can understand why management always is systematizing, routinizing, and proceduralizing marketing! To the extent management can put in sound structures, then to that extent high-priced marketing talent *doesn't have to* bridge the gaps in execution structures, thus allowing low-effort execution and high marketing effectiveness.

In an important sense, then, there are two ways to get marketing effectiveness, a "cheap" one and an "expensive" one. The cheap one is to routinize, proceduralize, and generally build structures to handle the implementation of many marketing tasks, programs, and plans. This has the advantage of requiring low effort, because the managers can rely on the structures to help them do their job.

The expensive way is to build, recruit, and train managers highly skilled at interacting, allocating, monitoring, and organizing. Then it doesn't matter if the structures are bad, because these men and women will act to get the job done anyway. This alternative is expensive because such highly skilled people are expensive, act in nonroutine manners, and usually don't allow systematization of what they have done.

The external danger that keeps the first approach from *always* being the better one is that marketing structures (and all management ones, for that matter) have a marvelous tendency to go awry, to become inappropriate for changed conditions and special circumstances, and to drive the firm toward failure. The trick for management is to find ways to know *when to structure* and when not to. Skilled managers always are needed, because sometimes the structures don't work.

3. Competitive reaction is associated with increased effort, and therefore with reduced effectiveness.

This simple, straightforward, and commonsense notion is not often factored into management's thinking about marketing effectiveness, but it needs to be. Effectiveness in any endeavor is relative to the latitude allowed by competitors as they respond to management's moves. As competitive response increases in magnitude or rapidity, effectiveness of marketing programs declines. Therefore, the marketer who produces his or her results in a highly competitive environment is more effective than the one with equally stellar achievements in a monopoly setting.

There are two other implications of this overall view of marketing effectiveness having equal utility to top managers viewing the outputs of their marketing efforts:

4. Effectiveness in marketing endeavors is measurable only piecemeal, over individual marketing programs. There is no "overall" statement of marketing effectiveness.

This implication follows directly from my line of reasoning about marketing effectiveness and management satisfaction. When management is more or less satisfied with its efforts in marketing implementation, it usually is evaluating its efforts to cope with specific problems besetting product lines, segments, and programs. One group's expectations, effort, and results may be quite different from another's. It is impossible to evaluate these groups using the same measure of effectiveness, because the basis of the comparison will not be the same.

Not only will effectiveness be calculated differently across marketing's programs, but marketing *quality will be variable* within the same firm or division. It is wrong to talk about "excellent" marketing groups but right to talk about "excellent" programs, actions, or projects *in* the marketing group.

This implication accounts nicely for the fact that, even in the best companies, marketing outcomes are uneven. Some managers expect much and deliver it with low effort, a pattern for high effectiveness. Others seem to expect less and deliver nothing by twenty-four-hour toil. This kind of "practice unevenness" is normal and to be expected; what the top manager wants to do is minimize the variability as much as possible between the best and worst outcomes.

5. Marketing effectiveness is not marketing efficiency.

The heart of quality in marketing practices is how effective management is at getting results consistent with its expectations for actions taken involving the customers and trade. Share, revenues, and the like are useful measures only in the context of management's expectations, effort, and competitive responses; by themselves, they represent nothing.

Moreover, *what is achieved* (marketing effectiveness) says little about *how it is achieved* (marketing efficiency). The latter allows choices between beefing up structures in order to achieve routinization and beefing up skills in order to achieve flexibility. This is the grand conflict of quality practices: routine-dominance or people-dominance?

Marketing Efficiency: Structural Soundness

What makes some companies able to work within sound structures, and thus able to get high unit outputs per management input? What factors throw others into disastrous disarray, leaving them in the position of executing their way out of regular implementation structure shortfalls or strategic failures?

There is little need to examine the negative side of the equation: Chapters 3 through 6 have detailed what goes wrong with execution structures in some depth. Basically, marketing (and management) structures, including systems, go awry because the world "slips away" dynamically from the static structures meant to make action easier, so that good practice becomes harder. This phenomenon is as visible in general management as it is in marketing. It is, however, more dangerous and more immediate in marketing, because it is this discipline which is at the cutting edge of translating customer preferences into the firm and marketing actions to the outside.

Indeed, I found one variant of structural calcification so frequently in my early implementation research that I was moved to name it "marketing inertia" and to write an article about it.[6] I thought I had stumbled onto the "mother lode" of implementation generalizations. As it turned out, I had found only a small piece of the efficiency puzzle.

The thesis of the inertia argument was that regular successes in the market place encouraged a firm and its management to start *believing* in its own structures and systems, allowing these to calcify in much the same way that a fish trapped in a net cannot see that it need only swim the other way to be free. Market place losers, I perceived, did not suffer from this inertia, for they had no investment in thinking their own beliefs about how to do things were the right ones.

What struck me in my early observations was the special case of the general principle being expounded here. I thought that when a company is regularly successful, it *inevitably* must "calcify" in such a manner that management had better *hope* that the world didn't change, because the company couldn't! I pointed out the large auto makers and a number of other companies that I thought suffered violently from this disease and spent time trying to simulate catastrophes to keep marketers flexible.

I now know it is *not necessarily true* that regular success has to lead to calcified systems and to eventual disaster, though that pattern occurs in the majority of instances I observe. There are firms that have been able to make strong structure work for marketing efficiency. The one characteristic of these high-structure successes I missed in my earlier work was that *they are precisely the same companies that have managers strongly skilled at implementation!*

This is the key rule for marketing efficiency: Structure can be built and maintained as long as there are managers with powerful personal implementation skills in the company who will yank the structure back as soon as it starts to give "funny" results, who will stay close to the customers, who will ride with routinization as long as it produces the choices they themselves would have made, and who will not hesitate to substitute their own judgments when the structure starts showing signs of cracking. As in the rest of life, they can best afford to structure marketing who have the least need to, for they have a built-in insurance policy against disaster.

The key to building powerful structures and to reaping the benefits of routinization is having the "insurance" provided by managers with strong implementation skills. The P&Gs, the IBMs, and the Frito-Lays get their consistently effective results not because they have a "systen." and religiously follow "The Book," though they do. Rather consistency of output comes from the presence of sharp-eyed and sharp-skilled implementers who constantly help revise, revamp, and tune the structures to changing marketing conditions, and who are not afraid to substitute their own judgments for structural shortfalls.

The "answer" to the efficiency problem in marketing practices, then, appears to be: "Routinize some, but keep your implementation skills sharp. Judging from the experience of even the best of firms, structures degrade over time, and you shall need them."

CONCLUSION

Good marketing practice is quality performance in *coping with the inevitable execution crises that arise in every firm*, which threaten to short-circuit strategy's impact on the market place. "Quality performance," in turn, is dependent both on management's expectations of what results will accrue from its practices and on the effort expended to achieve them. Marketing effectiveness involves the "peace of mind" that comes from expecting much and getting it.

Marketing efficiency concerns management's ability to routinize implementation acts, programs, systems, or policies in such a way that they are less effortful. Here the companies that can afford the risks of routinization, and the corresponding dangers this presents in terms of structural inflexibility, are precisely the same ones that have strongly skilled managers.

The "keys to the kingdoms" of effectiveness and efficiency, then, turn out to be already in the manager's pocket. Marketing quality is the peace of mind that comes from effectively coping with the myriad execution crises that threaten strategic viability. Often this implies managing the expectations of the marketers to be sure their goals are high enough, and their efforts as stream-lined as possible.

Because of the nature of marketing, with its simultaneous within-firm and extra-firm job requirements, execution crises come in two flavors. The first kind concern what needs to be done inside the company to allow quality actions to occur. The second involves the consequences of those actions (or more correctly, manage-ment's *satisfaction* with the consequences of those efforts) among customers and trade.

Marketers can cope with internal and external crises in two manners. The first is through the application of personal execution skills by managers, and the second through strong systems. The former is expensive but flexible, and the latter cheap but vulnerable to market changes.

The *real* key to effectiveness *with* efficiency is as simple as start-ing with strongly skilled managers, then carefully building struc-ture to take over for them "under most circumstances." The im-plementers, though, must remain present and sharp to take over at a moment's notice from the structural routinization when it ap-pears those structures are leading to bad decisions. Then they will be doing what they are paid to do—manage.

Research Appendix

THIS RESEARCH APPENDIX surveys the continuing four-year research project I have undertaken on marketing practices. It describes the research questions and objectives, the clinical case investigation method, the case data, and some synergies that have occurred among the data, the classroom, and consulting projects.

RESEARCH CAUSES AND QUESTIONS

As I argued in Chapter 1 and throughout the book, marketing for a number of years has been long on advice about *what to do* in a given competitive or market situation and short on useful recommendations for *how to do it* within company, competitor, and customer constraints. Yet my experiences with both managers and students argues strongly that these parties often are strategy-sophisticated but implementation-bound. That is, they know quite well *what* it is they want to do in marketing; usually, however, there are real problems in *getting the marketing job done*. The research project was undertaken to:

- Identify the components of marketing practices, called "marketing implementation," as these occurred across companies, industries, and managers
- Learn whether commonalities existed across companies and

industries in the practice of marketing, both regarding problems encountered when strategies are implemented and concerning rules for good marketing practice
- Attempt to improve the practice of marketing as done by the operating manager in the same way that two decades of strategy-development work in marketing have improved his planning.

My research philosophy and background also underlay the research question set and served as powerful causes for it. Because of my professional training as a social psychologist, I see the world as primarily a place where the complex interdependencies between people and groups determine outcomes. Understanding these dependencies has been paramount for me; thus it is only natural that I would emphasize the *relationship* between buyer and sellers in marketing.

Yet as I consulted the marketing literature, I was profoundly unimpressed with what I felt was an overemphasis on the customer's reactions to marketing moves made by impersonal and faceless "corporations" and an underemphasis on the managers who made the moves. It seemed as if the accepted models of marketing consisted of (1) formulating a strategy and then (2) watching for customer response. These models, in my view, left out the "other half" of the interaction, the managers who put strategies into practice. Consequently they ignored a terribly important topic of interest, how those strategies were implemented. Whether because marketers were striving for simplicity, had their hands full just studying strategy, or simply found it easier to ignore the "slips 'twixt the cup and the lip" that occur whenever plans are executed, no attention was being paid to marketing execution or its rules.

Further, as I examined my own consulting practice and managerial contacts, it seemed to me that the managers with whom I came in contact were generally strategy-sophisticated. This meant that clever strategy less and less would be able to serve as the "enduring competitive advantage" talked about by the consultants, because many were strategically clever.

At the same time, however, most executives seemed to have problems making their strategies work; it was the implementation that was problematical, not the plans. It occurred to me that execution excellence might become a new basis for competitive advantage in the 1980s. On the negative side, it struck me that unless we focused on how *well* the marketing job got done and learned a science of execution to go along with our plethora of plans, marketers would be rightly accused of becoming more and more elegant in thought and less and less able in action. It was to refocus attention on this action, implementation, execution, and practice component of *doing marketing* that I undertook my study.

THE CLINICAL METHODOLOGY FOR THE STUDY OF PRACTICE

There is no doubt that proposing to investigate how marketing is *practiced*, as opposed to how it is planned, poses special research problems. It would not do to give sophomore students who had never managed anything a set of scenarios and claim their responses are "just like" what managers would have done,[1] for example. Nor could I rely on some quick and dirty mail survey sent to a thousand managers in hopes that a hundred would not be too busy to reply and would be motivated to do anything but "make smoke" in their answers. Besides, I had no idea of what questions to ask.[2]

On reflection, it seemed that learning about marketing practices meant a unique requirement to go out to where marketing *was practiced,* to "hang around" and try to learn something about what was going on. The hope was that by trying to understand how marketing and general managers made sense of their practice problems, a "deep knowing" that perhaps traded off statistically reliable numbers for the wisdom of individual situations and events-as-they-happened might result. If it was nothing else, a research project into marketing implementation was distinctly *clinical* in its information needs. I needed to go to school in the field to see what was what.

The Case Method for Research

Fortunately, the institution where I work has for seventy-five years been perfecting a kind of clinical investigation method that seemed especially well suited to the research questions[3] puzzling me. It is also a place with extensive management contacts and has a strength of reputation that makes busy presidents at least consider letting a professor sell Fritos from the truck.

The case method is known by generations of students and managers as an excellent teaching vehicle that provokes managerial competency by making participants experience the problems with which managers struggle daily and by forcing them to create their own learning templates to deal with the vast array of different dilemmas they are confronted with. It is less well known as a legitimate part of scientific inquiry called "qualitative method," used by large numbers of social scientists and medical researchers to inform themselves on the operation of complex phenomena.[4] Since the phenomena I proposed to investigate certainly were complex, and since the clinical methods of case research seemed to fit the problem, it was this method that I used to investigate marketing implementation.

A case is a description of a management situation. In compiling this description, the case researcher "goes out to where the situation is," to management, and attempts to write a complete and current account of management's *current experience* with a problem of interest. For instance, Manac System's difficulties with selling its legal software was a current problem being experienced by president Lynne Verchere at the time that case was compiled. The case researcher's job is to document, as fully as time, ability, and data allow, the relevant aspects of the problem in a manner not dissimilar to the anthropologist's investigation of an island culture or a physician's tracking of symptoms to causes.

Cases are the research analog of the physician's (or the detective's—see Edgar Allen Poe or Conan Doyle, for instance) clinical examination and rely on many of the same multiple data sources found in that technique. While a physician may ask questions, look at vital signs, and check on family history in order to make a determination of whether headache symptoms indicate stressful living or a more immediately life-threatening cause, the case researcher also asks questions (interviews managers), looks at vital signs (market share, margins), and checks on family history (industry structure, company and product line history) to allow an equivalent determination to be made about a management problem.

While most case studies focus on a specific problem of current interest to management, it is legitimate and eminently possible to construct useful research cases without a specific problem focus (e.g. some of the Frito-Lay materials referred to in the text) to illustrate the operation of healthy marketing practices, just as sports medicine physicians study those in especially good physical condition.

Case construction always employs multiple data sources in compilation. While cases, like other qualitative methods available

to the investigator, rely heavily upon verbal data (personal interviews) and what are called "naturalistic observations" (watching
what is going on), they are distinguished from other methods by
their use of many other data sources. These include examining
financial data like budgets and operating statements, market performance data, competitive data, and customer data. Such data are
almost always reported to the case researcher in undisguised,
"real" numbers, and only after the case is compiled is some
disguise applied to the real numbers to protect proprietary information. "Doing" a case study is a collaboration between management and research and involves a remarkable degree of disrobing
on the part of management, a high degree of trust for the case
writer, and a real commitment to the research.[5]

Ordinarily the development of each case study in my sample required 120–200 man-hours of work from the case writer, and
perhaps a third of that amount of time from management. The
resultant document averaged twenty-two pages in length; involved interviews with perhaps ten to twenty managers, not
counting customers, distributors, and other parties; and represented an in-depth clinical examination of the company and industry as this pertained to a problem management was experiencing in marketing. Only twenty to forty hours of time was spent
"on-site," usually doing the interviewing and collecting docu-
ments. The remainder was spent in talking with customers, competitors, and industry experts and mostly in trying to make sense
of the mass of company memoranda, interview notes, and competitive reports, as well as putting in days "selling" in the field
with company salespeople and the like to form a coherent picture
of the problem under investigation.

The Case Research Cycle

Clearly the topics, companies, and managers selected for case investigation will, to a great degree, determine the findings and
shape resultant understanding. Whether done for research or
teaching purposes, case site selection is by no means either a random or a thoughtless process. First, case selection is constrained by
the topic of investigation. Second, it is constrained by the case site
opportunities. Third, it is regulated by a process not unlike that
which guides all other kinds of scientific inquiries.

On the first point, topic of interest guidance, I specifically
sought out situations where marketing strategy seemed sound but

problems had cropped up in the execution of a low-level function, program, system, or policy. Often the chief executive or top marketing manager of a company was most helpful in identifying areas of marketing implementation interest, as opposed to marketing strategy interest. At other times the business press or contacts with colleagues produced viable case leads. Not a few came from consulting contacts and past students.

Still, it would be wrong to assert that all companies were searched and somehow systematically sampled for marketing implementation problems. That was not true; perforce, the sample of companies was neither random nor disinterestedly selected. Rather, a dynamic process guided the case research process.

Case research proceeds through four distinct stages that I call "drift," "design," "prediction," and "disconfirmation."

In the "drift" stage of case research the investigator isn't quite sure what the right questions are, who should be studied, or, indeed, how to think about his research problem very well. The early stages of any managerial research project, a case research one in particular, is largely a matter of "going to school" on willing managers so the researcher can learn the dimensions of his problem and how to think about it.

In the marketing implementation research project, the managers taught me quickly that there were *structures* for implementation (actions, programs, systems, policies) and also *skills* (interacting, allocating, monitoring, organizing) brought to the job by the managers. They also taught me that these dimensions weren't independent but could be used to categorize marketing practice problems in a neat way that could shape the investigation and suggest what cases needed to be collected.

In the "design" stage the investigator has a pretty good idea of what the elements of the problem might be (our four levels by four skills implementation matrix), and wishes to flesh out his understanding of the concepts and drive to the surface any generalizations that might appear across industries and companies. For example, once the four-by-four typology given in Chapter 1 was discovered, I knew I had to look at low-level problems of marketing actions (like trade show management), programs (like national accounts management), marketing systems, and marketing policies issues. Consumer, industrial, and service industry cases had to be collected as well, in order to gain a perspective on the applicability of these categories across industries and thus on the typology's generalizability. Case collection in the design stage largely is a matter of "fleshing out the matrix" of preliminary understanding gained from the drift stage.

As cases were collected to fill in the marketing implementation taxonomy, certain generalizations about marketing practices started to make themselves clear to me. For instance, early in the research project it became clear that actions-level soundness coupled with a clear marketing theme was preferable to a profusion of programs. The research then entered the "prediction" stage; even more case sites were selected to see if these beginning generalizations held across small versus large companies, different stages in the corporate life cycle, and other variables.

The prediction stage generated a set of "useful digressions" in case collection as well. For instance, it became clear about midway through the research process that marketing systems and policies, ordinarily *very* difficult to observe in firms, became ripe candidates for examination when management had taken a decision to perform a "marketing audit" on its activities. Consequently, I compiled four different cases on the marketing audit and learned more about doing this important evaluation task than I had ever expected, because of my interest in making predictions about marketing systems and policies. It was in this digression that the generalization that marketing execution requires strong management leaders became evident, for example.

Finally, toward the end of the research collection effort, and continuing even now, came the "disconfirmation" stage. Here, cases were deliberately collected in unusual or unfamiliar settings (e.g. international, governmental, and venture start-up) to test the limits of the generalizations revealed. The generalizations had come to appear with almost boring regularity in case sites, and it was desired to learn their limits.

The result of all of this case collecting, puzzlement, testing, and disconfirmation-seeking is a kind of "rolling knowledge" about marketing practice over the course of the research. One generalization will be regarded as firm, and attempts will be made to test its limits, while another is just coming to the fore. It is only after findings "settle down" into a clear pattern (this took more than three years in the present project) that any confidence can be placed in what is known.

Further, like most managerial knowledge, "what is known" remains purely and simply *currently useful generalization*. That is to say, what I have unearthed as true today may not be true tomorrow; what I have found useful for managers in some companies may or may not be useful for those in others; and the findings we are talking about throughout the book are "generalizations," not some sort of absolute and immutable "truth." This is the nature of all research findings, not just those produced by the case method.

A summary of the casework[6] is given in Table A–1 (pp. 211–226), which contains synopses of the thirty-eight case studies collected from twenty-two different companies in this research project. Most of the cases are available to readers unrestrictedly, either from HBS Case Services,[7] or in the companion book to this volume, called *Managing Marketing: Text, Cases, and Readings*. You are encouraged, even exhorted, to look at the cases in their "raw form" to derive your own insights about marketing practice.

Some Case Statistics

It is worthwhile to look at the cases in somewhat more detail to (1) make sure that the waterfront of industries, companies, and market situations has been covered and (2) to ask how the findings differ when different situations are studied.

Table A–2 (pp. 227–228) shows each case categorized by (1) industry, (2) size of operating unit studied, (3) market growth rate, (4) competitive position in its industry, (5) consumer/industrial marketing situation, and (6) product or service classification.

As can be seen from Table A–2, the set of industries in which at least one marketing practice problem was investigated is especially large, as befits the far-ranging research questions asked in this project. The sample competes in industries as different as commodities (e.g. zinc) and high technology, and as distinct as business jets versus crayons.

Similarly, the sample has good coverage of small, medium, and large operating units. The smaller companies especially have not been neglected in this project, and indeed, if the sample could be "beefed up" in some regard, I should add a few more $50–$200 -million companies to the list to make surer that the generalizations offered are applicable to medium-size units. Though it is not indicated on the table, privately held companies as well as publicly held ones are well represented in the data.

Again, good coverage of market growth rates is evidenced in the case sample, with a number of slow-growth industries (e.g. light bulbs, coal mining equipment) covered, several medium-growth situations (crayons, aluminum), and quite a few high-growth market situations as well (mostly high technology). Similarly, the continuum of competitive positions has been studied across companies, from weak to dominant. I shall try to collect a few more cases in case sites where the operating unit enjoys a weak position in its market to be surer of the applicability of the generalizations found in that subsegment.

If anything, this case sample errs on the side of industrial as opposed to consumer marketing focus, and again on the side of products and "hard goods" as opposed to services. This is not surprising considering the fact that I am an industrial marketer and, again, considering that product marketing problems routinely are more easily available to the case writer than are services ones.

Considering the overall sample, if there were any sets of situations in which I would caution *against* applying the generalizations offered throughout the book, they would be in services, not-for-profit, and governmental marketing. Though I have every confidence that the same rule of good marketing practices apply there as in more traditional marketing settings, I cannot offer the empirical evidence to back up this faith.

At several points during the case study project I attempted statistical comparisons of consumer, say, versus industrial companies regarding type of marketing implementation problem experienced and other differences that possibly could be found. Although some exist, they generally are not worth the space it takes to discuss them. Overall, (1) the problems inherent in practicing the marketing job seem to be similar for large and small companies, weak and strong ones, old and young ones. Further, (2) if anything is striking when such a comparison is done, it is the ease with which the generalizations offered in the chapters above adapt themselves to such different settings, and not the differences between them.

Unexpected Synergies

It would be an incomplete account of this research project if I did not mention the linkage between this research and the Harvard Business School classroom. As the cases were compiled for use in the research project, they also were compiled for use in our second-year classroom in a course on marketing implementation. This course, which has proved popular with students at the school, does just what this book does: It provides a forum for inquiry into the nature of marketing practices and an arena in which the requirements for good marketing practices can be carried out. Its "raw data" are the case studies themselves, presented without commentary or analysis from me.

The reason it is important to know about the classroom effort paralleling the research one is that much of what I have learned about marketing implementation I have learned in vigorous discussion from my students as they "tore apart" each case situation to lay bare its essentials. Many of the generalizations included in this book originally came from the students or else were first thought of in concert with them and then further confirmed in the field.

Limitations of Case Research

There are many limitations to any research project, and mine is no exception. Two general limitations come to mind.

Perhaps the most critical comment that could be made about the present project is that it is pitched too broadly to attack the implementation specifics of any one industry in sufficient depth to solve them in detail. As a result it might be claimed that my research simply has reconfirmed commonsense notions about marketing practices repackaged as new generalizations.

There are two ready defenses against this criticism. The first is that many of the generalizations found in the research are in no way commonsensical, at least to my mind. For instance, that a profusion of marketing programs is likely to lead to implementation difficulties came as quite a surprise to me. But it is also true that some of the generalizations (strong leaders, poor followers) *are* commonsensical.

The second defense against a charge of platitude admits it cheerfully, but takes it as compliment rather than criticism. Frankly, I think there's not nearly enough common sense in management, or marketing, to produce good practice regularly. If my research has contributed to more of it in some way, that's useful indeed.

Finally, in light of the fact that my sample has investigated only a limited set of firms and industries, it might be claimed that there are classes of corporations or industry groups for which the rules of good marketing practice posed may not apply. That may be so, but there appears to be a great commonality of general (not specific) implementation problems and solutions across marketing functions no matter in what size or type of company they are found. While specific practice problems faced do differ considerably, the general ones have a remarkable similarity, which, to my way of thinking, is encouraging. It means that there truly is room for a "science of practice" to go along with the science of strategy with which marketers have become so familiar in the last two decades. It is at initiating this study that the research was targeted.

Table A–1. Case Abstracts and Site List

NAME	NUMBER[a]	ABSTRACT
Alcan Aluminum Corp: Building Products Division	9-583-034*	Alcan Aluminum Corp., the lowest-cost producer of aluminum in the world, was confronted with the rising use of vinyl siding. Because it was cheaper to produce vinyl, vinyl siding had made substantial inroads into the aluminum siding market. In view of vinyl's increased popularity, Alcan authorized a small vinyl siding operating in 1980. The vinyl siding was to be sold only defensively, that is, to distributors who would otherwise drop Alcan's aluminum line. John Edwards, president of Alcan's Building Products Division, wonders how to effectively manage the placement of vinyl siding along with aluminum to distributors. He has been instructed to sell vinyl only "defensively."
Applicon, Inc.	9-581-010*	Applicon is a large manufacturer of sophisticated computerized designing and drafting equipment. Its national account manager, Thomas Norbury, needs to determine the nature, procedures, and support systems for a sales program that will allow the company to sell key accounts more effectively. To date Applicon

[a] All cases starting with a "9" are available from HBS Case Services, Soldiers Field, Boston, MA 02163, for a nominal fee. Cases starred (*) are contained in the companion volume, *Managing Marketing: Text, Cases and Readings* (New York: The Free Press, 1984).

(continued)

Table A–1   (continued)

NAME	NUMBER	ABSTRACT
		has been more successful with smaller users and has had difficulties selling and servicing large accounts.
Applied Materials, Inc.	9-585-003	AMI makes gas etchers, which produce silicon chips. It has a postsale service problem. The equipment AMI vends is used in a manufacturing process resembling art more than science and besides is highly maintenance-sensitive. Customers buy AMI etchers, attempt self-maintenance, then complain of poor machine up-times. AMI needs to attack the service problem head on to avoid "bad press" on its equipment's reliability for service problems that its customers cause.
Atlantic Aviation Corp.: Westwind Division	9-581-142*	This case raises issues of monitoring and controlling flight demonstration costs for the Westwind business jet. Atlantic's marketing vice president is concerned about rising demonstration costs but does not wish to deny solid prospects an evaluation ride. He asks the general manager of the division to formulate a policy meeting both of these goals.
AT&T Long Lines Dept.: Charter Financial Corp.	9-582-085*	Mr. Chris Johnson, national account manager for AT&T, has inherited a national account that just doubled in

Table A–1 (continued)

NAME	NUMBER	ABSTRACT
		size by acquiring another firm. The parent account, Charter Financial Corp., has had an uneven relationship with Bell and Mr. Johnson's predecessor. The new acquisition, Alliance Insurance, is much more favorable than Charter toward Bell but must be integrated into the Charter telecommunications structure. Mr. Johnson must reorganize and restaff his team. Also, he must plan for an account meeting with Charter in three weeks.
AT&T Long Lines Dept.:[b] National account selling (A)	9-578-119*	On December 6, 1977, Mr. Michael Murphy, AT&T Long Lines National Account Manager responsible for the Amalgamated Manufacturing Company account, received some bad news. One of six AMC divisions was about to issue an RFP (request for proposal) tailored with a competitor's equipment in mind. This was especially distressing to Murphy because in October 1977 another AMC division had chosen to upgrade its telecommunications system with the latest Bell equipment. The RFP was important because of the revenue involved but especially because of the impact it might have on the future of the account. AMC provided

[b]This case was prepared by Professor Benson P. Shapiro of the Harvard Business School.

(continued)

Table A–1 (continued)

NAME	NUMBER	ABSTRACT
		over $1 million of annual revenue to the Bell system. The (A) case provides extensive background on the Bell system, on AT&T's approach to national account selling, and on the competitive threats to Bell's future in 1978.
AT&T Long Lines Dept.: National account selling (B)	9-581-032*	This case depicts a meeting between AMC management and national account representatives from the Bell Telephone System. Intended for use with AT&T Long Lines Dept.: National Account Selling (A); the (C) and (D) cases are also marketing implementation cases that must be used in conjunction with the (A) case.
AT&T Long Lines Dept.: National account selling (C)	9-581-033*	This case depicts an equipment demonstration in which Bell has received good attendance from the AMC management team to hear a well-organized presentation of what Bell is about, the functions of the account team, and certain issues relative to AMC's management needs. Intended for use with AT&T Long Lines Dept.: National account selling (A), (B), and (D).
AT&T Long Lines Dept.: National account selling (D)	9-581-034*	This case presents the text of a letter from Leon Gradowski, vice president in

Table A–1 (continued)

NAME	NUMBER	ABSTRACT
		charge of information systems. The letter confirms an order for DIMENSION equipment at the Atlantic Division and also confirms authorization for a negotiated purchase of a competitor's equipment in Dallas. Must be used with AT&T Long Lines Dept.: National Account Selling (A).
Benco, Inc. (A): Arch-flow	9-581-127*	Benco, Inc., a family firm, competes in the agricultural drainage market with several near-commodity types of plastic pipe. The company has invented a new arch-shaped drainage pipe that uses 30 percent fewer materials in production, is 180 percent as efficient as existing products, and offers significant installer benefits. A newly appointed marketing vice president is concerned about pricing the new pipe. Equally important, he wishes to change the marketing culture of Benco top and sales management to ensure the product's success.
Benco, Inc. (B): Marketing organization	9-581-128*	Benco's marketing vice president gets a consultant's evaluation advising Benco to implement a matrixed marketing organization. Five new staff positions will be needed at a cost of $250,000. The vice presi-

(continued)

Table A–1 (continued)

NAME	NUMBER	ABSTRACT
		dent is uncertain about the merit of some of the plan's aspects but is favorable overall to the proposed changes. The company's chairman wishes to implement only part of the reorganization and is generally not in favor of adding to staff functions.
Benco, Inc. (C): Marketing operations audit	9-582-084*	The chairman of Benco, a $70-million agricultural drainage pipe producer, performs a marketing operations audit on his marketing department. To be used with Benco (A) and (B).
Binney and Smith, Inc.: The Fun Center program	9-583-033*	Binney and Smith (B&S) is a $94 million company best known for Crayola Crayons. In 1980 B&S developed the Crayola Fun Center, a multishelf merchandising unit intended for food and drug chains, mass merchandisers, and service merchandisers. The unit was designed to hold most of the Crayola brand items in a single display. The vice president of marketing must decide on immediate plans to service the 1,500 units currently in retail outlets and plan for servicing the projected 16,000 units by 1986. The concept of retail servicing is new to B&S, as art materials traditionally are shipped to and serviced by retailers.

Table A–1 (continued)

NAME	NUMBER	ABSTRACT
Boston Whaler, Inc.: Managing the dealer network	1-584-036	Mr. Joseph Lawler, newly appointed president of Boston Whaler, Inc. (BWI), believes that better dealer management is the key to his company's continued growth. BWI manufactured a high-price, high-performance line of power and other boats for the recreational and commercial markets. Its 250 dealers were serviced by a small force of regional managers. Most dealers were not exclusively Whaler distributors, and Whaler sales ordinarily did not account for the majority of dealer revenues. Mr. Lawler wants dealer "commitment" to BWI increased, whether through new dealer agreements, training, minimum stocking requirements, or whatever other device will help increase the importance of the BWI relationship to the dealers. The case presents a relatively complete account of distribution management problems and additionally allows a key account analysis of BWI's top 50 dealers.
Capital Cities Communications, Inc.	9-584-128	CCCI owns a number of television stations and uses a sales representation firm, John Blair and Company (JBC), to sell the advertising time available from these stations. CCCI is concerned

(continued)

Table A–1   (continued)

NAME	NUMBER	ABSTRACT
		about some recent reorganizations at JBC and wishes to do a complete evaluation of the services provided by this manufacturer's rep and the pros and cons of "owning" its sales force.
Cole National Corporation	0-585-104	Dan Siewert, president of the Optical Division at Cole National Corporation, has just received authorization from corporate management to open the first in what Siewert hopes will be a new national chain of eye care department stores. However, he also needs to maintain the rapid growth of his 500+ optical departments in Sears stores and to avoid cannibalization of the leased outlets by the new stores. Corporate is watching closely, and important decisions will be taken as a result of next year's performance.
Computer Devices, Inc.: Selling intelligent terminals	9-581-146*	This case raises issues of sales force and sales management adequacy for the introduction of a new product line requiring systems selling. A sales "blitz" designed to increase sales of CDI's new 1206 portable computer fails. Management is convinced that portable computers will be a strong growth area in the 1980s and suspects an implementation problem.

Table A–1 (continued)

NAME	NUMBER	ABSTRACT
Concept Devices, Inc.: International market entry	9-582-052*	Concept Devices, Inc., is a start-up vendor of a new design in distributed data-processing computers. In its infancy, the firm has nonetheless received a great deal of international interest. Management wants to penetrate England and France but is uncertain about how to enter the international market. Concept's management has just about decided to open a wholly owned subsidiary in Great Britain. The best way to gain entry to France, however, whether by direct entry, a joint venture with a major European computer company, or by granting an exclusive license to the dominant French competition, is not clear.
Frito-Lay, Inc. (A)	9-582-110*	The president, executive vice president, and vice president of marketing and sales give differing accounts of what makes Frito-Lay, Inc. (FLI) excel at marketing. The case gives an overview of the snack industry, FLI's position in it, and the company's marketing methods. The case concludes with a day in the truck with a FLI driver–salesperson. The (A) case may be analyzed alone as an inquiry into marketing excellence, or it may be used as the first case in the Frito-Lay series with (C) and (D).

(continued)

Table A–1   (continued)

NAME	NUMBER	ABSTRACT
Frito-Lay, Inc. (C)	9-582-111*	This case concerns the preliminary rollout of GrandMa's Cookies and Snack Bars. This is FLI's $20-million gamble to play its distribution strengths into a $120-million sweet snack franchise. The initial data show some preliminary problems with supermarket placements of GrandMa's. The decision issue is whether and how to modify the rollout in a new FLI zone.
Frito-Lay, Inc. (D)	9-582-112*	This case gives three months' additional placement data from the test zones.
Frito-Lay, Inc.: GrandMa's "ready-to-eat" cookies	9-583-152*	Mr. Kenneth Treece, marketing director of Frito-Lay's GrandMa's® Cookie division, has received the final test market figures for the new supermarket line of GrandMa's ready-to-eat cookies. One set of data, the Kansas City test results, were extremely encouraging; market share was 50% higher than management had projected. Although the results of the Northwest region test were not positive, they seemed to justify continuing the rollout. In light of these conflicting test figures and the previously less than satisfactory performance of GrandMa's in single-serve packages, Mr. Treece wonders how he can change the rollout specifics

Table A–1 (continued)

NAME	NUMBER	ABSTRACT
		to better ensure the success of the new packaged Grand-Ma's line.
Gillette Co.: Personal Care Division Silkience Shampoo	9-581-103*	This case illustrates marketing and managerial issues raised by questions of how brand management should relate to and manage an aggressive advertising agency during a new product introduction.
Hertz Corp: Guaranteed pricing	9-582-126*	The Hertz Corp., a $1.3-billion subsidiary of RCA, has instituted a "no mileage charge, ever" price program in response to competitive pressures. Pro forma revenue and profit projections, however, show the firm to be even farther away from its corporate plan than before the move. The president asks for a contingency plan to go back to time-plus-mileage charges, just in case.
Inter-Footwear, Ltd.	9-584-129	IFL, a British company, has lost its "Inter" brand name for its line of sport shoes and has done a good job of changing customer and track perceptions over two years to the new "Hi-Tec" brand name. Now the president is concerned that retailers who are still holding significant stocks of the old "Inter" shoes may dump them on the market if he goes ahead with a brand termination notice.

(continued)

Table A–1 (continued)

NAME	NUMBER	ABSTRACT
Macon Prestressed Concrete Co., Inc. (A)	9-182-175*	This case provides background information on the prestressed concrete industry and Macon Prestressed Concrete Co. in particular. This case is useful as background information for the (B), (C), and (D) cases.
Macon Prestressed Concrete Co., Inc. (B)	9-182-176*	This case describes a sales and marketing audit conducted by a consulting firm. It covers both what the auditors did and what they recommended. This case is designed to be used with the (A) case and also the (C) and (D) cases.
Macon Prestressed Concrete Co., Inc. (C)	9-182-177*	This case describes a consulting assignment to design a marketing and sales control system. The need for an improved control system was discovered in a marketing and sales audit described in the (B) case. A summary of the consultants' report is provided.
Macon Prestressed Concrete Co., Inc. (D)	9-182-266*	This is the fourth case in a series concerning the auditing of the marketing function in a small ($20-million) privately held firm. The case depicts a meeting between the president and the consultant. The president has only partially implemented the consultant's recommendations to install marketing controls. The consultant feels that the control system will

Table A–1 (continued)

NAME	NUMBER	ABSTRACT
		allow management to segment the market better and to sell more productively. This case should be analyzed with Macon (A) through (C).
Manac Systems (A): Selling legal software	9-584-037	Ms. Lynne Verchere, president and founder of Manac Systems International, Ltd., a small company that produces and sells software to law firms, needs to formulate a method to sell the software successfully. Manac's systems are high quality; 50 systems have been sold to date. But sales are successful only when Ms. Verchere has had direct involvement in the selling process. The company has had consistent employee turnover in the sales and marketing areas, and so far these individuals have been unable to sell the software systems. Raises issues of how to sell a product with a lengthy buying process to organizations that are often resistant to change, and allows a detailed "win/loss" analysis to be done on the factors involved in successful and unsuccessful sales attempts.
Merrill Lynch Pierce Fenner and Smith Inc.: Marketing audit (A)	9-583-031*	Mr. Daniel Tully, executive vice president of marketing, and Mr. John Fitzgerald, vice president of marketing services for MLPF&S, feel that the company should

(continued)

Table A–1 (continued)

NAME	NUMBER	ABSTRACT
		become more marketing-oriented as opposed to sales-driven in light of the present and probably future developments in the financial industry. They recommend a marketing audit and consider how it should be done. What are the specifics involved? Should the evaluation be done by an outside consulting firm? What are the costs and political ramifications involved?
Merrill Lynch Pierce Fenner and Smith Inc.: Marketing audit (B)	9-583-032*	Mr. Tully, executive vice president of marketing, decides to approve a continuation of the marketing evaluation being conducted by an outside firm. He also received a copy of a memo written by the director of the institutional sales division requesting a significant reorganization. As the reorganization would have an impact on the marketing orientation of the company, as well as on company morale, Mr. Tully wonders whether to recommend immediate implementation of the proposal, or to wait until additional information is gathered by the consulting firm. Must be used with Merrill Lynch Pierce Fenner and Smith (A).
National Mine Service Co. (A)	9-581-055*	National Mine Service Co. (A)–(C), raises marketing implementation issues in the design, introduction, and promotion of a new

Table A–1 (continued)

NAME	NUMBER	ABSTRACT
		underground mining machine. The (A) case describes the coal industry and company background, the competitive environment, and company organization.
National Mine Service Co. (B)	9-581-056*	Raises issues in the implementation of industrial new product design and introduction. Issues of the organization, allocation, control, and behavior of a new product design group are raised as a semicustom new product, the 2460 continuous miner, is brought to market. Intrafirm conflicts (and cooperation) between the design function, manufacturing, sales, and top management are illustrated.
National Mine Service Co. (C)	9-581-057*	A new continuous miner is introduced at a trade show. Participation costs the company $500,000. Has the money been well spent?
National Mine Service Co. (D)	9-581-148	The chairman of National Mine is concerned about the firm's marketing and sales performance. He wishes to audit NMS's performance in this area and to establish a marketing reporting system.
North American Philips Lighting Corp.: Project Shopping Cart	9-582-100*	Mr. John Hayes, marketing director at North American Philips Lighting Corp. (NAPLC), must decide his

(continued)

Table A–1   (continued)

NAME	NUMBER	ABSTRACT
		next steps after the failure of Project Shopping Cart, a program to introduce Norelco brand light bulbs to grocery stores via novel product packaging displays and an extensive trade relations program. The grocery channel traditionally supported only Westinghouse and General Electric bulbs in addition to private label goods produced in high volume by NAPLC. Norelco remains committed to the retail distribution strategy, however, and feels it must penetrate the branded retail segment or eventually be driven from the business entirely.
United States Zinc Co.: Marketing raw materials for galvanizing	9-580-087	The U.S. Zinc Co. case primarily concerns ''around-the-corner'' industrial marketing. U.S. Zinc Co. mines and refines zinc primarily for sale to customer galvanizing houses but is attempting to stimulate user or owner demand for its lagging sales and profits. The case raises secondary but analyzable issues of research into industrial buying behavior, marketing strategy decision-making, and implementation policies. Promotional strategies are researched and presented for debate as well as issues of market selection and foreign competition.

Table A–2. Case Situation by Salient Characteristic

CASE NAME	INDUSTRY	SIZE[a]	MARKET[b] GROWTH	COMPETITIVE[c] POSITION	CONSUMER/ INDUSTRIAL[d]	PRODUCT/ SERVICE
Alcan Aluminum	Aluminum	Medium	Slow	Dominant	Industrial	Product
Applicon, Inc.	Computer	Small	Rapid	Strong	Industrial	Product
Applied Materials, Inc.	Silicon etchers	Medium	Rapid	Strong	Industrial	Product
Atlantic Aviation	Business jets	Medium	Moderate	Moderate	Industrial	Product
AT&T–AMC (A)–(D)	Telecommunications	Large	Moderate	Dominant	Industrial	Prod./Serv.
AT&T–Charter	Telecommunications	Large	Moderate	Dominant	Industrial	Prod./Serv.
Benco (A) (B) (C)	Drainage	Medium	Slow	Strong	Industrial	Product
Binney & Smith	Crayons	Medium	Mod./Slow	Dominant	Consumer	Product
Boston Whaler, Inc.	Boats	Small	Slow	Variable	Consumer	Product
Capital Cities Communications	Television	Large	Moderate	Strong	Consumer	Service
Cole National Corporation	Eye care	Medium	Moderate	Strong	Consumer	Prod./Serv.
Computer Devices	Terminals	Small	Rapid	Weak	Industrial	Product
Concept Devices	Computers	Small	Rapid	Weak	Industrial	Product
Frito-Lay (A) (C) (D)	Salty snacks	Large	Moderate	Strong	Consumer	Product
Frito-Lay Ready-to-Eat	Cookies	Large	Slow	Weak	Consumer	Product
Gillette	Shampoo	Large	Mod./Rapid	Moderate	Consumer	Product
Hertz	Rental cars	Large	Moderate	Strong	Industrial	Service
Inter-Footwear, LTD.	Sport shoes	Small	Moderate	Weak	Consumer	Product
Macon Prestressed (A)–(D)	Concrete	Small	Slow	Strong	Industrial	Prod./Serv.

(continued)

Table A–2 (continued)

CASE NAME	INDUSTRY	SIZE[a]	MARKET[b] GROWTH	COMPETITIVE[c] POSITION	CONSUMER/ INDUSTRIAL[d]	PRODUCT/ SERVICE
Manac Systems	Legal software	Small	Moderate	Variable	Indus./Cons.	Prod./Serv.
Merrill Lynch (A) (B)	Financial service	Large	Mod./Rapid	Strong	Consumer	Service
National Mine (A) (B) (C) (D)	Mine equipment	Medium	Slow	Weak	Industrial	Product
North Am. Philips	Light bulbs	Small	Slow	Weak	Consumer	Product
U.S. Zinc Company	Base metals	Large	Slow	Weak	Industrial	Product

[a] Size is of operating unit, not company:

Small = <$50 million sales
Medium = $51–$200 million
Large = >$201 million

[b] Market Growth:

Slow = <10%
Moderate = 10–20%
Rapid = >20%

[c] Competitive Position:

Dominant = Clear market leader
Strong = Leader with others
Moderate = Significant competitor, not leader
Weak = Low share or new entrant

[d] Consumer/Industrial:

Industrial = Sale not to ultimate end user
Consumer = Sale to ultimate end user

CASE COUNT: Number: 38
Companies: 22

Notes

Chapter One INTRODUCTION

1. Many case examples are used in this book. Usually, they are actual management situations studied in depth by me (see "The Research Project" in this chapter or the Research Appendix). Sometimes, as in this example, company names have been disguised. Often the managers' names have been changed. Proprietary data like market share have been disguised, but relationships between data have been preserved.

2. See Peter F. Drucker, *Management: Tasks, Responsibilities, Practices* (New York: Harper & Row, 1974), p. 61. Drucker adds the innovation function as the only other non–cost-center activity of a business. He concludes: "Marketing and innovation produce results; all the rest are costs."

3. See Drucker, *Management*, pp. 62–64, on customer creation as the central purpose of a business.

4. Two good discussions of marketing strategy can be found in Robert D. Buzzell, Robert E. M. Nourse, John B. Matthews, Jr., and Theodore Levitt, *Marketing: A Contemporary Analysis*, 2d edition (New York: McGraw-Hill Book Company, 1972), pp. 315–43, and in Philip Kotler, *Marketing Management: Analysis, Planning and Control*, 3d edition (Englewood Cliffs, NJ: Prentice-Hall, 1984), pp. 45–65.

5. Professor E. R. Corey has found the same strategy-constraining effects from execution in his ongoing study of how distribution is done

in a number of industries. What we do comes to affect what we can plan.

6. A "standard" scientific account of the research project can be found in my paper with Kenneth Wong, "A Case Study in Case Research," Harvard Business School *Working Papers*, 1984.

Chapter Two MANAGING MARKETING

1. Much of the material in this chapter originally appeared as "Making Your Marketing Strategy Work," *Harvard Business Review*, 62 (1984): 69–76.

2. Robert Pirsig, *Zen and the Art of Motorcycle Maintenance* (New York: Bantam Books, 1974).

3. This is the obverse of Peters and Waterman's "try it, fix it" rule, encouraging experimentation among companies wishing excellence in management. See Thomas J. Peters and Robert H. Waterman, Jr., *In Search of Excellence: Lessons from America's Best-Run Companies* (New York: Harper & Row, 1983). Where experimentation is supported by necessary analysis and homework, this is a good rule. Where it is not, my research suggests Peters's advice can be a dangerous route to follow.

4. A good book on management culture, relevant for the marketer, has been written by my colleague Vijay Sathe, *Managerial Action and Corporate Culture* (Cambridge: Harvard Business School, 1982).

5. See Chapter 10 for more on this topic.

Chapter Three BLOCKING AND TACKLING— MARKETING ACTIONS

1. Some of these already have been written. See, for example, my "Get More Out of Your Trade Shows," *Harvard Business Review*, 61 (January/February, 1983): 75–83 (order # 83101), and "Major Sales: Who *Really* Does the Buying?" *Harvard Business Review*, 60 (May/June, 1982): 111–19 (order # 82305).

2. A very good treatment of selling and sales management, with guidelines for executing this subfunction well, can be found in Benson P. Shapiro, *Sales Program Management* (Englewood Cliffs, N.J.: Prentice-Hall, 1977).

3. The final panel on the diagram shows a third logical "breaking" of the marketing pipeline. In this case the sales force is well attuned to market needs and buying patterns, but the product they are given to sell does not meet customer demands. This may or may not have been a factor with CDI's new microcomputers.

4. It is a sad but true report that training in most corporations, where sales representatives or sales management is involved, is a low- to no-productivity endeavor. Similarly, it is my experience that incentive-compensation-without-thought is a weak palliative that management frequently throws at structural contradiction problems in selling.

5. The Hertz case, though I use it as a pricing-by-assumption illustration, also shows the immense power of marketing theme in directing all that is done in the marketing function. See Chapter 6.

6. Advertising effectiveness correctly has been compared to the old "You don't see any sharks, do you?" joke. In the joke, a man in a bar claims his tie keeps away sharks. When questioned, he cites the punch line as evidence that the tie is an effective shark-repellent. Often current advertising levels are used in much the same way, as "protection money" to keep the current number of customers coming in, even though nobody knows whether it works.

7. See my article, "Making Your Marketing Strategy Work," *Harvard Business Review*, 62 (March/April, 1984): 67–76.

8. Management, needless to say, would dispute each of these assertions vigorously.

9. See Thomas J. Peters and Robert H. Waterman, Jr., *In Search of Excellence* (New York: Harper & Row, 1983).

Chapter Four MARKETING PROGRAMS

1. This is a bad example because it is offensive to two-year-olds. *They*, at least, can improve their skills with practice and maturation. That is not necessarily true of the management that reformulates programs repetitively but cannot execute them.

2. The "marketing mix," a tailored setting of product design, pricing levels, and promotion and distribution tactics, is nothing more than an incomplete recommendation for program construction in marketing.

3. This discussion should not be taken to imply that a firm never can undertake an unfamiliar marketing program. But there is a right way and a wrong way to do this, as we shall see later. In NAPLCO's case, it involved eventually buying another company's skills at consumer bulb marketing.

4. The somewhat irreverent label for this style of program management comes from the story of a man who needed an ox to pull a plow, but only had rabbits. Mating them assiduously, he was in time suffocated by their offspring, but never once succeeded in breeding an ox!

5. I shall have more to say about this deceptively simple construct in later chapters.

6. This finding should not be read to say that good implementers don't experiment with new programs. They do, but they (1) experiment with many at once, often (2) in a way that isolates the experimentation (e.g. off-site, "special" division) from the mainstream of the company, and (3) let such experimental ventures run for awhile before one is added to the firm's "mainstream" marketing endeavors. The history of "high experimentation, few programs" firms confirms this cycle: IBM's treatment of the Personal Computer Division as a physical and reporting stepchild until that division had "proved itself" is a case in point.

Chapter Five MARKETING SYSTEMS

1. Work had to offer a margin that exceeded a standard cost multiplier applied by MPCC. This multiplier, needless to say, took quite a beating in bad times.

2. The term "control" is used too loosely by managers when they mean "monitor." A firm I recently read about has designed a clever plan to market low-cost telescopes to customers in anticipation of the arrival of Halley's Comet. While this corporation may well *monitor* the said heavenly event and even base its marketing strategy on its occurrence, in no way can they claim to *control* it. Much the same could be said about many marketing phenomena. Therefore I prefer the term "monitor" instead of control to encompass both what is watched and what is changed.

3. See the classic work on marketing organization by Corey and Star for a number of insights about type of organization and resultant marketing outcomes. E. R. Corey and S. H. Star, *Organization Strategy: A Marketing Approach* (Boston, Mass.: Division of Research, Graduate School of Business Administration, Harvard University, 1971).

4. By rate of change I don't necessarily mean industry change or even market change, though those two certainly often play a big part when marketing systems are inconsistent with the reality they hope to routinize. Even when management's internal ways of doing things change, marketing systems can become inappropriate and constraining.

5. See Max Boas and Steve Chain, *Big Mac: The Unauthorized Story of McDonald's* (New York: E. P. Dutton, 1976), for a now somewhat dated but still powerful account of marketing in this retail chain.

6. There is a great deal of difference between the terms "data" and "information." The former is a set of facts; the latter is an analyzed and understood set of facts. There is an abundance of data crossing the general manager's desk and very little information.

7. Some good academic work on this topic has been done by Ian Mitroff. See his book *The Subjective Side of Science* (New York: Elsevier, 1974).

8. Although Peters and I disagree on some details, we essentially "pray in the same church." See Thomas J. Peters and Robert H. Waterman, Jr., *In Search of Excellence: Findings from America's Best-Run Companies* (New York: Harper & Row, 1983), for a very good overall account of good practice in general management.

9. The statement often is made that consumer marketing is "more advanced" as regards systems of all sorts than industrial marketing. That isn't quite right; consumer marketers generally work with larger markets that are more predictable in the aggregate and more standard product lines with a high degree of standardization. Thus the consumer marketer's job is more suitable to systematization than the industrial marketer's job in many instances.

Chapter Six MARKETING POLICIES

1. Most of the actors mentioned here are no longer at Frito-Lay but have moved on without and within the PepsioCo system to bigger and better things. Current management, though, seems as able as its predecessors at the general principles enunciated here.

2. Three useful treatments of culture in management life can be found in Vijay Sathe, *Managerial Action and Corporate Cultures* (Boston: Harvard Business School, 1982); Terrence E. Deal and Allen A. Kennedy, *Corporate Cultures: The Rites and Rituals of Corporate Life* (Reading, Mass.: Addison Wesley, 1982); and, indirectly, Thomas J. Peters and Robert M. Waterman, Jr., *In Search of Excellence: Lessons from America's Best-Run Companies* (New York: Harper & Row, 1982).

3. The office is instructive in the symbols and "meeting the hero" sense. The best way to learn what Siewert has done with the Optical Group is to "go selling" with one of his regional managers, however.

Chapter Seven BRIDGING THE GAP

1. This terminology of motorcycles and mechanics is taken from Robert Pirsig's *Zen and the Art of Motorcycle Maintenance* (New York: Morrow Books, 1974), which, the reader will have noted, I am fond of quoting. Pirsig suggests that it is impossible to divorce the motorcycle from the mechanic who fixes it, an idea remarkably akin to my own about execution structures and the managers operating within them. We shall return to Pirsig in a substantive way in Chapter 11.

2. Several good pieces have been written on the marketing audit, an unfortunate term because of the eyeshade mentality it suggests. See

Philip Kotler, William Gregor, and Will Rodgers, "The Marketing Audit Comes of Age", *Sloan Management Review*, 18 (1977): 25–43. Also see Chapter 10 for more on audit *process*.

Chapter Eight INTERACTING AND ALLOCATING SKILLS

1. We could discuss the *monitoring* aspects of this situation as easily as the interacting ones, and will do so in the next chapter. Often more than one personal execution skill is seen at one time.

2. The shampoo did not fail in the market; nor did it do as well as management had hoped it might.

3. More correctly, whatever structural constraints existed existed equally and identically for *both* programs.

4. To suggest that *only* my marketing implementation research observations have led me to conclusions about interacting would be false. I have been a social psychologist for more than a decade, and what I "saw" in the field was influenced as much by my psychological work as by what was there. Besides, consulting contacts not in the formal research sample figure in this and the following chapter more than in the remainder of the book.

5. Bubbapsychology is the psychology of grandmothers ("bubbas"), which is to say a clever and commonsense understanding of how relationships (and people) work.

6. See, for example, John W. Atkinson and Joel O. Raynor, *Motivation and Achievement* (Washington, D.C.: H. V. Winston & Sons, 1974), or any basic psychology text for an explanation of achievement motive research. Many of these books, however, are written not for the manager but rather for the scientist.

7. Again, this reference is not really suitable managerial reading in large part. See Julian B. Rotter, June E. Chance, and E. Jerry Phares, *Applications of a Social Learning Theory of Personality* (New York: Holt, 1972). A good source of much of the psychological work I refer to in this chapter and the next is my book with Zaltman. See Thomas V. Bonoma and Gerald Zaltman, *Psychology for Managers* (Boston: Kent, 1981).

8. I have written previously about these skills as they affect major account selling. See Thomas V. Bonoma, "Major Sales: Who *Really* Does the Buying?" *Harvard Business Review*, May/June 1982, pp. 110–15.

9. Logrolling is an under-studied political technique in which issues relevant to one party but not another are tied to issues relevant to

that second party so that both get what they want. An amendment for completion of a new Boston tunnel tacked onto a federal highway bill is an example of logrolling.

10. See Peters and Waterman, *In Search of Excellence*, for a good explanation of how excellent managers have a "bias toward action."

11. I should not overpaint this "going over budget" phenomenon. What was authorized in fact was a small additional allocation of monies, plus some "rearranging" of already committed monies to permit the advertising to be "pulsed" in a way that effectively doubled it when the impact was needed.

12. When I shared this particular finding with a colleague, he was quick to point out that companies like 3M are rightly held up for encouraging experimentation, starting many ventures, and, indeed, embodying an entrepreneurial spirit that suggests an almost uncritical acceptance of new programs. That's true, of course, if one is considering the initial $30,000 or so seed money a manager may request at a company like 3M to pursue a promising new idea. What it leaves out is the careful and thorough review process done by management after these projects are initiated and the *very* thorough weeding out of unsuitable ones that is done. It is eminently possible to encourage entrepreneurship and still to be *very* picky about which of those many little projects management wishes to make a major investment in.

Chapter Nine MONITORING AND ORGANIZING

1. Thomas J. Peters, "Moving Toward Excellence: Attention, Symbols, Calendar, Drama, Celebration . . . and Small Wins," unpublished, 1984.

2. This is stated very strongly, but is one of the few incontrovertible truths I know.

3. One of the most frequently forgotten principles of *good* theory is parsimony, or the ability to explain the most complex data with the simplest and fewest principles.

4. See John B. Miner, *The Human Constraint: The Coming Shortage of Managerial Talent* (Washington, DC: Bureau of National Affairs, 1974). Miner's book, written in the middle of the "apathy generation," is as worth reading now as it was when it was originally done.

5. Before the reader jumps to libelous conclusions, I had not, to the best of my knowledge, lost my mind. I performed perfectly on the examination.

Chapter Ten STRATEGISTS AND IMPLEMENTERS: ARE THEY DIFFERENT?

1. The self-help books *never* bring up the possibility that the disease with which they wish to scare us is not fixable, because then why would we need self-help books? But it is true that some management ills do not get whisked away with either a training seminar or issuance of a top management edict.

2. For some very interesting and very scary (if you're Type A) reading, see Meyer Friedman, M.D., and Ray H. Rosenman, M.D., *Type A Behavior and Your Heart* (Greenwich, Conn.: Fawcett Publications, 1974).

3. A good discussion of line–staff research can be found in A. C. Filley and Robert J. House, *Managerial Processes and Organizational Behavior* (Glenview, Ill.: Scott, Foresman, 1969), especially Chapter 9.

4. The social psychologists Stephen V. Jacobs and Mark A. Rhodes of Harvard University helped me with the research I'll summarize here. A fuller description, in scientific terminology, is contained in Thomas V. Bonoma, Stephen V. Jacobs, and Mark A. Rhodes, "Thinkers and Doers: Strategists and Implementers in the Marketing Discipline," unpublished, Harvard Business School, 1984.

5. See Thomas V. Bonoma and Dennis P. Slevin, *Executive Survival Manual* (Boston: CBI Publishing Company, 1978).

6. The managers agreed to let me use disguised scales with them; all were debriefed fully about the study's purposes and findings after they had supplied data.

7. See, for example, John Kotter, *The General Managers* (New York: The Free Press, 1983), for a good account of how general managers spend much of their time implementing strategies, not formulating them. Professor Daniel Isenberg at the Harvard Business School also has reached conclusions similar to mine about the importance of implementation to top management on the basis of his clinical work with chief executive officers.

Chapter Eleven MARKETING QUALITY

1. A search of the ABI/Inform electronic data base reveals that of the more than ten thousand articles catalogued on marketing topics, only a meager 383 concern marketing productivity. A careful search of *these* shows that fully 20 percent of the writings are *calls* for more work on marketing productivity! Clearly, to a great extent marketing productivity research has been a sterile and difficult concern for the marketing scholar.

2. I cannot summarize Pirsig's arguments justly here. It is worth reading them in the original.

3. It is definitely worth reading Gilbert's book, *Human Competence* (New York: McGraw-Hill, 1978).

4. There is nothing new about this suggestion. The psychologist Kurt Lewin made it in the late 1940s.

5. For an overview of this literature, see my "Notes Toward Industrial Marketing Productivity," to appear in David A. Wilson and Richard Spekman, eds., *New Developments in Industrial Marketing* (Chicago: American Marketing Association, forthcoming).

6. See Thomas V. Bonoma, "Market Success Can Breed 'Marketing Inertia'," *Harvard Business Review*, 59 (September–October 1981): 111–16.

RESEARCH APPENDIX

1. The tendency to use undergraduate or graduate students in academic research to simulate the behavior of industrial buyers or even general managers is rampant in marketing research. It is an unfortunate and often counterproductive tendency.

2. There is a place for widespread surveys in the study of marketing implementation, and we are proceeding with them as part of the ancillary research described in Chapter 10.

3. I skip much in the interests of conciseness. For almost a year I went around talking to (1) top managers, (2) Harvard and non-Harvard colleagues, and (3) my students about whether marketing practices *could* be studied and about how one could think about them. The managers know who they are; HBS colleagues Theodore Levitt, Benson Shapiro, and E. Raymond Corey, to name just a few, were generous with their time and insights in the way only the truly rich in ideas can be throughout this early phase and this entire project.

4. I have written at some length in another place about the role of clinical case research in science generally and in marketing's arsenal of research tools specifically. See Thomas V. Bonoma and Kenneth Wong, "A Case Study in Case Research," Harvard University Graduate School of Business Administration *Working Papers*, Number 84-41, 1984.

5. Needless to say, this research project could not have been conducted without the able and willing cooperation of many senior and not so senior managers in corporations. To them I'm very grateful, and I hope that this book repays their efforts in some small way.

6. I was aided in case compilation by several able case writers and students. Karen Carlson and Margaret Kane both did yeoman service in case preparation throughout the research project.

7. HBS Case Services, Soldiers Field, Boston, MA 02163.

Index